Influencer

The
**Power
To Change**
Anything

**Kerry Patterson • Joseph Grenny
David Maxfield • Ron McMillan • Al Switzler**

McGraw-Hill

New York   Chicago   San Francisco
Lisbon   London   Madrid   Mexico City
Milan   New Delhi   San Juan   Seoul
Singapore   Sydney   Toronto

The *McGraw·Hill* Companies

3 4 5 6 7 8 9 0 DOC/DOC 0 9 8 7

ISBN 13: 978-0-07-148499-2
ISBN 10: 0-07-148499-X

McGraw-Hill books are available at special quantity discounts to use as premiums and sales promotions, or for use in corporate training programs. For more information, please write to the Director of Special Sales, Professional Publishing, McGraw-Hill, Two Penn Plaza, New York, NY 10121-2298. Or contact your local bookstore.

This book is printed on recycled, acid-free paper.

Library of Congress Cataloging-in-Publication Data

Influencer : the power to change anything / by Kerry Patterson. . .   [et al.].
    p. cm.
ISBN 978-0-07-148499-2 (alk. paper)
1. Influence (Psychology) I. Patterson, Kerry, 1946-
    BF774.I54 2007
    153.8'5–dc22

                                                                2007025382

*We dedicate this book to influencers everywhere—
to the tenacious scholars and practitioners who, through the
careful blending of theory and experience, have not only
added to an ever-growing knowledge of how things work, but
have also curbed the cynic's smirk, restored hope, and made it
possible for each of us to become a powerful agent of change.*

Contents

Influencer

Authors' Note

For more than two decades we've felt an obligation to write this book. But the thought of capturing the strategies of influence masters worldwide was a daunting task, so we did what many authors have done under similar circumstances. We put off writing as long as we could.

Then three experiences convinced us that we had to write the book. The first took place in 1997 when we were practically knocked over by the results of an influence project we'd been working on for the previous 18 months at the Fort Worth Tactical Aircraft Division of Lockheed Martin—home of the F-16 fighter jet. Not only had the intervention been successful, but it had been *remarkably* successful. We had assisted leaders in attempts to influence a handful of key behaviors and, sure enough, the behaviors had improved substantially. More importantly, so had key outcomes ranging from productivity, to costs, to quality, and employee satisfaction.

With the completion of this successful change project, we had now demonstrated on over two dozen separate projects that when leaders apply sound influence theory to vexing organizational problems, they can dramatically improve results. By 1997 over a quarter of a million employees from these two dozen companies had been touched in ways that improved not only their organizations, but also their personal lives.

We received a second nudge to write a book about influence when we initiated a study to uncover every intervention we could find that had successfully influenced behavior change in organizations. As we pored over the rather massive body of literature, we learned there were embarrassingly few examples of leaders who had been successful at influencing employees to act in new ways. Most of the influence books and articles we found sounded as if they had been penned by prophets of doom rather than professors of change.

But this didn't make any sense. It wasn't as if behavior change was a new topic. For more than five decades social scientists and skilled practitioners had amassed an impressive literature that demonstrated that influence efforts, when based on sound theory and implemented by a knowing practitioner, had routinely led to lasting improvements. Perhaps it was time we located these individuals and shared their methods.

When we eventually tracked down the best of the seasoned influencers, we received our third and final nudge to write this book. Their work was simply too intriguing not to share. The journey to find them took us far beyond our corporate roots to points scattered all over the world, but the trip was well worth it. From Bangkok to Boston, we found quiet but tenacious influencers who had solved world-sized problems in world-class ways—solely by influencing how people behave.

We were ultimately compelled to write this book when it became clear that the influence strategies every one of these impressive change agents employed were based on the same set of theories and principles we had been applying in organizations for over 20 years. These are ideas we learned at the feet of renowned scholars and that we now introduce as a unified theory of influence.

We apologize for our procrastination. At long last, meet the influencers.

Part

1

The Power to Change Anything

If you're like most people, you face several influence challenges that have you stumped. For instance, at work you're fighting an uphill battle. You've given your heart and soul to a quality-improvement program, but your best efforts to make quality part of the everyday culture have yielded no improvements whatsoever. None.

At the personal level, you're fighting a weight problem that has gone on for years. Actually you have a *metabolism* problem. It turns out your body doesn't burn 6,000 calories a day. Talk about bad luck.

At the family level, your oldest son just turned 13, and he hangs out with a pretty frightening-looking crowd that appears to have lost all interest in civility, decency, and hair care. You've tried reasoning and bribing and even a well-timed threat, but when you talk to him, there's no one home. It's as if the day he turned 13 your ability to influence him expired.

At the community level, you have a neighbor who allows three vicious, three-foot-tall pit bulls to wander his backyard with impunity. The problem is his four-foot fence. It's just a matter of time until the dogs break out and run wild, but the local animal control people won't do a thing about it. According to them, someone has to suffer before they can take action. To cap the whole thing off, your region of the country is going through a five-year drought because apparently the world is heating up like a meatball in a microwave.

And you can't fix any of this.

3

Fortunately you've learned to follow the words of a well-known prayer: Every day you ask for the *serenity* to accept the things you cannot change, the *courage* to change the things you can, and the *wisdom* to know the difference. Somehow that gets you through.

THE SERENITY TRAP

And that's the problem. It's everyone's problem. We've come to believe that when we face enormous challenges that can be solved only by influencing intractable behaviors, we might attempt a couple of change strategies. When they fail miserably, we surrender. It's time to quit and move on. We tell ourselves that we're not influencers, and that it's time to turn our attention to things that are in our control. We seek serenity.

This would be a good tactic were it not for the fact that the problems we've listed—along with everything from changing the culture of an organization to eliminating HIV/AIDS transmission to reducing drug addiction to limiting divorce—can be and have been resolved by someone somewhere. That's right. There are actual people out there who—instead of continually seeking the "wisdom to know the difference"—have sought the wisdom to *make* a difference. And they've found it. They've discovered that when it comes to changing the world, what most of us lack is not the *courage* to change things, but the *skill* to do so.

The promise of this book is that almost all the profound, pervasive, and persistent problems we face in our lives, our companies, and our world can be solved. They can be solved because these problems don't require solutions that defy the laws of nature; they require people to act differently. And while it's true that most of us aren't all that skilled at getting ourselves and others to behave differently, there are experts out there who do it all the time.

In fact, one of the best-kept secrets in the world is that over the past half century a handful of behavioral science theorists and practitioners have discovered the power to change just about anything. So instead of pleading for the wisdom to know when to give up, we should be demanding the names and addresses of the influencers who have found solutions to the problems we face every day. We should be seeking to expand the list of things we can change so that we don't need to seek serenity so often.

Not everyone will become influencers with a capital "I," but everyone can learn and apply the methods and strategies the world's best influencers use every day. In fact, that's the purpose of this book—to share the principles and skills routinely employed by a handful of brilliant and powerful change agents so that readers can expand their set of influence tools and bring about important changes in their personal lives, their families, their companies, and even their communities.

Unlike most books on the topic, we don't draw upon the traditional way of thinking about how to exert influence by suggesting that the best way to help propel others to change is through the power of verbal persuasion. Wouldn't it be great if you could encourage others to stop their bad behavior with just the right combination of words? We've certainly tried. Legions of leaders have attempted to turn around their latest acquisition by preaching on the need to "do what's best for the larger good." Unfortunately, it's a rare leader who has seen this verbal volley alone change behavior in any noticeable way. Influence requires a lot more than the right combination of words.

For example, as you bite into a burger the size of a toaster, wouldn't it be nice if one more reminder from your spouse about how you're digging your grave with your teeth would actually inspire you to swear off fast food forever? But it's not going to happen.

Instead of merely drawing on the power of persuasion, we explore the full array of strategies successful influencers use every day (often in combination) to change lifelong habits and bring about improvements. That means we don't offer influence methods that apply only to specific problems such as: "How to potty-train your Chihuahua" or "Six ways to motivate left-handed coal miners." Instead we look for high-leverage strategies and skills that can be applied across the vast array of human challenges.

For example, consider the following ongoing tragedy. Every year over 3,000 Americans drown—many of them in public pools. This ugly statistic remained unchanged until a team of tenacious leaders from the YMCA and Redwoods Insurance decided to abandon serenity and search for a workable change strategy. It wasn't long before they reduced fatal accidents at YMCA pools by two-thirds simply by employing a few of the influence strategies we're about to study.

To reduce the senseless loss of lives, the team found a way to encourage YMCA lifeguards to alter how they performed their job. Now that's no easy challenge because it requires the ability to exert influence over hundreds of teenage employees across the organization. However, when it came to guarding, the team discovered that one vital behavior—something they called "10/10 scanning"—was a key to saving lives. By using a few of the principles we cover in this book, they were able to zero in on and change a key behavior.

It turns out that traditional lifeguards spend much of their time greeting members, adjusting swim lanes, picking up kickboards, or testing pool chemicals. However, when lifeguards stand in a specific spot and scan their section of the pool every 10 seconds and then offer assistance to anyone in trouble within 10 seconds, drowning rates drop by two-thirds. To date, scores of communities have been spared the devastating loss of a life because a handful of clever influencers looked for a way to change behavior rather than accepting the existing reality.

And while we're talking about saving lives, let's take a look at an influence effort that has saved—and created—tens of thousands of *jobs*. In 2006 alone (during the writing of this book), the chronic influence failures of the leaders of Detroit auto companies resulted in the cumulative dismissal of tens of thousands of career employees. Yet at the same time, Toyota added tens of thousands of jobs not just in Japan, but in *North America*. Toyota has grown consistently while U.S. auto companies have declined because Toyota's leaders have perfected a system of influence that engages all employees in continuous improvement.

CHOOSING INFLUENCE

The reason most of us pray for serenity rather than doggedly seeking a new solution to what ails us is that, left to our own devices, we don't come up with the big ideas that solve the problems that have us stumped. We fall into the serenity trap every time we seek solace when we should be seeking a solution. To bring this problem to its knees, we first have to see ourselves as influencers. This revised self-image calls for a deviation from the existing norm. Rarely do people say that they currently are, or that one day they will be, an influencer.

"When I grow up, I'm going to move to New York City, where I plan on being a professional influencer!"

"Who me? I work for IBM. I'm the chief influence officer."

"Yes, I'm married with two children, so I guess I'm working pretty much full time as an influencer."

We typically don't think of ourselves as influencers because we fail to see that the common thread running through most of the triumphs and tragedies of our lives is our ability to exert influence. If we did, we'd invest enormous energy in looking for new and better ways to enhance our influence repertoire. For instance, every time we tried to exert influence over others with a few well-chosen words and nothing happened, we'd stop talking and try something new. Every time we tried an incentive and it failed, we'd try something new. We wouldn't move from talking to carping and from offering incentives to making threats. Instead, we'd try something new.

The fact that many of us don't realize that it's our duty to become good at exerting influence causes us a great deal of grief. Instead of owning up to our responsibility of becoming effective agents of change and then going about the task of improving our influence repertoire (much like an athlete running laps or a chess player learning moves), we grumble, threaten, ridicule, and, more often than not, find ways to cope.

WE'RE BETTER AT COPING THAN AT EXERTING INFLUENCE

People tend to be better copers than influencers. In fact, we're wonderful at inventing ways to cope. For instance, at work we abandon our quality-control program and install full-time inspectors. Nobody will listen. Instead of fixing lousy schools, we complain to our friends and then backfill by tutoring our children. It's the best we can do. And when it comes to diet and exercise, we own two or three different-sized wardrobes. It's impossible to stick to a diet.

Consider the following international example of coping. Not long ago the world celebrated the birthday of one of the smallest yet most successful organisms on the planet—a terrifying organism called HIV. A review of the proceedings of its birthday party in Toronto—the 16th International AIDS Conference—demonstrates our universal lack of confidence that we can actually change what people do. Of the speeches, classes, and activities that took place at that conference, over 90 percent dealt with how to cope with the effects of AIDS.

Of course, helping AIDS sufferers is essential. We *should* spend time talking about how to reduce discrimination against sufferers and how to dramatically increase access to medicines. But it's indicative of our collective sense of powerlessness that less than 10 percent of the speeches at the international AIDS conference even speculated on how to change the behavior that drives the disease in the first place. Here we have a disease that would never infect another human being if people simply thought and behaved differently, and yet the central forum for discussing the pandemic hardly touched on the topic of human behavior.

To cite an often-spoken metaphor that helps us understand what's happening with this ongoing tragedy, it's as if a steady stream of automobiles is hurtling toward a cliff and then plunging to destruction. A community leader catches sight of the devastating carnage and springs into action. However, instead of rushing to the top of the cliff and finding a way to prevent drivers from speeding toward disaster, the bureaucrat parks a fleet of ambulances at the bottom of the cliff. When the vast majority of our efforts go to after-the-fact treatment rather than avoidance of AIDS, we've quietly announced that we don't know how to influence thoughts and behavior, so we've given up.

You can see evidence of coping everywhere. What's the solution to, say, a gambling addiction? Current efforts are aimed at developing an antiaddiction pill. IT department isn't performing? Outsource it. Spouse giving you fits? Legislate an easy off-ramp to no-fault divorce. Are recently released convicts leaping too quickly back into crime? Don't free them so soon. Build bigger penitentiaries, and put in a revolving door. Then pray for serenity.

THE WISDOM TO *MAKE* A DIFFERENCE

Over the last year U.S. airlines lost over $10 billion and shed tens of thousands of jobs. At the same time, Southwest Airlines racked up its 14th straight year of profits and double-digit growth. What do Southwest's leaders do that others haven't figured out? They engage everyone in doing more with less. They turn planes faster at the gates. They treat customers better. And they get a higher percentage of bags and passengers to arrive at the same location. In other words, they've perfected an influence strategy that produces the behaviors that drive stellar results across their entire company.

While this has been going on in the business world, another influence genius in Dhaka, Bangladesh, helped over 4 million of the Developing World's poor to emerge from poverty.

Likewise, thousands of previously overweight Americans declared victory in the battle of their bulges by developing sustainable influence strategies over their own unhealthy behaviors.

And finally, in Thailand alone, over 5 million people avoided contracting HIV because of a remarkably effective influence strategy developed by a quiet but enormously effective influence genius who has a lot to teach us all.

So there is hope. In a world filled with those content with seeking serenity, there are people who know exactly what it takes to exert influence over human behavior—and change the world in a good way. We (the authors) know because we've tracked them down. We've traveled to Addis Ababa, Mexico City, Johannesburg, Bangkok, Boston, Burkina Faso, Denver, Dhaka, and other rather exotic-sounding places, and we've studied what they've done.

And what has this rather comprehensive search revealed? Every time we interview these influencers, we're both awed and humbled. Carefully, systematically, and with no fanfare whatsoever, a small group of tenacious gurus has been able to achieve everything from eradicating diseases to eliminating gender discrimination to turning around companies. One of the wizards we discovered influences hardened criminals and drug addicts to eventually become productive citizens—every single day.

And here's what qualifies these remarkable individuals as master change agents rather than as merely lucky. They have all successfully applied their influence strategies to problems that others haven't been able to solve for years—often centuries. None has succeeded through serendipity, nor have any of their results been idiosyncratic. Through years of careful research and studied practice, they've developed a handful of powerful influence principles and strategies that they themselves can and do replicate and that others can and do learn.

This book shares their combined knowledge. By sharing the principles and strategies of a handful of brilliant influencers, we (the authors) hope to help you expand your own sphere of influence—and thus change your own life for good.

In this book you'll meet a few of the influencers who are changing the world.

1
You're an Influencer

*I wanted the influence. In the end I wasn't very good
at being a [university] president. I looked out of the window
and thought that the man cutting the lawn actually
seemed to have more control over what he was doing.*

—*Warren Bennis*

To get a glimpse of what it takes to exert profound influence, to literally change anything, we first travel to San Francisco and look in on influence master Dr. Mimi Silbert. Consider what Silbert has been able to do by applying the best of today's influence strategies to one of today's most noxious problems. She is the founder of the Delancey Street Foundation, a one-of-a-kind organization with headquarters at an upscale address on San Francisco's Embarcadero. Silbert's company is part corporate conglomerate and part residential therapy. It consists of several dozen businesses, all headed by Silbert.

What's unique about the institution is the employee population. In Silbert's words, "They're nasty, racist, violent, and greedy. They're thieves, prostitutes, robbers, and murderers." Then she adds: "When we started 30 years ago, most were gang members. Today many are third-generation gang members." According to Silbert, "These guys get letters from Grandma saying, 'Get back here—the gang needs you!'"

Dr. Silbert's typical new hires have had 18 felony convictions. They've been homeless for years, and most are lifetime drug addicts. Within hours of joining Delancey, they are working in a restaurant, moving company, car repair shop, or one of the many Delancey companies. And other than Silbert herself, these felons and addicts make up the entire population at Delancey. No therapists. No professional staff. No donations, no grants, no guards—just a remarkable influence strategy that has profoundly changed the lives of 14,000 employees over the past 30 years. Of those who join Delancey, over 90 percent never go back to drugs or crime. Instead they earn degrees, become professionals, and change their lives. Forever.

MEET JAMES

One of the employees we met is a well-scrubbed, affable but steely-eyed fellow we'll call James. James's story is typical of Silbert's staff. Like many of the 500 residents living on the San Francisco campus, James was a career criminal and drug addict before coming to Delancey. And like most, he started young. After four years as a regular runaway, criminal, and drug abuser, James turned 10. By that time Illinois was fed up with his shenanigans and had tracked down James's father—who abandoned him at age one. State justice authorities wished James good luck as they stood at a gate at the O'Hare airport while making sure he understood that he was no longer welcome in Chicago.

James flew to Oakland, California, where he took up residence with his father near the docks. The first lesson his dear old dad taught him was how to shoot heroin. The next 25 years consisted of an uninterrupted period of violent crime, drug abuse, and prison time. Six years ago he was convicted of yet another violent offense and sentenced to 18 years with no hope of parole for 16 years. That's when he asked to join Delancey rather than serve his full sentence.

James changed in ways that are hard to imagine. When we first visited Delancey, he was professionally dressed and had not used drugs or alcohol in two years. To learn how Dr. Silbert influences this kind of change, we touch base with her work throughout this book. She draws from the principles and practices of every one of the influence geniuses we've studied to date.

Combining principles learned in Tanzania, practices honed in Mexico City, and theories developed in Palo Alto helps us understand how Ralph Heath in Marietta, Georgia, was able to influence the behavior of 4,500 engineers and craftsmen to move a stalled product from design to production, resulting in billions of dollars in needed sales; why Mike Miller was able to change the culture of a massive IT group in order to dramatically improve performance; and what makes it possible for an individual who has struggled to lose weight for years to finally turn the corner. But most importantly, these proven concepts, principles, and theories will help you, your family, your company, and your community develop an influence repertoire of enormous power.

SOME AMAZING CASES

Leaving San Francisco for warmer climes and more far-reaching methods, we head to Mexico City to visit TV producer Miguel Sabido. He has created a method for influencing hundreds of thousands of people at a time.

Sabido has perfected strategies for changing how people think and behave by producing life-changing soap operas—of all things. At one point, when Sabido aimed his popular TV show *Ven Conmigo* ("Come with Me") at improving literacy (a problem that had remained intractable for decades), his TV characters propelled over a quarter of a million viewers into the streets of Mexico City—all in search of free literacy booklets that were shown on the program. Sabido's work in entertainment education has now been replicated in dozens of countries with remarkable success. A careful review of his work helps us understand how to use one of the world's best tools for helping others *willingly* change their minds.

Switching our attention to Ithaca, New York, we see Brian Wansink explore how the physical world can either help or hinder people in their quest to shed unwanted pounds. By learning how Wansink and others enlist the "curious power of propinquity," we are able to apply the same methods to, say, propel your kids to read more books, or encourage coworkers to collaborate.

To learn how to develop one of the most important of all influence methods, we travel to Atlanta, Georgia, and meet Dr. Donald Hopkins and his staff at The Carter Center. Their work across Africa and Asia teaches us how to identify a handful of vital behaviors that help change the habits of millions of people. In this case, he and his colleagues help change the dangerous water-drinking habits of millions of remote villagers. Hopkins's work on applying principles of "positive deviance" helps us all understand what it takes to discover a handful of high-leverage behaviors that drive virtually every change effort we'll ever undertake.

Try this for a challenge. Since 1986, Dr. Hopkins and his team at The Carter Center in Atlanta have focused on the eradication of the Guinea worm disease. The Guinea worm is one of the largest human parasites (it can grow to three feet long), and it has caused incalculable pain and suffering in millions of people. When West Asian and sub-Saharan villagers drink stagnant and unfiltered water, they take in the larvae of Guinea worms, which then burrow into abdominal tissues and slowly grow into enormous worms.

Eventually the worms begin to excrete an acidlike substance that helps carve a path out of the host human's body. Once the worm approaches the skin's surface, the acid causes painful blisters. To ease the horrific pain, victims rush to the local water source and plunge their worm-infected limbs into the pond for cooling relief. This gives the worm what it wanted—access to water in which to lay hundreds of thousands of eggs, thus continuing the tragic cycle.

Sufferers cannot work their crops for many weeks. When parents are afflicted, their children may drop out of school to help out with chores. Crops cannot be cultivated. The harvest is lost. Starvation ensues. The cycle of illiteracy and poverty consumes the next generation. Often, secondary infections caused by the worm can kill. Consequently, for over 3,500 years the Guinea worm has been a major barrier to economic and social progress in dozens of nations.

In 1986 Dr. Hopkins and his colleagues declared war on the worm. Hopkins was interested in this particular disease because he knew that if 120 million people in 23,000 villages would change just a few vital behaviors for just one year, there would never be another case of the infection. Ever. But imagine the audacity of intending to influence such a scattered population in so many countries—frequently faced with corrupt or nonexistent health systems or fragile political stability.

And yet this is exactly what Hopkins's team has done. Soon he and his colleagues will have laid claim to something never before accomplished in human history. They will have eradicated a global disease without finding a cure. Despite this enormous disadvantage, Hopkins and his small band of intrepid change agents will have beaten the disease with nothing more than the ability to influence human thought and action.

The implications of Hopkins's work for individuals, businesses, and communities are enormous. Everyone has a version of a Guinea worm disease: some self-defeating behaviors that, if changed, could unlock a whole new level of performance. Hopkins teaches us first how to find success where others have failed, and second, how to locate a handful of key actions that, if routinely enacted, will guarantee our own success.

Who can't benefit from learning how to locate strategies that routinely succeed in the face of widespread failure?

STUDY WITH THE BEST SCHOLARS

Hopkins, Silbert, Sabido—in fact, virtually all the influencers we studied—draw on the same sources: a handful of brilliant social scientists you'll meet in this book. For now, let's meet the one almost all cited as the scholar of scholars: Albert Bandura. He's a genius whom influence masters routinely study. When we first entered the offices of the practitioners we studied, most displayed Dr. Bandura's works on their bookshelves. His name leaped out at us because our history with him goes back over 30 years.

We first encountered Bandura in the mid-1970s in his modest office at Stanford University. There we met a mild-mannered and brilliant man who was already legendary as the father of social learning theory. When we reconnected with him three decades later, at an energetic 83, Dr. Bandura was still up to his neck in influence research that continues to tilt the world. He can still lay claim to the fact that he's the most cited psychologist alive.

Here's how Bandura's work fits into the world of influence and can be of enormous help to all of us. In his early years, Dr. Bandura generated a remarkable body of knowledge that led to rapid changes in behaviors that other theorists had dawdled over for years. Phobics who'd spent years on a couch were freed in hours. Addicts who had used drugs for decades became clean in weeks and were well on their way to making the transforma-tive changes in their lives that would keep them clean. Individuals struggling with obesity for a lifetime developed new habits in months.

One of Bandura's classic studies demonstrated, for exam-ple, how powerfully our behavior is shaped by observing oth-ers. This came at a time when most psychologists believed that behavior was solely influenced by the direct rewards and pun-ishments people experienced. This was the age of strict behav-iorism. And yet Bandura's intense curiosity about how to change human behavior made him impatient with such simplistic explanations. So he took a daring swing at the established dogma and began an exodus toward a much more powerful theory.

Seeing a rise in violence corresponding with the diffusion of television, Bandura thought it worthwhile to examine whether juveniles were learning violent behaviors by watching TV characters smack, kick, and shoot one another. To explore the effects of TV violence, Bandura and a team of graduate students watched closely as nursery school children played in a small room packed with toys—dolls, tiny stoves, balls, and so forth. Among this tempting array of playthings was a "Bobo doll"—a large plastic blow-up doll with a weight in the bottom. If you punch the doll in the nose, it bounces right back so you can punch it again.

Left to their own devices, children played with several of the toys, moving from one to the next—occasionally giving Bobo a punch or two. But what if researchers demonstrated novel aggressive behavior for the children? Would kids learn through simple observation? To answer this question, Bandura showed a different group of children a short movie of a woman modeling novel aggressive behavior. She pummeled the Bobo doll with a mallet. She flung the plastic toy into the air, kicked it repeatedly, and eventually sat on it and beat it. That seemed novel enough.

The children who watched the film were then released one at a time into the toy room. Would simple modeling influence their behavior? You only have to watch the black-and-white film segments taken of the experiment for a few seconds to answer the question. A little girl wearing a dress—complete with a 50s-style poofy petticoat—enters the room, digs through the toys until she finds the mallet, and starts whaling on Bobo. She and the dozens of other nursery school kids who followed her demonstrate all the aggressive behavior they had seen modeled—including inventive new forms of aggression such as beating the doll with a cap gun. In Bandura's own words,

"They added creative embellishments. One girl actually transforms a *doll* into a weapon of assault." There she is—that cute little girl in the frilly outfit—smacking Bobo with Raggedy Ann.

In addition to demonstrating that humans are influenced by watching the behavior of others, Bandura was able to prove that the violence pumped out by the television networks was likely to exact a terrible toll on viewers. Dr. Bandura caps his review of his classic study by stating with a twinkle: "This research didn't get me onto the Christmas-card list of the broadcast industry." But it did put him smack dab in the center of influence research.

This work, when combined with hundreds of other Bandura studies that have been aimed at fixing an ailing world, teaches us the very first thing we need to know about influence. Influence strategies can indeed be studied, tested, and mastered. Bandura also taught us where *not* to waste our time. For instance, if you want others to change, you don't have to put them on a couch for 10 years to learn about their critical childhood moments. You also need not trouble yourself by laying a trail of Reese's Pieces in front of others to propel them through a maze. Humans aren't simple-minded pawns who can be readily manipulated to do whatever you like—even if you have the right amount of candy.

In fact, Bandura found humans to be quite complicated. It turns out that they *think*. Humans observe, cogitate, draw conclusions, and then act. All this is important to know because if you want to change the world, you eventually have to change how people behave. And if you want to change how they behave, you have to first change how they think.

WHAT THIS MEANS TO YOU

There's good news in all of this. Since our ineffectiveness at influencing others stems from a simple inability rather than a character flaw or lack of motivation, the solution lies in continued learning. We can become powerful influencers. We don't have to wait for everyone else to miraculously change. We won't have to constantly seek serenity.

It also means that the changes we need to make won't be too intrusive. We don't need a lobotomy, a pep talk, or an infusion of tenacity. Instead, we simply need to expand our self-image by seeing ourselves as influencers; it's the one job that cuts across every domain of our life. In addition, like any dedicated person, we need to study the works of the influencers who are already good at the job. As we learn the strategies influence masters have been implementing for the past five decades, we'll be in far better shape to take on the profound and persistent problems that have been plaguing us for years.

Notice that we have used the word "strategies." We've chosen the plural because there is no one strategy—no silver bullet—for resolving profound, persistent, and resistant problems. When it comes to the problems that have us stymied, it takes an entire set of influence methods. We'll help you create your own set of tools by sharing the strategies used by every influencer we've studied.

These influence strategies, by the way, are value-neutral. They can be used either to break or to cause a heroin addiction. They can be used either to create or to destroy a customer-driven corporate culture. Naturally, the influencers we studied routinely aimed their strategies at deserving, even noble causes. But not everyone does or will. We knowingly share the powerful methods of the world's best influencers as a way of making them both accessible and transparent. To the degree that people understand new strategies, their ability to make their own life better grows exponentially. To the degree that people understand the forces that are already influencing their behavior, they are more empowered to choose their response.

Any one of the influence strategies we explore, combined with what you already know, could be enough to put you on the road to creating lasting change. Put into play several methods, and your chances for improvement only grow. Find a way to combine all the methods, and you'll be able to create changes that most of us have only been able to imagine.

So join us as we do our best to answer: How can I learn to change *anything?*

2

Find Vital Behaviors

*It is not enough to do your best; you must
know what to do, and THEN do your best.*

—W. Edwards Deming

Before you can influence change, you have to decide *what* you're trying to change. Influence geniuses focus on behaviors. They're universally firm on this point. They don't dive into developing influence strategies until they've carefully identified the behaviors they want to influence.

And now for the big idea: A few behaviors can drive a lot of change.

The breakthrough discovery of most influence geniuses is that enormous influence comes from focusing on just a few *vital behaviors*. Even the most pervasive problems will often yield to changes in a handful of high-leverage behaviors. Find these, and you've found the beginning of influence.

THE KING'S BIRTHDAY PRESENT

To see how tenaciously searching for vital behaviors can make an important difference, meet Dr. Wiwat Rojanapithayakorn (or, as he is known around the world, Dr. Wiwat). He learned the value of searching until you find the right behaviors the hard way.

In 1988, King Rama IX of Thailand turned 60. To honor the event, he gave the country a gift. Unfortunately, the king's well-intended present actually unleashed a horrendous plague on his people. Prior to the king's birthday, AIDS in Thailand had been restricted to prisoners who passed the disease from one to the other by sharing used needles. For several years the disease stayed incarcerated with its hosts. But in 1988, in a birthday-inspired act of compassion (in keeping with a national tradition for momentous occasions), the king granted amnesty to over 30,000 prisoners. Released from its confinement, the AIDS virus celebrated its new freedom by rampaging through a much larger intravenous drug-user community. In just a few months almost half the users nationwide were infected.

The country's infectious disease experts watched in horror as month by month the disease spread from one community to another. Close on the heels of IV drug users, sex workers fell prey. Within only a year, as many as one-third of the sex workers in some provinces tested HIV positive. Next, married men carried the scourge home to their unsuspecting wives, who frequently passed it to newborn babies. By 1993 an estimated 1 million Thais were infected with HIV. Health experts worldwide predicted that in just a few years Thailand would lead the world in infections per capita—with as many as one in four adults carrying the virus.

But it never happened. Within two years the virus hit a wall, and then it retreated. By the late 1990s—largely because of a remarkable influence strategy implemented by Dr. Wiwat—new infections had been cut by 80 percent. The Thai government estimates that as of 2004, over 5 million people who *should* have been infected weren't.

But the solution didn't come easily, and it certainly didn't come after the first attempt. While AIDS was taking Thailand by storm, Dr. Wiwat battled the plague alongside a handful of his colleagues in the Ratchaburi province. His training had taught him that the key to fighting the spread of any disease lay in making the public aware of the threat. The experts who were advising Wiwat (people who had thought about the transmission problem but who hadn't actually solved it) argued that diseases thrive in ignorance; therefore, you have to spread the word.

With this idea in mind, when Dr. Wiwat accepted a position with Thailand's Ministry of Public Health, specializing in venereal diseases, he approached the task of informing an ignorant public in much the same way corporate executives try to improve quality, customer service, or teamwork. Wiwat's team distributed posters. They held education sessions. They convinced celebrities to broadcast television and radio spots.

Despite their best efforts, Wiwat and his teammates failed. After a couple of exhausting, hectic, and expensive years, Thai researchers found that they had accomplished nothing. The problem had actually grown far worse. That's when Wiwat threw out the handbook. Rather than accepting the word of people who had never actually succeeded in eliminating the rapid transmission of the disease, Dr. Wiwat decided to conduct a more intensive search for a strategy. He started by poring over data about the transmission cycle of AIDS through Thailand.

It didn't take Wiwat long to realize that 97 percent of all new HIV infections came from heterosexual contact with sex workers. This statistic might seem a bit odd until you learn that Thailand has over 150,000 sex workers—about one for every 150 adult men. Induced by low prices and a permissive culture, the vast majority of Thai men periodically visit brothels.

This statistic gave Dr. Wiwat the focus he needed. If contact with sex workers was causing the pandemic, he had no choice but to focus his attention there—despite the fact that the government refused to admit that the massive sex-trade industry even existed. With over a million HIV infections in Thailand, Wiwat decided the time for political sensitivity and social niceties was long past. If the problem was born in a brothel, the solution would be found there as well.

After continuing his search for a solution, Wiwat surmised that if he could persuade 100 percent of the country's sex workers to demand that their clients use condoms, he could nearly stop the spread of HIV in Thailand. That became his primary strategy. He'd find a way to get every single sex worker to comply with the condom code. And much to the surprise of the world's epidemiologists, Wiwat's plan worked.

Later we explore how Dr. Wiwat successfully influenced sex workers to follow the plan (no easy task). The takeaway we want to focus on now is the fact that by carefully searching for and targeting a vital behavior, Wiwat was able to break from traditional untested methods and find something that actually succeeded.

SEARCH FOR *BEHAVIORS*

Wiwat's work teaches our first search principle: When faced with a number of possible options, take care to search for strategies that focus on specific *behaviors*. Once Wiwat settled on the exact behavior he wanted to influence (condom use), he knew precisely what he needed to motivate and enable others to do.

It turns out that all influence geniuses focus on behaviors. They're inflexible on this point. They don't develop an influence strategy until they've carefully identified the specific behaviors they want to change. They start by asking: In order to improve our existing situation, what must people actually *do*?

It's important to note that this concept is lost on individuals who misunderstand the meaning of the word *behavior*. Consider Henry Denton, who is currently trying to lose weight. He decided to lose a few pounds after overhearing his grandchildren speculate about his demise. One of them said: "He's so fat, he'll probably die of a heart attack pretty soon."

This terse comment gave birth to his strategy: "Eat fewer calories than I burn." His plan, while effective at explaining how weight is lost, doesn't exactly inform his daily actions. In fact, his strategy focuses on an outcome, not on behaviors. What he's really saying is that if he does *something* right, as a *result* of his efforts he'll burn more calories than he eats. What he has to *do* is still unknown.

Confusing outcomes with behaviors is no small issue. In fact, when you look at most failed influence strategies, you're likely to find at least one example of means/ends confusion. For instance, your neighbor attends a seminar on problem solving with teenagers. She's told that in order to commence the high-risk conversation on the right foot, she needs to "establish a good relationship." That's it. That's what she's supposed to do. She's given this counsel by a coach who actually believes that he's providing her with behavioral advice. In truth, your neighbor is actually being told what to *achieve*, not what to *do*. What the advice is really suggesting is: "Do something; we're not sure what it is, but do something that results in a good relationship."

In a sense, this was the problem Wiwat faced when he first started his campaign. He was told by the specialists he consulted to make sure that people understood the problem they were facing. Disease breeds in ignorance, so he set off on an information-sharing campaign.

"The dreaded disease is coming. Beware, the disease is coming. Soon one in four of us will be infected!"

What the enormously important campaign didn't clarify was what people were actually supposed to do. Without specific behaviors, Wiwat and his team were also unable to take steps to ensure that the public did whatever it was that they were supposed to do. It turns out that without a behavioral focus, people didn't choose to enact the right behaviors, and the spread of the disease only worsened. Based on the chilling information that was being blasted from every street corner, Thai citizens were indeed more worried; but the disease transmission rate actually escalated. It's no wonder that influence masters, no matter what challenge they face, always focus on behaviors.

SEARCH FOR *VITAL* BEHAVIORS

Perhaps the most important discovery from Wiwat's work is the notion that in addition to focusing on behavior, you should give special attention to a handful of *high-leverage* behaviors. Principle number two: Discover a few *vital* behaviors, change those, and problems—no matter their size—topple like a house of cards.

For example, relationship scholar Howard Markman took us into his Relationship Lab to show us how he learned that by focusing on only a few behaviors, he could predict with startling accuracy whether a given married couple is headed for divorce. More importantly, he found that if he could help couples practice a few similarly critical behaviors, he could reduce their chances of divorce or unhappiness by over one-third. You don't have to study what interests the couples share in common or how they were raised or any of a thousand different ways they treat each other. Merely watch how they argue. If Markman and his colleagues can watch a couple for just 15 minutes, they can predict with 90 percent accuracy who will and who won't be together and happy five years later! During those 15 minutes, Markman will invite a couple to discuss some topic about which they disagree. If the argument involves a significant amount of blaming, escalation, invalidation, or withdrawal, the future is bleak. If, on the other hand, the same couple opens tough conversations with statements that communicate respect and a shared purpose, and halts emotional escalation in a respectful way to take a time out, the future will be entirely different.

To see exactly how only a few behaviors can play an enormous role in both causing and solving profound problems, let's look in on Dr. Mimi Silbert, the influence wizard who heads up Delancey. She learned early on that if you're going to work with subjects who lack just about every skill imaginable, you have to limit your scope of influence by identifying only a couple of vital behaviors and then work on them. Otherwise you dilute your efforts and eventually fail.

As you chat with Dr. Silbert, she's quick to point out that if you want to change ex-cons' lives, you need to focus on behavior, not values, homilies, or emotional appeals. Just imagine Mimi Silbert giving a value-laden lesson to James on his first day at Delancey. James vividly describes what she'd be up against.

"When residents wake up in their dorm the first morning and you say, 'Good morning' to them, they assault you with profanity in return." A pep talk on courtesy just isn't going to cut it in this venue.

So Dr. Silbert focuses on changing behavior, not on preaching homilies. And, once again, a few behaviors, not dozens. During one interview, Silbert explained with a wry smile: "You can't succeed by trying to change 20 things at the same time!" So Silbert made a study of the behaviors that needed changing, hoping to find a few that would provide focus and leverage in transforming criminals into citizens. After working with over 14,000 hardened criminals, Silbert is now convinced that just a couple of behaviors open the floodgates of change. If you focus on these two, a whole host of other behaviors, values, attitudes, and outcomes follow. Silbert explains how it works.

"The hardest thing we do here is try to get rid of the code of the street. It says: 'Care only about yourself, and don't rat on anyone.' However," Silbert continues, "If you reverse those two behaviors, you can change everything else."

James elaborates: "Helping residents learn to confront problems is essential. We've got Crips, Bloods, white supremacists boarding with us, and they're all bunking together. As you might imagine, the tension runs high. Everything we try to change in here is about getting rid of the gang culture. So we *talk* a lot."

With this in mind, Silbert targets two high-leverage behaviors that help residents talk in ways that eventually destroy the gang culture. First, she requires each person to take responsibility for someone else's success. Second, she demands that everyone confront everyone else about every single violation.

To transform these ideals into realities, each resident is placed in charge of someone else the very first week. For instance, say you're a resident who was homeless and strung out on crack a week ago. During the seven days since coming to Delancey, someone who had been a resident for only a little longer than you would take you under his or her wing and teach you to set a table in the restaurant. A week later when someone even newer than you comes in, you're in charge of teaching that person to set the table. From that moment forward, people no longer talk to you about how *you're* doing. They ask you how *your crew* is doing.

Next, residents learn the second vital behavior: to speak up to people who are breaking rules, drifting off, becoming verbally aggressive, and otherwise behaving badly. For most ex-criminals, talking about these types of problems is like speaking a foreign language. Ultimately, Silbert helps residents change their values and attitudes—even their hearts—but she does so by focusing on two vital behaviors.

STUDY THE BEST

Silbert and Wiwat (in fact, all the influence masters we studied) make judicious use of vital behaviors. It's their trademark. Before they run off willy-nilly implementing the first influence strategy that comes to mind, they search for behaviors—*vital* behaviors.

How do legitimate researchers actually discover the handful of behaviors that typically lead to success? People will tell you that they've discovered the behaviors that lead to weight loss or increased productivity or whatever it is that you want to change, but how do you know if they've really found the high-leverage actions that lead to the results you care about? Fortunately, the science of identifying which actions lead to key outcomes—no matter the domain—has already been carefully developed by those who study "best practices." To learn what to watch for as you study the best practices others have uncovered, consider the following case.

MEET ETHNA REID

To see how one of these best-practice studies is completed, we'll visit Dr. Ethna Reid in Salt Lake City. She'll teach us how to identify which behaviors, from a list of hundreds, separate successful people from everyone else. The technique she routinely applies to schoolteachers sets the standard for how to search for vital behaviors.

Forty years before we met Dr. Reid, soon after she had completed her doctoral work and was teaching prospective educators how to improve students' poor reading habits, she turned to her academic mentor and asked, "Does any of what you're teaching me actually *work?*"

Her mentor explained that he didn't know for sure. He suspected it did. It certainly made sense. But nobody had actually studied the effects of the accepted methods.

Dr. Reid decided it was time to find out.

She began by calling a local school district and asking if anyone had records tracking, say, reading comprehension. The district experts actually had 20 years of data. Better still, they had conducted studies that were quite informative—and tragic. Based only on the first year's testing, researchers could predict how well students would do in the third year, the seventh, and so on.

"The model is highly predictive," explained the voice on the other end of the phone. Reid was thunderstruck. With cold, scientific precision, the researcher explained to her that the current education system essentially set kids on a course of success or failure beginning in the *first grade*—independent of what anyone did afterward.

Stunned and indignant, Reid was determined to find out if there was something teachers could do to make a difference. Weren't there teachers out there who started with children the model predicted would lag behind, but who helped the students beat the model? And, if so, what was the difference between those who were successful and everyone else?

Here's where Dr. Reid's mix of genius and dogged determination came into play. She pored over the data until she found teachers whose students did better in later years than before being taught by those teachers. Some did considerably better.

"These were the teachers who beat the projections," Dr. Reid explained. "For whatever reason, their students beat the model. We also were able to find teachers whose students did far worse than predicted after spending a year under their tutelage.

"I was curious as to what was going on with both groups," Reid continued, "so I gathered a dozen teachers whose students were achieving better results than the model predicted and asked them what methods they used to cause their students to read at a higher level than expected. They didn't know what had led to success. Later I gathered teachers whose students had done worse than predicted and bluntly asked: 'What are you doing that *prevents* the children from learning?' After an extended awkward silence, they confessed that they didn't know."

And now for the determination. For the next five years Reid watched both top and bottom performers in action in order to divine the vital behaviors that separated the best teachers from the rest. She codified, gathered, and studied data on virtually every type of teaching behavior she and a team of doctoral students could identify.

With still vibrant enthusiasm, Reid announced to us the findings. They had found certain behaviors that separate top performers from everyone else. They've proven to be the same behaviors across ages, gender, geography, topic, and anything else the researchers could imagine.

One of the vital behaviors consists of the use of praise versus the use of punishment. Top performers reward positive performance far more frequently than their counterparts. Bottom performers quickly become discouraged and mutter things such as, "Didn't I just teach you that two minutes ago?" The best consistently reinforce even moderately good performance, and learning flourishes.

Another vital behavior they found is that top performers rapidly alternate between teaching and questioning or otherwise testing. Then, when required, they make immediate corrections. Poor performers drone on for a long time and then let the students struggle, often leaving students to repeat the same errors.

After explaining the vital behaviors, Dr. Reid remarked, "You're probably wondering how we know for a certainty that these are the vital behaviors—the ones that separate the best from the rest." She then turned to a plain wooden cupboard attached to the wall behind her, opened it, and pointed to dozens of doctoral dissertations.

For over three decades, Reid and a constant stream of doctoral students had tracked the same topic: What vital behaviors set top teachers apart from the masses? She would pick the learning target she cared about—say, vocabulary. Then she'd find a data set and identify teachers who beat the predictive model along with those who trailed it. Finally, she would watch both groups in action, codify their actions, and tease out which behaviors worked and which ones didn't.

Dr. Reid now knows with a scientific certainty the specific behaviors that lead to the best results. This means that she now knows which vital behaviors to *influence* if she wants to improve the outcomes she desires.

The good news behind this story is that this type of best-practice research can be conducted in any organization. We (the authors) used similar techniques when trying to determine the behaviors that lead to high productivity in companies. We watched top performers at work, compared them with others who were decent but not quite as good, and identified two sets of behaviors that set apart the best from the rest—both of which we've written about in detail in our books *Crucial Conversations* and *Crucial Confrontations*.*

In each case, researchers compared the best to the rest and then discovered the unique and powerful behaviors that led to success. They didn't think up their ideas on the way to the mall. They didn't sit down and brainstorm techniques with their best friends. They didn't even ask top performers what they believed set them apart from their peers. Instead, they closely watched people with proven track records and discovered what caused them to succeed.

Of course, the real test of this and other forms of best-practice research comes when scholars take newly discovered vital behaviors and teach them to experimental groups. If they have indeed found the right behaviors, experimental subjects show far greater improvement in both the vital behaviors *and the desired outcome* than do control subjects. Consider Ethna Reid's success. Studies in Maine, Massachusetts, Michigan, Tennessee, Texas, North Carolina, South Carolina, Nebraska, Washington, Virginia, Hawaii, Alabama, and California have shown that, independent of the topic, pupils, school size, budget, or demography, changes in the vital behaviors Reid discovered improve performance outcomes that influence the entire lifetime of a child.

From this best-practice research we learn two important concepts. First, there is a process for discovering what successful people actually do. We know what to look for when examining others' claims that they've found vital behaviors. If the

---

*For more information on *Crucial Conversations* and *Crucial Confrontations*, visit www.vitalsmarts.com.

individuals who are offering up best practices haven't scientifically compared the best to the rest, found the differentiating behaviors, taught these behaviors to new subjects, and then demonstrated changes in the outcomes they care about, they're not the people we want to learn from.

Second, in many of the areas where you'd like to exert influence, the vital behaviors research has already been done. For example, if you want to learn how to live healthfully with type one diabetes, two vital behaviors have already been found: Test your blood sugar four times a day and adjust your insulin appropriately to keep your blood glucose in control. These two behaviors substantially increase the likelihood of a normal, healthy life. If you search carefully, you'll find that good scholars have found the vital behaviors that solve most challenges that affect a large number of people.

STUDY POSITIVE DEVIANCE

Let's add another tool that can help us in our search for vital behaviors. It draws from a long-tested methodology often used in social research and is known as *positive deviance*. To see how this method works, we look more closely at the Guinea worm efforts conducted in Africa and Asia.

The destructive pest has been largely eradicated by a strategy devised by a small team at The Carter Center and Centers for Disease Control and Prevention. Leaders from The Carter Center didn't have the luxury Ethna Reid had of conducting controlled laboratory experiments. It was simply not practical to study hundreds of villagers and perform statistical analyses on behavioral differences to arrive at the vital few they would then attempt to influence across the continent. They had to find a different strategy.

"Positive deviance" can be extremely helpful in discovering the handful of vital behaviors that will help solve the problem you're attacking. That is, first dive into the center of the actual community, family, or organization you want to change. Second, discover and study settings where the targeted problem should exist but doesn't. Third, identify the unique behaviors of the group that succeeds.

When members of The Carter Center team began their assault on Guinea worm disease, they used this exact methodology. They flew into sub-Saharan Africa and searched for villages that should have Guinea worm disease but didn't. They were particularly interested in studying villages that were immediate neighbors to locations that were rife with Guinea worm disease. Eventually the team discovered its deviant village. It was a place where people rarely suffered from the awful scourge despite the fact that the villagers drank from the same water supply as a nearby highly infected village.

It didn't take long to discover the vital behaviors. Members of the team knew that behaviors related to the fetching and handling of water would be particularly crucial, so they zeroed in on those. In the worm-free village, the women fetched water exactly as their neighbors did, but they did something different when they returned home. They took a second water pot, covered it with their skirts, and poured the water *through* their skirt into the pot, effectively straining out the problem-causing larvae. Voilà! That was a vital behavior. The successful villagers had invented their own eminently practical solution.

The team took copious notes about this and a handful of other vital behaviors. By studying the successful villagers, the team learned that water could easily be filtered without importing prohibitively expensive Western solutions.

To bring this a bit closer to home, let's briefly look at something many people have experienced—what seems like uncaring or insensitive medical care. In this case, a large regional medical center's service quality scores had been decreasing slowly and consistently for 13 consecutive months. Clinical quality was very good, but the scores showed that patients and their families didn't feel like they were being treated with care, dignity, and respect.

The chief administrator called the executive team together. He shared the data and made a proposal. The question he posed was this: "What do we have to do, all 4,000 of us, to fix this?" Two teams of respected employees, six to a team, were formed. Each team represented half the functions in the hospital. The teams were chartered with finding positive deviance. Locate those health-care professionals who routinely scored high on customer satisfaction in areas where others did poorly. They were not to worry about systems, pay, or carpet in the employee lounge, but behaviors they could teach others— behaviors that were both recognizable and replicable.

Each team interviewed dozens of patients and family members and sought ideas from colleagues in their hospital. They searched the Web and called colleagues in other hospitals. But mostly they watched exactly what top performers did to see what made them different from everyone else.

Eventually the teams identified the vital behaviors they believed led to higher customer satisfaction scores. They found five: Smile, make eye contact, identify yourself, let people know what you're doing and why, and end every interaction by asking, "Is there anything else that you need?"

The executives created a robust strategy to influence these behaviors. The result? As 4,000 employees started enacting these five vital behaviors, service-quality scores quit decreasing and improved dramatically for 12 months in a row. The regional medical center became best-in-class among its peers within a year of the executives' focus on these five vital behaviors.

SEARCH FOR RECOVERY BEHAVIORS

To explain the next search principle, we return to the Guinea worm problem The Carter Center tackled. In addition to discovering what the successful villagers had done to avoid contracting the parasite, the team also studied what the villagers did when an occasional worm did pop up in the village. Here team members exemplify our third search principle: Search for recovery behaviors. People are going to make mistakes, so you have to develop a recovery plan.

For instance, people in the healthier villages knew that they were most vulnerable to the spread of the parasite when a worm started to emerge from a person's body. As was stated before, the infected villager's only source of relief from the excruciating pain is to soak the limb in water. If the villager used the local water supply, it would be contaminated for yet another year.

The Carter Center team found that within the positive deviant villages, the locals took two recovery steps to cut off the disease cycle. First, villagers had to be willing to speak up when they knew their neighbor was infected. Once villagers realized that the worm came from unfiltered water, those who got the worm sometimes felt ashamed to admit their error. The vital recovery behavior, then, was that friends and neighbors had to speak up when the Guinea worm sufferer was unwilling to do so. Only when the community took responsibility for compliance could the entire village protect itself from the failure of a single villager. This crucial conversation triggered a response from village volunteers that enabled the second vital behavior: During the weeks or months it takes the worm to exit the victim's body, villagers had to ensure that he or she went nowhere near the water supply.

It turned out that if everyone in a village enacted these two recovery behaviors—speaking up and keeping infected people away from the water supply—for one full year, the worm would be gone forever. No new larvae would enter the water, and the Guinea worm would be extinct.

These same methods for discovering positive deviance can be applied almost anywhere. We (the authors) used the techniques to invigorate a massive quality effort in a large manu-facturing organization in the United States. A few hundred employees had been through several weeks of Six Sigma train-ing (a quality improvement program aimed at eliminating defects as completely as possible), but the company was seeing almost no benefit. For reasons that were hard to comprehend, Six Sigma graduates didn't appear to be applying any of the new tools they had spent weeks learning. To learn what was going on, two of the authors and a handful of managers went on a search for positive deviance. We were looking for the answer to two important questions: Had anyone in the company found a way to put the tools to work? And if so, could other teams apply the same techniques? It wasn't long until we found four teams that had enjoyed several Six Sigma successes despite the fact that most other teams were cynical about the effort and had given up on employing any of the new techniques.

What had the deviants done to avoid failure and the result-ant cynicism? When the researchers interviewed unsuccessful team members, they learned that their cynicism stemmed from three experiences. First, when they offered innovative ideas, their supervisor usually shot them down. Second, they had irre-sponsible teammates no one ever dealt with, and therefore they concluded that improvement ideas were a crock. And finally, they felt powerless to question management policies or deci-sions that appeared to obstruct their improvement efforts.

The successful teams were opposite in every respect. In these three dicey situations, they behaved in ways that kept them from becoming cynical. Their "recovery behaviors" involved stepping up to conversations their peers avoided. Team members vigorously but skillfully challenged their supervisor. They were candid with peers who weren't carrying their weight. And finally, they were capable of talking to sen-ior management—the same senior managers more cynical peers avoided—about policies or practices that they believed impeded improvements.

We concluded that the teams that had successfully implemented Six Sigma techniques did so not because they learned the methods better or had received more support from their bosses, but because they knew how to step up to crucial conversations.

The good news with positive deviance techniques is that these methods for uncovering vital behaviors are available to everyone. Start by examining the exact population and the setting you are interested in changing. Next, look for people who should be experiencing the problem but aren't. Then discover the unique behaviors that separate them from the rest. When applying positive deviance techniques to yourself, compare yourself to *you*. Think back to a time when you were successful, and figure out what you did that caused your success. Finally, take care to identify recovery behaviors as well.

TEST YOUR RESULTS

Let's add a word of caution. With standard research methods—such as the work done by Ethna Reid—scholars compare top performers to poor performers, codify and record behaviors, and then have the computer tease out the answer to what causes what. With positive deviance you typically don't have this luxury. Practitioners interview and watch successful subjects on site until they think they've discovered how top performers differ from their less successful counterparts. Then they draw conclusions about what causes success—in their heads.

There's the rub. Allowing one's brain to complete the final calculations can be dangerous. One can easily draw bogus conclusions. With Guinea worm disease, modern medicine explains the worm's entire life cycle, so when practitioners observed villagers filtering out larvae in their skirts or avoiding contact with their water source when the worm was emerging, they immediately and correctly concluded that these specific techniques eliminated the noxious worm.

With something as fuzzy as the ability to talk to others about high-stakes issues, it's less clear that this precariously "soft" interpersonal skill is the primary contributor to the Six Sigma training taking effect. Successful teams did report progress in this area as opposed to the cynical teams, but did the ability to talk openly actually *cause* the difference?

When you move from computer analysis to taking a guess on your own, you walk precariously close to the line that separates science from everything else. Crazy superstitions live off bogus conclusions. Whole companies can be brought to ruin when leaders respond to hunches.

Given the inherent dangers of watching and concluding on your own, it's essential to immediately follow up your conclusions about cause and effect with a test. Then you must teach your newly discovered vital behaviors to the failed groups and see if the behaviors you chose actually do cause the results you're trying to achieve. In the Six Sigma case, we (the authors) taught the three vital behaviors across the 4,000-person factory and saw immediate gains in the company's Six Sigma investments. With the Guinea worm, The Carter Center and CDC team has now eliminated the plague from 11 of the 20 countries that were afflicted when they began the campaign. Worldwide infections have dropped by over 99 percent because of an influence strategy that focused on three vital behaviors. Evidently, they were the right ones.

TRY THIS AT HOME

How about the home version of the search game? When you're not dealing with Guinea worms in sub-Saharan Africa or failed Six Sigma projects at a factory, you might wonder which search techniques, if any, could work for you personally. Henry Denton—our friend who is trying to lose weight—would certainly be interested in finding a handful of vital behaviors that would make it easier for him take the weight off.

A good starting point for Henry would be to search for experts who have already learned which actions are best for helping people lose weight and keep it off. He'd reject plans that focus on outcomes—that is, burn more calories than you eat—and he'd demand behaviors: vital behaviors.

If Henry did poke around, he'd discover that the National Weight Control Registry has identified vital behaviors for weight loss, using a method that compares the best to the rest. This institution tracks people who lose at least 30 pounds and keep it off for a minimum of six years. Their data reveal three vital behaviors. Successful people exercise on home equipment, eat breakfast, and weigh themselves daily.

These vital behaviors would give Henry a good start, but only a start. From there he'd need to ascertain which strategies work best for him given his unique circumstances. He could learn this by conducting his own version of a positive deviance study. That is, he would compare himself *to himself* by asking what makes a good weight day a "good weight day."

For example, as Henry considers times in his life when he's maintained a healthy diet, he realizes that lunchtime puts him in harm's way. When he goes out to a restaurant, if he thinks in advance about what he should order, he orders healthy food. If he doesn't, he splurges and eats all the wrong things. Shopping time is equally dangerous. He realizes that when he buys fatty foods, he eats fatty foods. It's far easier for him to resist buying unhealthy items than it is to resist eating them once they're in his home.

When Henry does indulge, he tends to feel depressed and to reason that since he's blown his plan, he might as well enjoy it. His one-time indulgence then expands to a week-long binge, and he packs on another five pounds. As he thinks about his vulnerabilities, Henry realizes that he needs to create a recovery plan when he does fall off the wagon or he'll continue to fall farther than if he had caught himself early. Next time he deviates, he'll reset his goals to accommodate his latest indulgence, and he won't try to play catch-up by eating too little or exercising too much. Instead he'll return immediately to his updated health plan and follow it carefully.

Finally, Henry will conduct dozens of mini experiments to learn what actually works for him. Rather than try any one thing and bet on it, he'll play with different exercise techniques, recipes, shopping patterns, restaurants, and so forth until he finds what suits him best.

SUMMARY: SEARCH FOR VITAL BEHAVIORS

Search for Behaviors. Take care to ensure that you're searching for strategies that focus on *behavior*. Don't let experts pass off outcomes as behaviors. You already know what you want to achieve; now you want to learn what to *do*. Be leery of vague advice. If you can't immediately figure out what the expert is telling you to do, then the advice is too abstract and could imply a number of possible behaviors—many of them wrong.

Search for *Vital* Behaviors. Master influencers know that a few behaviors can drive big change. They look carefully for the vital behaviors that create a cascade of change. No matter the size of the problem, if you dilute your efforts across dozens of behaviors, you'll never reach critical mass. If your problem is common, odds are the research has already been done for you.

When behaviors must be customized to your personal or local circumstance, look for vital behaviors by studying positive deviance. Look for people, times, or places where you or others don't experience the same problems and try to determine the unique behaviors that make the difference.

Search for *Recovery* Behaviors. People make mistakes, and yet some find a way to quickly get back on track rather than sink further into despair. Henry, for example, learned that failing to follow his dietary plan one day should cue him to look for where he went wrong and then to take corrective action—

and not to take the one-time failure as a sign that he won't be able to succeed and that therefore he should give in to his cravings.

Until Henry identified this and similar recovery behaviors, he was constantly taking two steps forward, followed by three steps back. Now when he runs into a problem, he stops his backward fall by using his mistake as a data point for learning and not as an indicator that he ought to give up. Recovery behaviors make up an important part of every change master's influence strategy.

Test Your Results. Finally, if you've conducted your own research and found candidates for what you think are high-leverage vital behaviors, test your ideas. Implement the proposed actions and see if they yield the results you want. Don't merely measure the presence or absence of the vital behaviors; also check to see whether the results you want are happening.

To make it easy to both surface and test vital behaviors, conduct short-cycle-time experiments. Don't hypothesize forever or put massive studies into place. Instead, develop the habit of conducting rapid, low-risk mini experiments.

Whether you conduct best-practices studies on your own, search for positive deviance, conduct mini experiments, or simply look for those who have already identified the vital behaviors for you, the point is the same. Don't glance around, take the first piece of advice from a friend, or rely on a hunch. Instead, follow the lead of influence geniuses everywhere. Conduct a genuine search for vital behaviors. If you don't, it won't be long before you'll be searching for serenity.

3

Change the Way You Change Minds

*There are three kinds of men, ones that learn
by reading, a few who learn by observation,
and the rest of them have to pee on the electric
fence and find out for themselves.*

—Will Rogers

O nce you've identified the behaviors you want to change, you're ready to do what most people are looking to achieve when they buy a book on influence— to convince others to change their minds. After all, before people will change their behavior, they have to want to do so, and this means that they'll have to think differently. But as you might suspect, when it comes to profound and resistant problems, convincing others to see the world differently isn't easy. In fact, others are very likely to resist your attempts to reshape their views. They may tenaciously hold onto outdated, irrational, or even crazy opinions.

To get at the heart of why people resist efforts to influence their view of the world—despite massive amounts of disconfirming data—let's return to Dr. Albert Bandura. He set out to create a theory of why people do what they do so that he and his colleagues could then come up with a method for getting them to act differently. Just like the rest of us, he was interested in exerting influence.

LEARNING FROM PHOBICS

When we last visited Dr. Bandura, he was watching a little girl in a frilly dress straddling a Bobo doll and whacking it with a mallet. His goal had been to demonstrate that humans can learn from observing others, thus averting the often tedious and painful school of trial and error. Having found that people do in fact learn from watching others in action, Bandura next turned his attention to helping people who suffered from highly inaccurate views. Albert turned his academic eye on finding a way to cure snake phobics.

Phobics provide a perfect set of beliefs for learning how to change people's thinking. First, phobics' feelings are not accurate, and they would benefit from having them changed. Second, phobics resist change at every turn. Learn how to alter the inaccurate beliefs of people who have clung to a wild idea for years despite the constant nagging of friends and loved ones, and you've got something to crow about.

To find plausible subjects, Bandura ran an ad in the *Palo Alto News* asking people who had a paralyzing fear of snakes to descend into the basement of the psychology department to get cured. He had hoped that at least a dozen subjects would respond. Despite the creepy tone of the ad, hundreds of people made their way to the research site. All had been seriously debilitated by their unreasonable fear of things that slither. Most had horrible nightmares, many were veritable shut-ins, and since their irrational fear extended to even harmless garter snakes, the possible subjects suffered endless ridicule and indignity. It's little wonder that they showed up for therapy; they were desperate.

HONEST, SNAKES ARE OUR FRIENDS!

With the stage set, Dr. Bandura and his team were ready to explore influence techniques. They could now study what it takes to convince people that some of their views are unfounded—thus propelling them to change their behavior. Success would be achieved when subjects could sit with a six-foot red-tailed boa constrictor draped across their lap. How hard could that be?

None of the subjects would so much as enter the room containing a snake in a covered terrarium.

Bandura did not start with the method most of us would have chosen—he did not lecture. When it comes to confronting people who hold unrealistic fears (or just plain stupid ideas), we've all done it. We figure that words, well chosen and expertly delivered, can set the record straight. Bandura knew that the best way to overcome a phobia is to confront what one fears and then to be enabled to exercise control over it, but he also recognized that lectures and coercion would only reinforce the phobic's dread and inability to act.

It turns out that phobics typically remain phobics because they rarely disconfirm their unfounded fears by approaching them head-on. Since lectures don't work with phobics and you can't get them to conquer their fear through personal experience, you have to find something in between—something more than words and less than personal action. This "in between" thing turns out to be one of the most highly valued tools in any influence genius's arsenal. It's referred to as *vicarious experience*.

Here's how vicarious experience works. When you expose subjects to other people who are demonstrating a vital behavior, the subjects learn from the surrogate's successes and failures. Watching others in action is the next best thing to experiencing something on your own. It's also far safer than, say, touching a six-foot nocturnal predator. In Bandura's case, he asked subjects to watch the therapist handle a snake in order to see what happened.

Bandura asked subjects to watch from the doorway of the room—or if that was still too difficult, to watch through glass—as the therapist walked into the room containing the snake, took a look at it, opened the terrarium, petted the snake, and finally removed the boa and placed it on his or her lap. After the subjects watched someone else handle the snake, Dr. Bandura then asked them to follow similar steps. First they had to simply walk into the room.

But this wasn't enough to put everyone at ease. Some of the subjects asked for protective gear—hockey goalie gloves, a baseball catcher chest protector and mask, and so on. Now, dressed like a samurai warrior, subjects entered the room and stood next to the enclosed tank. Gradually, after several tries they worked up to removing the terrarium cover and then quickly retreated from the room. No harm done. After a bit more experience, they finally touched the snake. Later still they touched the snake without gloves and so forth. Eventually subjects sat in the room by themselves with the six-foot constrictor draped across their lap.

And now for the real miracle: The entire process took only three hours! People who had been debilitated most of their lives by a paralyzing fear were completely "cured" in a single morning. And the results lasted a lifetime. Once the phobics had a personal and positive interaction with the snake, they never regressed, and it improved their lives forever.

In Dr. Bandura's own words, "It was surprising to see how liberating it was for the subjects to be freed from the phobia. Their whole life seemed to open up before them now that they didn't have to worry about snakes. In addition, they gained confidence about their ability to make personal changes. Since they had been able to conquer their fear of snakes, perhaps now they could overcome other problems."

WHAT DO WE LEARN FROM THIS?

Let's see what Bandura's work teaches us about human behavior. His theory of learning provides the underpinnings for virtually all the influence geniuses we've studied. Equally important, it helps us discover what we're trying to extract from this chapter—how to get people to change their minds.

People choose their behaviors based on what they think will happen to them as a result. First and foremost, humans are thinking creatures who can and do learn in a variety of ways. The thoughts that most profoundly affect behavior are composed of mini maps of cause and effect. For instance: "*If* I touch the snake, *then* it will wrap around my arm, drop me to the floor, crush me, and eat me like a large human Twinkie. *Therefore*, I'll stay away from the snake." At work an employee might believe that if she comes in late, nobody will care, leading to an erratic start time. Your daughter may believe that if she experiments with a party drug, it will be fun and that she'll only do it this once. So she gives it a try.

If you want to change behavior, any behavior, you have to change maps of cause and effect.

Many thoughts are incomplete or inaccurate, leading people to the disastrous, unhealthy, and inconvenient behaviors that are causing some of the problems they currently experience. It's important to note that people's interpretations of events trump the facts of any situation. And once again, not all interpretations are anchored in reality. Humans routinely create myths, fairy tales, silly misunderstandings, and phobias.

The factors influencing whether people choose to enact a vital behavior are based on two essential expectations. When trying to influence people into changing their behavior—by encouraging them to think differently—you don't have to unseat all their thoughts. For instance, believing that Sydney is the capital of Australia, while inaccurate, probably isn't going to be anyone's undoing.

When it comes to altering behavior, you need to help others answer only two questions. First: Is it worth it? (If not, why waste the effort?) And second: Can they do this thing? (If not, why try?) Consequently, when trying to change behaviors, think of the only two questions that matter. Is it worth it? (Will I be safe and become cured, or will the snake hurt me?) Can I do it? (Can I touch the snake, or will I hyperventilate and pass out when I enter the room?) If you want to change behavior, change one or both of these expectations.

The most common tool we use to change others' expectations is the use of verbal persuasion. We employ verbal persuasion as our first influence tool because not only is it enormously convenient (we carry our mouths with us everywhere), but it also serves us well because it works a great deal of the time. When people trust both our knowledge and our motives, they generally comply with our requests.

When it comes to resistant problems, verbal persuasion rarely works. Verbal persuasion often comes across as an attack. It can feel like nagging or manipulation. If people routinely enact behaviors that are difficult to change, you can bet that they've heard more than one soliloquy on what's wrong with them—and to no effect.

If the behavior you're attempting to get the other person to change is personally rewarding (as is the case with, say, most addictions) or linked to a deeply held belief system (as is the case with most traditions and credos), others will be particularly creative in coming up with arguments that support their existing view. People aren't about to give up what gives them intense pleasure or what constitutes an important window into their view of self simply because of a well-turned phrase.

Consequently, whenever you use forceful and overt verbal persuasion to try to convince others to see things your way, they're probably not listening to what you say. Instead, they're looking for every error in your logic and mistake in your facts, all the while constructing counterarguments. Worse still, they don't merely believe you're wrong; they need you to be wrong in order to protect the status quo. And since the final judge exists in their own head, you lose every time.

The great persuader is personal experience. With persistent problems, it's best to give verbal persuasion a rest and try to help people experience the world as you experience it. Personal experience is the mother of all cognitive map changers. For instance, even after watching others touch the snake, Bandura's phobics didn't completely change their views. After all, the stranger messing with the snake could easily have been a professional snake handler. Only after the subjects had handled the boa themselves to no ill effect did they change their minds.

Let's take a moment to consider the most profound and obvious implications of what we've just learned. When trying to encourage others to change their long-established views, we should fight our inclination to persuade them through the clever use of verbal gymnastic and debate tricks. Instead, we should opt for a field trip—or several of them. Nothing changes a mind like the cold, hard world hitting it with actual real-life data.

For example, a large U.S. manufacturing firm the authors once worked with was struggling to keep up with its Japanese competitors. The competitors produced more finished product per employee because their employees often worked faster and always worked more consistently. As a result, during an eight-hour shift, the Japanese workers completed around 40 percent more finished product than the American workers.

When the big bosses gathered the American employees in a large tent and told them that they had to work harder and faster if they wanted to keep their jobs, the speech almost caused a riot. Not only didn't employees believe the argument, but they turned on the bosses. "We're on to your tricks! You want to work us to death so you can earn your big fat bonuses!" was the common complaint.

After several more influence attempts that used snappy charts, multimedia effects, and well-rehearsed speeches, the employees still didn't believe that their competitors were 40 percent more productive. Realizing that words were cheap and that the hourly troops simply didn't trust the messengers anyway, the plant leaders arranged for a team of 10 hourly employees to get unprecedented access to a Japanese manufacturing plant. It was time for a field trip.

The leaders hoped that once the employees watched their hard-working Japanese competitors in action, they could see and hear for themselves just how serious the threat was. As you might guess, the hourly employees had their own agenda for the trip. They climbed into the jumbo jet for the sole purpose of exposing the bald-faced lie. There was no way that the Japanese employees worked harder than they did!

Ten minutes into the Japanese plant tour, the fact-finding team decided that it was all a sham. People were working hard, no question, but they were laboring at a pace that was far faster than normal because they were being watched. From that point on, nothing could convince the visitors that they were observing a normal day at work.

Later that night the team hatched a plot to uncover the lie. Team members quietly entered the plant unannounced and watched the Japanese night shift at work. Instead of catching their competitors plodding along and messing around (as they themselves often did back in the United States), the night-shift employees appeared to work, if anything, faster than the day-shift employees.

Now the visitors believed the threat. They didn't like it, but they believed it. Consequently, the born-again team members returned home with the mission of convincing their teammates that if they didn't find a way to work harder, one day they would all lose their jobs. But how could they convince their peers with anything other than a heartfelt trip report (read verbal persuasion on steroids)?

Create a surrogate for actual experience. Create a vicarious experience. The only way Bandura was able to convince phobics to do anything with a snake was through a surrogate. By watching what happened to other people, subjects were able to experience the outcomes almost as if they were their own. Nobody said a word to the phobics, and they were required to do nothing themselves, but when they watched others in action, they discovered that if a person touches a boa, nothing bad happens.

This is what the manufacturing fact-finding team would eventually have to do with their colleagues. They'd have to drop verbal persuasion as their primary influence tool and create a vicarious experience that worked with their peers.

CREATE PROFOUND VICARIOUS EXPERIENCES

Bandura and his team had discovered something profound. First, if you want people to change their persistent and resistant view of the world, drop verbal persuasion and come up with innovative ways to create personal experiences. Second, when you can't take everyone on the field trip, create vicarious experiences. This not only helped Bandura's team cure phobics in a matter of hours, but within a couple of years it became the primary technique for driving large-scale change efforts. In fact, over the past few decades, when aimed at social change, the effective use of vicarious models has saved millions of lives and improved the quality of life for tens of millions more.

And now the good news. Since most of you won't be leading a worldwide change effort any time soon, it's important to note that vicarious modeling is also one of the most accessible influence tools a parent, coach, community leader, or executive can employ.

Earlier we alluded to the work of Miguel Sabido and others who had clogged the streets of Mexico City with people in hot pursuit of adult literacy pamphlets. Previously, every attempt to encourage people to improve their lives by learning how to read and write had failed to produce more than a handful of interested people. Sabido changed that in a matter of weeks by creating a TV show that used protagonists to teach viewers important social lessons—not through speeches, but by living out their lives in front of everyone.

As you will recall, Sabido (a fervent student of Bandura) created a five-day-a-week soap opera called *Ven Conmigo* ("Come with Me"). At one point, a protagonist struggled over daily problems that largely stemmed from his inability to read and write. Eventually several of the characters decided to visit the country's adult education headquarters where they'd receive free adult literacy materials. To everyone's surprise, the next day over a quarter of a million people poured into the streets of Mexico City trying to get their own literacy booklets.

How did something as artificial as a TV soap opera yield such profound results? It created that all-important vicarious experience. When programs are presented as realistic stories dealing with real-life issues, viewers lower their defenses and allow the program to work on their thoughts in much the same way as they might experience the world for themselves. But this still left an important question unanswered. Was the vicarious modeling actually causing the changes?

To test the impact of vicarious models on human behavior, change advocate David Poindexter worked with Martha Swai, the program manager for Radio Tanzania, to transport serial dramas to Tanzania. There a local version of a *radio* play (not enough TVs in the area) was aired to certain parts of the population, but not others. By dividing the populace into experimental and control groups, researchers would be able to test the actual impact on such modeled behaviors as spousal abuse, family planning, and safe sex.

In 1993 when the show *Twende na Wakati* ("Let's Go with the Times") first aired, Swai and the producers chose to address HIV/AIDS transmission. This wasn't going to be easy because many of the locals held completely inaccurate beliefs about AIDS. For instance, some thought that you could be cured of AIDS by having sex with a virgin. To demonstrate the cause and effect of AIDS, writers created a flamboyant, macho, and highly controversial truck driver named Mkwaju. He abused his wife, wanted only male children, drank excessively, engaged in unprotected sex with prostitutes along his route, and bragged about his escapades. His wife, Tutu (a model for female independence), eventually leaves him and succeeds in her own small business.

The philandering Mkwaju (who eventually dies of AIDS) became so real to the listening audience that when the actor playing him went to a local vegetable market, villagers recognized his voice and women actually threw stones at him!

To see the emotional and behavioral impact firsthand, we (the authors) interviewed several listening groups just outside Tanzania's capital city. One family group consisting of a father, mother, grandmother, aunt, and five grown children had religiously tuned in to the wild antics of Mkwaju and had been enormously affected. When we asked them exactly how the program had influenced them, the father explained that at first he had admired Mkwaju, but with time he concluded that the truck driver's reckless behaviors were causing pain to his wife, Tutu, and their children.

After tuning in to the show for several weeks, the father had come to sympathize with all the characters, and one day when sweet Tutu was hurt by her alcoholic husband, a light went on—his own wife was also suffering from similar treatment. Although this avid listener wasn't a truck-driving philanderer, he had abused alcohol. A part of him was Mkwaju. From that moment on he stopped abusing both alcohol and his family members. It seemed strange that this self-discovery would come through a contrived radio show, but as the transformed father finished his story, everyone in his family nodded in energetic agreement. He had truly changed.

This touching account, along with similar interviews, provided anecdotal evidence that vicarious modeling appeared to be having an effect. But is there more than just anecdotal support for the power of this influence strategy? The answer is yes, and we know with a certainty because *Twende na Wakati* was the first controlled national field experiment in the history of the world. Since the Dodoma region of Tanzania was excluded from the evening radio broadcasts, researchers could explore the effect of the vicarious models offered over the radio. From 1993 to 1995 all regions experienced a variety of HIV/AIDS interventions, but only half were exposed to the radio drama.

In their award-winning book, *Combating AIDS: Communication Strategies in Action*, Everett Rogers and Arvind Singhal report that one-fourth of the population in the broadcast area had modified its behavior in critical ways to avoid HIV—and attributed the change in behavior to the influence of the program. The impact was so remarkable that the controlled experiment had to be stopped after two years in order to make the intervention available to everyone. Within a year, similar results were seen in Dodoma.

Rogers and Singhal proved with rare scientific certainty that exposing experimental subjects to believable models affected not only their thoughts and emotions but also their behavior. People who tuned in to *Twende na Wakati* were more likely to seek marital counseling, make better use of family planning, remain faithful to their spouses, and use protection than were their neighbors who didn't listen to the serial drama.

Change agents don't merely aim vicarious models at audiences in the developing world. Readers may not be aware of how effectively the same methods have been deployed in the United States. Before David Poindexter and others exported serial dramas to Africa, Poindexter met with Norman Lear—producer of popular TV sitcoms such as *All in the Family* and *Maude*. As part of their agenda to reduce worldwide population growth,

Poindexter, Lear, and others routinely injected family planning messages into their programming.

It was no coincidence that in 1972, with 41 percent of those watching TV in America tuned in to his show, Lear created an episode ("Maude's Dilemma") in which the star—a middle-aged woman—announced that she was considering an abortion. This was the first time this topic was inserted into a primetime plot line, and it wasn't included by accident. Love it or hate it, it was part of a systematic plan of using vicarious models to influence social change. And according to public opinion surveys, it did just that, as have dozens of other programs that have since made use of vicarious modeling.

USE STORIES TO HELP CHANGE MINDS

The implications of this discovery should be obvious. Entertainment education helps people change how they view the world through the telling of vibrant and credible stories. Told well, these vicariously created events approximate the gold standard of change—real experiences. And we all have our stories. That means we don't have to be a TV producer or serial-drama writer to exert influence. We merely need to be a good storyteller. We can use words to persuade others to come around to our way of thinking by telling a story rather than firing off a lecture. Stories can create touching moments that help people view the world in new ways. We can tell stories at work, we can share them with our children, and we can use them whenever and wherever we choose.

But not every story helps change minds. We've all been cornered by a coworker or relative who couldn't spin a tale to save his or her life. We've all attempted to tell a clever story only to have it come across as a verbal attack. What is it that makes certain stories powerful tools of influence, while mere verbal persuasion can cause resistance or be quickly dismissed and forgotten?

Understanding

Every time you try to convince others through verbal persuasion, you suffer from your inability to select and share language in a way that reproduces in the mind of the listener exactly the same thoughts you are having. You say *your* words, but others hear *their* words, which in turn stimulate *their* images, *their* past histories, and *their* overall meaning—all of which may be very different from what you intended.

For example, you excitedly tell a group of employees that you have good news. Your company is going to merge with your number-one competitor. When you say the word "merge," you're thinking of new synergies, increased economies of scale, and higher profits. It'll be lovely. When the people you're talking to hear the word "merge," they think of expanding their back-breaking workload, working with semihostile strangers, and layoffs. It'll be hell. Making matters worse, the inaccurate images being conjured up by the employees you're chatting with are far more believable and vivid than the lifeless words you used to stimulate their thinking in the first place.

Words fail in other ways. For example, we (the authors) met with Dr. Arvind Singhal, a distinguished professor of communication and social change at the University of Texas, El Paso. One of his doctoral students, Elizabeth Rattine-Flaherty, shared how verbal persuasion suffers from an even simpler translation problem. Sometimes others simply can't comprehend your words—even when you think your verbiage is crystal clear. While working with locals in the Amazon basin, Rattine-Flaherty learned that in the past, health-care volunteers had explained to the locals that if they wanted to reduce diseases, they needed to boil their water for 15 minutes. None of the villagers complied despite the fact that the contaminated water was obviously harming their health. Why? Because as volunteers learned later, the locals didn't know what the volunteers wanted them to do; they had no word in their language for "boil" or any way of thinking about and measuring time in minutes.

Verbal persuasion suffers in still another way. Instruction methods almost always employ terse, shorthand statements that strip much of the detail from what the messenger is actually thinking. Unfortunately, when we're trying to bring people around to our view of the world, intellectual brevity rarely works. In an effort to cut to the chase, we strip our own thoughts of their rich and emotional detail—leaving behind lifeless, cold, and sparse abstractions that don't share the most important elements of our thinking.

Effective stories and other vicarious experiences overcome this flaw. A well-told narrative provides concrete and vivid detail rather than terse summaries and unclear conclusions. It changes people's view of how the world works because it presents a plausible, touching, and memorable flow of cause and effect that can alter people's view of the consequences of various actions or beliefs.

Believing

Very often, people become far less willing to believe what you have to say the moment they realize that your goal is to convince them of something—which, quite naturally, is precisely what you're trying to achieve through verbal persuasion.

This natural resistance always stems from the same two reasons—both are based on trust. First, others might not have confidence in your expertise. Why would anyone listen to a moron? Parents experience this form of mistrust when their children roll their eyes at their outdated and irrelevant guardian who can't figure out something as simple as how to store a phone number in a cell phone. Since dad is incompetent in all things technical, why should anyone trust his dating advice or his constant warning about running up too much credit-card debt?

Second, even when others find you to be perfectly competent, they may mistrust you in the traditional sense of the word—they may doubt your motive. You offer up a sincere explanation, but others figure that you're trying to manipulate them into doing something that will harm them and benefit you. For instance, in Tanzania many of the locals believed that when Western social workers encouraged them to use condoms, it was a trick to actually pass HIV/AIDS to anyone who was naive enough to believe the propaganda. They hadn't originally believed that condoms caused AIDS, but now that the recommendation was coming from suspicious outsiders with questionable motives, perhaps they did indeed cause the disease.

Stories mitigate both forms of mistrust. Told well, a detailed narration of an event helps listeners drop their doubts as to the credibility of the solution or the change being proposed. When they can picture the issue in a real-world scenario, it helps them see how the results make sense.

Stories take advantage of a common error of logic. We've all heard people make lame arguments such as: "Wait a minute. My uncle smoked cigars, and he lived to be a hundred!" When we know for certain that a real person stands as evidence against a factual argument, we tend to discount the hard data—even when the data are based on far more information than a single case.

To test the memorability and credibility of stories, one of the authors, along with Dr. Ray Price and Dr. Joanne Martin, provided three different groups of MBA students with exactly the same information. In one case, the students were given a verbal description that contained facts and figures. Another group was given the same information—only it was presented through charts and tables. The final group was provided the very same details presented as the story of a little old wine maker.

To the researchers' surprise, when tested several weeks later, not only did those who had heard the story recall more detail than the other two groups (that was predicted), but they also found the story more credible. MBA students gave more credence to a story than to cold hard facts.

But why? Why do even the most educated of people tend to set aside their well-honed cynicism and critical nature when listening to a story? Because stories help individuals *transport themselves* away from the role of a listener who is rigorously applying rules of logic, analysis, and criticism and into the story itself. According to creative writing expert Lajos Egri, here's how to transport the listener into a story.

> *The first step is to make your reader or viewer identify your character as someone he knows. Step two — if the author can make the audience imagine that what is happening can happen to him, the situation will be permeated with aroused emotion and the viewer will experience a sensation so great that he will feel not as a spectator but as the participant of an exciting drama before him.*

Concrete and vivid stories exert extraordinary influence because they transport people out of the role of critic and into the role of participant. The more poignant, vibrant, and relevant the story, the more the listener moves from thinking about the inherent arguments to experiencing every element of the tale itself. Stories don't merely trump verbal persuasion by disproving counterarguments; stories keep the listener from offering counterarguments in the first place.

Motivating

And now for the final dimension that sets stories ahead of plain verbal persuasion: human emotions. Finding a way to encourage others to both understand and believe in a new point of view may not be enough to propel them into action. Individuals must actually care about what they believe if their belief is going to get them, say, off the comfortable couch and into a gym. At some point, if emotions don't kick in, people don't act.

As Lajos Egri suggested, not only do vibrant stories transport the listener into the plot line, but when they're told well, stories stimulate genuine emotions. When they're transported into a story, people don't merely *sympathize* with the characters—having an intellectual appreciation for others' plight— they *empathize* with the characters. They actually generate emotions as if they themselves were acting out the behaviors illuminated in the story.

To understand how this transportation mechanism might work, let's examine, of all things, monkey brains. In an effort to understand how actions affect localized brain neurons, Italian researchers Giacomo Rizzolatti, Leonardo Fogassi, and Vittorio Gallese placed electrodes into the inferior frontal cortex of a macaque monkey. As the researchers carefully mapped neurons to actions, serendipity stepped in.

Rizzolatti explains: "I think it was Fogassi, standing next to a bowl of fruit and he reached for a banana, when some of the neurons reacted." The monkey hadn't reached, but the monkey's neurons associated with reaching fired anyway. These weren't the neurons that reflect thinking about someone else reaching; these were the neurons that supposedly fire only when the subject reaches.

The "mirror neurons," as Rizzolatti labeled them, were first identified as relatively primitive systems in monkeys. It was then discovered that such systems in humans were sophisticated and "allow us to grasp the minds of others not through traditional conceptual reasoning, but through direct stimulation—by feeling, not by thinking."

It's little wonder that the group of Tanzanian women who had listened to *Twende na Wakati* threw stones at the main actor when saw into him in person. They didn't run up to him and ask for his autograph or chat with him about the villainous character he portrayed. Since the listeners had experienced, right along with the faithful and devoted wife Tutu, the actual emotions connected to her husband Mkwaju's abusive philandering (mirror neurons firing away), they did what a lot of victims might have done under the circumstance—they tried to get even with the lout who had wronged them.

This empathic reaction also explains why thousands of television viewers and radio listeners around the world routinely write letters to the characters in serial dramas and soap operas thanking the characters for giving them hope or for teaching them valuable lessons. In very real ways, these vivid stories create vicarious experiences that become both intellectual and emotional parts of the viewers' lives.

MAKE STORIES WORK FOR YOU

Let's review what we're trying to achieve. To emulate the work of influence masters worldwide, we're trying to create changes in behavior by helping people alter their mental maps of cause and effect. When we find a way to change how individuals think, they're well on the way to changing their behavior. Equally important, we've learned to limit our change targets by aiming at two important maps that help people answer the questions: "Will it be worth it?" and "Can I do it?" Change one or both of these maps, and people change their behavior.

To help people come to a more accurate view of cause and effect, we've argued that it's best to set aside one's preference for verbal persuasion and to use methods that are far more understandable, believable, and compelling than your standard lecture or pep talk. This calls for the judicious use of actual and vicarious experience. Finally, since most of us aren't going to be in the phobic-curing or radio-drama business any time soon, we should become experts in the use of the most portable and readily available map-changing tool around—the poignant story.

Become a Master Storyteller

We start by returning to the manufacturing task force whose members came racing back from Japan because they wanted in the worst way to tell their coworkers that if they didn't work harder, they'd all be out of a job. And that's exactly what they did: They told them in the worst way! They gathered a group of their peers together and announced their finding— their competitors actually did produce 40 percent more per employee by working faster and more consistently. At the end of this rather terse and unpopular announcement, the members of the task force were booed off the stage by their own union brothers and sisters.

Undaunted, the world travelers brought another group together and told them the shortened version of what had happened. More boos. Finally, the team leader selected the best storyteller and set him loose on the next assembly of employees. He didn't ruin the message by quickly cutting to the chase—"Workers unite or we're dead!" Instead, this gifted storyteller took a full 10 minutes to narrate in vivid detail what had taken place.

The members of the task force had arrived in Japan, and to a person they were absolutely certain the foreigners they would soon observe would put on a show. Sure enough, they did (jeers). But the task force wasn't fooled (cheers). Next, the storyteller related how they had sneaked into the plant after hours and spied on the enemy (more cheers). But wait a second; the employees were working even faster (silence). This was depressing. If the Japanese workers continued to outperform the American workers, the Japanese companies could keep their costs down and dominate the market. American companies would downsize, and American workers would lose their jobs.

After they spied on the Japanese workers, the members of the task force returned to their hotel and tried to figure out how to beat their competitors at their own game. Then it hit them. Why not work on the Japanese line and see if they could handle the jobs? For the next couple of days they stepped into a variety of the jobs on the Japanese production line and performed them quite readily. It was work, but nothing they couldn't handle (more cheers). And finally the punch line: "If we take the right steps, we can take our fate back into our own hands and save our jobs" (raucous applause).

Now employees were ready to listen to the improvement plan that called for them to work harder. By sharing what had happened in narrative form, the narrator was able to communicate that, first, they could do what was required (hadn't the task force proven that by working the line?), and second, it would be worth it (by articulating the consequences of not working harder, the storyteller helped the audience see that it would be worth it). By telling a vivid story, he was able to share these two all-important messages in a way that was understandable, credible, and motivating.

Tell the Whole Story

Note that the task force members first tried to influence their colleagues by short-cutting the story—stripping it of its compelling narrative and leaving out much of the meaning and all of the emotion. Unaware of the limitations of verbal persuasion, the eager employees offered up what amounted to a verbal attack. As human beings, we do this all the time. Even the well-intended designers of national social programs fail to make the best use of stories. Not on purpose, of course, but when change agents attempt to tell a compelling story and inadvertently leave out key elements of the narrative, they render it impotent.

Consider what happened with the much vaunted program *Scared Straight.* As part of this "American success story," law-breaking teens were transported to prisons where hardened criminals shared horror stories about the evils of life in the big house. As the title of the program suggests, the young people were supposed to be completely horrified by the stories and thus scared straight.

Only it didn't work that way. When researchers took a closer look at the program, they learned that teenagers who had been given the scare tactics had no fewer encounters with the law than their counterparts who stayed home. Why? Because the *Scared Straight* program left out an important part of the story. By the end of the inmate show-and-tell, it was clear that prison was bad. The delinquents were convinced. They never wanted to go to prison.

What the inmates didn't make clear was that if the teenagers continued doing what they were doing, they would eventually be caught and sent to prison. And since most teenagers harbor an illusion of personal invulnerability, they didn't connect the dots on their own. They didn't create the full cognitive map: "If I keep doing what I'm doing, I'll get caught, and, if I get caught, I'll then go to prison. Therefore, I'll straighten out my life now." Instead, they believed that they would continue committing crimes and never get caught, so the whole prison ordeal was irrelevant.

Provide Hope

The takeaway here is that you don't want to merely share poignant and repulsive negative outcomes. Make sure that your story also offers up an equally credible and vivid solution.

For instance, consider what happened to a team of Stanford researchers who told only the negative part of a story to their subjects. The researchers showed subjects disgusting pictures of rotting gums as a means of compelling them to floss their teeth. That should keep them brushing and flossing, right? It turns out though that viewing the pictures had no long-term effect on the subjects. The researchers didn't offer any corrective steps—subjects were not given the solution to the problem.

In the short run subjects made minor adjustments, but fear itself didn't lead to lasting change.

The same is very likely to be true for a current spate of TV ads that show shocking scenes of people in body bags or vivid pictures of lungs that have been destroyed by smoking. These poignant commercials, no matter how many video awards they may garner, are also unlikely to change long-term habits if they don't offer viewers an option for the next steps to take to avoid these terrible ends. Although the pictures are vibrant, they fail to tell the whole story. They don't tell people how to solve the problem, and when you leave out the solution, people typically block out the message.

So, when trying to help people view the world in a more complete and accurate way, couple your stories of the harsh realities you're facing with equally concrete and vivid plans that offer hope. Tell the whole story. Provide hope.

Combine Stories and Experiences

We've focused a lot here on the power of stories to change minds. However, frequently the story may be enough to help people open their minds, but may not entirely *change* their minds. In these cases, master influencers use stories as a first step to inviting others into sharing personal experiences. Personal experiences are far less efficient at creating change since they often take substantial resources to orchestrate. But as we saw with the cynical manufacturing team, you can combine the direct experience of a few with the stories *they* can then tell to others to magnify a modest influence investment.

Vicarious narratives can be used in combination with actual experience to great advantage. In fact, stories are often told for the sole purpose of propelling people into their own personal experience. Consider the work of Dr. Don Berwick, clinical professor of pediatrics and health care policy at Harvard Medical School, and head of the Institute for Healthcare

Improvement (IHI). In a recent interview, Berwick shared an alarming statistic: The National Academy of Science reported that 44,000 to 98,000 people are killed by their health care every year, placing medical injury as the eighth largest public health hazard in America.

In December 2004, Dr. Berwick stood in front of a group of thousands of health-care professionals and issued an audacious challenge: "I think we should save 100,000 lives. I think we should do that by June 14, 2006." Pause. "By 9 a.m." The success of the 100,000 lives campaign is now in the record books. At the time of the writing of this book, IHI upped the ante with a 5 million lives *worldwide* campaign.

One of Berwick's greatest challenges is to help caring professionals recognize that their own health-care systems might be causing harm—prolonging hospital stays and even killing patients.

As you might imagine, telling physicians that they may be inadvertently putting patients in harm's way isn't an easy message to share. These are folks whose purpose in life (to which they take a sacred oath) is to provide assistance, to cure, and if nothing else, to do no harm. These are highly skilled professionals who often fail to recognize how their individual actions play out in a large, complex human system. So how can Berwick engage energy and curiosity without provoking defensiveness?

He tells stories. For example, the story of Josie King is one for which Berwick and his colleagues have a deep reverence.

MEET JOSIE KING

Josie King was a little girl who loved to dance. She was 18 months old, had brown eyes and light brown hair, and she had just learned to say, "I love you." In January of 2001 Josie stepped into a hot bath and burned herself badly. Her parents rushed her to Johns Hopkins Hospital where she was admitted into the pediatric intensive care unit. Much to her parents' relief, Josie recovered quickly. She was transferred to the inter-mediate-care floor and was expected to be released within days.

But Josie's mom noticed that something was wrong. "Every time she saw a drink, she would scream for it, and I thought this was strange. I was told not to let her drink. While a nurse and I gave her a bath, she sucked furiously on a washcloth." Josie's mom told the nurse Josie was thirsty, and asked her to call a doctor. The nurse assured her that everything was okay. She asked another nurse to check on Josie, but this nurse con-firmed that everything was fine.

Josie's mom called back twice during the night and was at her daughter's bedside by 5:30 the next morning. By then Josie was in crisis. In her mother's words, "Josie's heart stopped as I was rubbing her feet. Her eyes were fixed, and I screamed for help. I stood helpless as a crowd of doctors and nurses came running into her room. I was ushered into a small room with a chaplain." Two days before her scheduled release, Josie had died of thirst. Despite her mother's repeated pleas for help, this sweet little girl died of misused narcotics and dehydration.

This story makes dedicated physicians and other health-care professionals cry out, "How could this happen?!" In fact, this story is so powerful that it fills doctors, nurses, and administra-tors with outrage. But it often falls short of generating enough reflection. While everyone concludes, "How could they let this happen?" too few take the next logical step and ask, "Are we letting this happen?"

When Berwick hears "I'm certainly glad it doesn't happen here," he wisely steers clear of accusation or judgment—some-thing he is adamant would be wrong. "The problem is not bad people; it's bad systems." So he invites the system's constituents to form a story into an experience.

At this point Dr. Berwick asks, "Are you sure? Could we check that out? Let's count back the last 50 deaths in your hos-pital and answer the following questions: How did the patients die? Were they expected to die? What could have been done to prevent the deaths?" Finally, Dr. Berwick asks leaders to do their *own* detective work (they can't assign someone else the task) and return to tell the stories they've uncovered.

Many from the audience bring back their own Josie King stories. Berwick describes a group of senior executives (each led entire health-care systems) reporting back their results at a Harvard round table. One after another, they told their stories and broke down in tears. They described their personal experience as "life changing." For the next decade some of these executives became leaders in the effort to improve safety within hospitals.

CHANGING MINDS WORLDWIDE

As a way of pulling together everything we've discussed, let's return to The Carter Center's Guinea worm eradication program and watch how use is made of both stories and experiences as a way of changing minds at a global level—one village at a time.

Consider what the team did in Nigeria. To begin with, former President Jimmy Carter recruited General Gowon to join the Nigerian team. Former President-General Gowon is beloved by Nigerians for bringing stability and democracy to their country, so the day the general visits a village is one of the most important in its history. After dances, songs, and a tour, General Gowon explains that he brings great news! He asks how many in the village suffer from the "fiery serpent." He then explains that he has come to teach them how to rid themselves of the serpent forever.

The general then asks the villagers to bring him water from the pond. They bring him a clay jug full of water. He pours water into a clear quart bottle for all to see. This is a new experience for most villagers who carry their water in buckets or pots. Now they're examining their murky water for the first time.

The general shows them a magnifying glass, and asks them to use it to look at the water and tell him what they see.

Someone describes the many tiny fleas swimming and darting around. Everyone gets a look, and most are disgusted. As they watch, the general covers another glass bottle with a cloth filter, pours the pond water from the same pot through the filter into the second bottle, and invites everyone to take a look. Not only are all the insects gone, but the water has changed from a cloudy yellow color to a clear liquid.

The beloved general then asks the villagers which they would rather drink. Everyone points to the clear water. He hands it to the chief who drinks the filtered water and reports that it is good.

While holding everyone's absolute attention, the general now tells them about a village not too far away. It too suffered horribly from the Guinea worm. Many of these neighboring villagers could not work. Their crops rotted in the field. Many died. Then the general taught them how to destroy the worm by filtering the water. The nearby villagers followed everything the general instructed them to do for two full years. After one year, no one in the village had the serpent. After the second year, they knew for sure it would never come back.

"You can do what they did and be free of the fiery serpent forever," the general promises them.

The villagers nod thoughtfully. They are not entirely convinced. But the compelling experience and convincing story have brought them to at least suspend their disbelief. General Gowon has begun to change their minds. This is the first step in helping them change their behavior.

SUMMARY: CHANGING MINDS

People will attempt to change their behavior if (1) they believe it will be worth it, and (2) they can do what is required. Instill these two views, and individuals will at least try to enact a new behavior or perhaps stop an old one. To change one or both of these views, most people rely on verbal persuasion. Talk is easy, and it works a great deal of the time. However, with persistent and resistant problems, talk has very likely failed in the past, and it's time to help individuals experience for themselves the benefits of the proposed behavior. It's time for a field trip.

When it's impossible to create an actual experience, it's best to create a vicarious experience. For most of us, that means we'll make use of a well-told story.

Stories provide every person, no matter how limited his or her resources, with an influence tool that is both immediately accessible and enormously powerful. Poignant narratives help listeners transport themselves away from the content of what is being spoken and into the experience itself. Because they create vivid images and provide concrete detail, stories are more understandable than terse lectures. Because they focus on the simple reality of an actual event, stories are often more credible than simple statements of fact. Finally, as listeners dive into the narrative and suspend disbelief, stories create an empathic reaction that feels just as real as enacting the behavior themselves.

Tell the whole story. Make sure that the narrative you're employing contains a clear link between the current behaviors and existing (or possibly future) negative results. Also make sure that the story includes positive replacement behaviors that yield new and better results. Remember, stories need to deal with both "Will it be worth it?" and "Can I do it?" When it comes to changing behavior, nothing else matters.

Part

2

Make Change Inevitable

Who shall set a limit to the influence of a human being?
—*Ralph Waldo Emerson*

L et's say that you've discovered the vital behaviors that need to be enacted to help resolve a profound and persistent problem you're facing. You've also helped everyone involved see the need for change. Now how do you actually go about making that change happen?

To answer this question, let's return to Guinea worm disease eradication efforts in North Africa—this time to a town in Nigeria. Imagine that you're following General Gowon. He has been to this village to help dislodge the flawed beliefs that have kept villagers from changing their behavior. Minds have been changed. Certainly changing behavior will be a snap. So what's the next step?

Most of us have our favorite influence methods—just pass a law, just threaten a consequence, or just offer a training program. The problem with sticking to our favorite methods is not that the methods are flawed per se; it's that they're far too simplistic. It's akin to hiking the Himalayas with only a fanny pack. There's nothing wrong with Gatorade and a granola bar, but you'll probably need a lot more. Bringing a simple solution to a complex and resistant problem almost never works.

Nevertheless, people bet on single-source influence strategies all the time. For instance, ask leaders how they're planning to change their employees from being clock-punchers to quality zealots, and they'll point to their new training program—the same one that they're convinced drove General Electric's stock through the stratosphere in the 1990s. The training content might provide a start, but when it comes to creating a culture of quality, it'll take a great deal more than a training class. Ask politicians what they're doing to fight crime, and they'll tell you that they're working hard to secure harsher sentences for felony convictions. Also not enough to have much of an impact. Ask community leaders what steps they're taking to stem the growing plight of childhood obesity, and they'll sing the praises of their latest pet project—removing candy machines from schools.

And let's be honest. How many of us haven't yearned for a quick fix for our own problems? A miracle diet pill, a magical marriage solution, or a $500 set of DVDs that promises financial freedom. Just give us that *one thing*, and we're ready to roll.

But it takes a combination of strategies aimed at a handful of vital behaviors to solve profound and persistent problems. In fact, this is the core principle demonstrated by virtually all the change masters we studied. No single strategy explained their success. In fact, it became quite evident that individuals who succeed where others have routinely failed *overdetermine* success—that is, they bring more influence strategies into play than they might assume would be the minimum required for success. They leave nothing to chance.

This could sound discouraging. In Chapter 2 we shared the good news that it often takes only a few vital behaviors, routinely enacted, to bring about massive and lasting changes. Now we're adding the idea that, while you need to affect only a few behaviors, behind each you'll uncover a number of forces that either encourage or discourage the right action and an equal number of forces that either enable or block the correct behavior. Ignore these varied and sundry forces at your own peril.

Fortunately there's additional good news. We now know enough about the forces that affect human behavior to place them into a coherent and workable model that can be used to organize our thinking, select a full set of influence strategies, combine them into a powerful plan, and eventually make change inevitable.

MASTER SIX SOURCES OF INFLUENCE

Here's how the model works. As we've said before, virtually all forces that have an impact on human behavior work on only two mental maps—not two thousand, just two. At the end of the day a person asks, "Can I do what's required?" and, "Will it be worth it?" The first question simply asks, "Am I able?" The second, "Am I motivated?" Consequently, no matter the number of forces that affect human action—from peer pressure in a junior high school to making citizens aware of the cost of illiteracy in a barrio to offering a class on anger management in Beverly Hills—all these strategies work in one of two ways. They either motivate or enable a vital behavior. Some do both.

Motivation and ability comprise the first two domains of our model.

We further subdivide these two domains into personal, social, and structural sources. These three sources of influence reflect separate and highly developed literatures—psychology, social psychology, and organization theory. By exploring all three, we ensure that we draw our strategies from the known repertoire of influence techniques.

Let's quickly look at the range of influence sources effective influencers draw upon. Don't worry if they aren't crystal clear at this point. Over the next six chapters, we explain the various influence methods in detail. In fact, you're likely to see how many of them account for improvements you've made in your own life. But for now, you'll know how to consciously draw upon this robust set of sources any time you need.

At the personal level, influence masters work on connecting vital behaviors to intrinsic motives as well as coaching the specifics of each behavior through deliberate practice. At the group level, savvy folks draw on the enormous power of social influence to both motivate and enable the target behaviors. At the structural level, top performers take advantage of methods that most people rarely use. They attach appropriate reward structures to motivate people to pick up the vital behaviors. And finally, they go to pains to ensure that *things*—systems, processes, reporting structures, visual cues, work layouts, tools, supplies, machinery, and so forth—support the vital behaviors.

With this model at the ready, influence geniuses know exactly which forces to bring into play in order to overdetermine their chances of success.

Pictorially, we can display these six sources of influence in the following model.

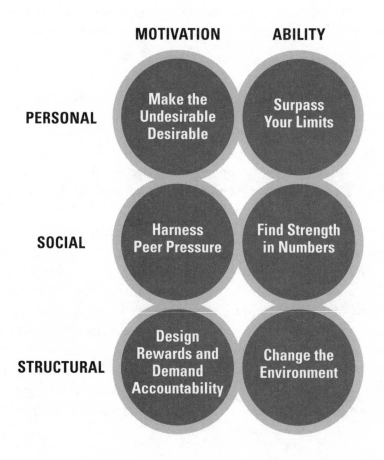

To better understand how each of these six sources operates, let's return to the village in Nigeria where we show up with visions of annihilating the nasty Guinea worm. We know that villagers need to enact only three vital behaviors in order to eliminate the worm. First, people must filter their water. How hard could that be? Second, should someone still become infected, he or she must not make contact with the public water supply until the infection has run its course. Just stay away from the water. And third, if a neighbor is not filtering water or becomes infected, the villagers must confront him or her.

Since we know the three behaviors that will eradicate the Guinea worm, it sounds as if our influence project won't be particularly complicated. However, before we start giving heartfelt speeches and handing out four-color pamphlets, let's see how each of the six sources of influence affects this actual project.

Source 1: Personal Motivation. When the Guinea worm is exiting a victim's body, the pain is absolutely excruciating. Since victims can't merely yank the worm out of their arm or leg without the worm breaking and causing a horrific infection, they're forced to wind the parasite around a stick and slowly edge it out over a couple of weeks—or even a couple of months. There's only one source of relief during this prolonged ordeal, and that's for victims to soak their painful sores in water. That means that individuals are personally motivated to do exactly the opposite of one of the vital behaviors—stay away from the water. If you don't deal with *personal motivation*, your influence plan will fail.

Source 2: Personal Ability. Many of the villagers don't know how to properly filter water. They've been trying since General Gowon left, but the Guinea worm disease is still rampant. When they take the steps to filter the water, they'll carelessly slop over a splash here and a drop there, infecting the water supply and continuing the infestation. Or they'll transfer filtered water into a pot that's still moist with unfiltered water. They'll need training to enhance their *personal ability*.

Source 3: Social Motivation. Next, when you sit down with the locals to teach them how to eliminate the Guinea worm, nobody is going to pay very much attention to your advice. You're an outsider and as such simply can't be trusted. You may be in good with the chief, but there are three tribes in the village, two of which resent the chief and will resist anything you offer *because* he's behind it. Unless circumstances change, you have a serious problem with *social motivation*.

Source 4: Social Ability. People in a community will have to assist each other if they hope to succeed. When it comes to an outbreak, nobody can make it on his or her own. If ever there was a circumstance where the expression "It takes a village" applies, this is it. For example, if someone comes down with the worm, others may have to fetch water for him or her. And when it comes to filtering, locals often have to buddy up in order to have enough pots to both fetch and filter water. If locals don't enlist the help of others, you'll be missing the key factor of *social ability*.

Source 5: Structural Motivation. Given the villagers' current financial circumstances (living hand-to-mouth), individuals who become infected can't afford to stay away from work. This forces them to labor in and around the water supply. Quite simply, to put food on the table, they'll need to fetch water for both their crops and livestock. This means that the formal reward system is at odds with the three vital behaviors. Infected people earn money only if they work near the water source. If you don't compensate for the existing reward structure, victims will be compelled to serve their families at the expense of the entire village. Try to move forward without addressing *structural motivation,* and your influence won't reach far.

Source 6: Structural Ability. Lastly, locals don't have all the tools they need to filter the water or to care for their wounds in a way that keeps them away from the community water source. Worse still, the layout of the village makes access to the public water supply so easy and natural that it's enormously tempting for victims to merely plunge their aching arm or leg into the water—at the peril of everyone else. If you don't work on this last source of influence, *structural ability*, you're also likely to fail.

MAKE USE OF ALL SIX SOURCES

Now that we've explored how all six sources of influence came into play with the Guinea worm project, it's easy to see why influence geniuses take pains to address each source when going head to head with a profound and persistent problem. Leave out one source, and you're likely to fail.

Throughout the remainder of this book—to demonstrate how the six sources can be applied in combination—we explore what Dr. Silbert has done with each of these influence tools to help transform lifelong felons into productive citizens. At the home level, we follow an individual who is trying to lose weight and see how each of the six sources might apply to this widespread (pun intended) problem. Finally, we'd ask you to pick a challenge of your own and read each of the six chapters with that problem in mind. Then fashion your own six-source influence strategy. Do it correctly, and like Dr. Silbert and dozens of other successful influencers, you'll solve problems that have had you and others stumped for years.

4

Make the
Undesirable Desirable

PERSONAL MOTIVATION

Hard work pays off in the future. Laziness pays off now.
—Steven Wright

In this chapter we examine the first and most basic source of motivation—intrinsic satisfaction. This source of influence asks the question: Do individuals take personal satisfaction from doing the required activity? That is, does enacting the vital behavior itself bring people pleasure? If not, *how can you get people (yourself or others) to do things they currently find loathsome, boring, insulting, or painful?*

For example, how could you ever convince a lifetime drug addict to withstand the pain of withdrawal long enough to get clean? Or for that matter, how might you motivate a terrified nurse to tell an intimidating doctor that he needs to wash his hands more thoroughly before examining patients?

If you can't find a way to change a person's intrinsic response to a behavior—if you can't make the right behaviors pleasurable and the wrong behaviors painful—you'll have to make up for the motivational shortfall by relying on external incentives or possibly even punishments. You know what that's like. Your son hates taking out the garbage, so you load on the "pretty pleases" or threaten to ground him through puberty. Your employees despise completing quality checks, so you have to harp on them every few hours. The guy who owns the empty lot next to your house hates keeping it neat (as required by the community code), so you have to keep ratting him out to the local authorities. And guess what. If you stop grounding, harping, or ratting folks out, they'll stop doing what they're supposed to be doing because *they don't like doing it.*

The point? If we could only find a way to make a healthy behavior intrinsically satisfying, or an unhealthy behavior inherently undesirable, then we wouldn't need to keep applying pressure—*forever.* The behavior would carry its own motivational power—forever.

So here's our first question. Can you actually change how humans experience a behavior? Naturally, we're not talking about simply adding a spoonful of sugar. That's cheating. We're asking whether it's possible to change the meaning of a behavior itself from loathsome to gratifying, from pleasurable to disgusting, or from insulting to inspiring.

It sounds impossible, but if you ask gifted influencers, their unequivocal answer will be, *of course you can.* And you *must.*

TUESDAY AFTERNOON

It's 3:17 Tuesday afternoon. Terri is carrying a CD loaded with financial data from the accounting office to the Delancey Street Restaurant. The manager asked her to bring it over ASAP, so she logged into her computer, burned the data onto the disc, and headed for the restaurant.

What surprises Terri is how quickly her feet are moving. She can't recall the last time they moved this fast. From the time she was nine, she had perfected a purposefully casual gait. She took great pride in her "I'm okay/you suck" approach to life. No matter that this attitude had landed her in jail for most of her adolescent years. No matter that it earned her a manslaughter conviction after someone looked at her sideways in a bar. Nobody was going to tell her what to do. Nobody.

So why is Terri walking so fast now? It's been 19 months since she was offered a tour at Delancey Street rather than serving her last five years in prison. Every semester, Terri has attended Delancey's graduation ceremony. It's a grand gathering where all 500 residents of the San Francisco campus crowd into the main hall to celebrate each other's progress. The first two times Terri was recognized for her accomplishments, she stared at the floor and ignored whatever they were saying about her. *"Who gives a flying leap that I now know how to set a frigging table? This is all a stupid game, and I'm not playing it!"* When the applause for Terri had died down, she walked back to her chair, unaffected.

But last week they talked about her diploma and her promotion to crew boss. She looked over at Dr. Silbert, who was waving her arms and barking out Terri's amazing accomplishment. And Terri made the mistake of listening to what Silbert said—just for a second. Then came the wave of applause. Terri looked around the room and caught the eyes of a few of her crew members. Then she looked quickly back down at the floor. Her legs felt weak when she walked back to her chair.

"I'm not sure what that is," she mumbled to herself. "I'm probably just hungry." She ate a candy bar.

Now as Terri rushes to the restaurant, she looks down again, only this time at her legs. They're moving so fast it's as if they have a mind of their own. And then she lifts her hand to her cheek and feels something wet. *"I don't do this. What the hell is this?"* Terri is crying.

MAKE PAIN PLEASURABLE

So, what has happened to Terri? Is she actually enjoying work that she once despised? It's almost as if she *enjoys* accomplishing something. She's found pleasure in her work. Better still, she's learned to care about something. In Terri's own words, "After thinking about it all afternoon, I finally realized, I was crying because *I cared*. I cared that I got the disc to Lionel. I cared."

If that's true, if Terri has found a way to enjoy something that she had previously disliked, what might your average person extract from this? For example, what mysterious trick might you pull in order to help your son *want* to do his chores? Could this same magic potion make a team *enjoy* the work involved in reducing errors to below 3.4 per million? And can you use Terri's mystical elixir to make eating mini carrots as enjoyable as wolfing down a slice of chocolate cream pie?

Actually, people do learn ways to take pleasure from almost any activity, even if an activity isn't inherently satisfying. Psychiatrist M. Scott Peck makes this point rather bluntly:

> *Just because a desire or behavior is natural, does not mean it is . . . unchangeable. . . . It is also natural . . .*

to never brush our teeth. Yet we teach ourselves to do the unnatural. Another characteristic of human nature—perhaps the one that makes us more human—is our capacity to do the unnatural, to transcend and hence transform our own nature.

The promise here is significant. If we can find a way to change the feeling associated with a vital behavior, we can make compulsive bad habits feel as disgusting as going to bed with gritty teeth. And we can make formerly unappealing activities become as satisfying as brushing our teeth. And if you miss this important concept, whenever you try to motivate yourself or others to change behavior, you'll turn to perks and wisecracks rather than find ways to make the activity itself more inherently attractive.

To see how to accomplish all of this transcending and transforming, we must first understand where our likes and dislikes come from. Once we have a handle on the origins of pleasure and pain, savvy influencers will teach us what to do with this knowledge.

Many of our preferences come from our biology. We have powerful desires for things like food, drink, warmth, rest, sex, and air. But biology isn't always destiny. Despite our hardwiring, some biological drives—or at least their impacts on our preferences—are surprisingly easy to change. You'll recall that back in the early 1900s, students of Ivan Pavlov completed dozens of studies that used buzzers, metronomes, or bells to signal dogs that food was coming. After being fed on cue several times, the dogs would begin to salivate whenever they heard the signal.

This kind of learning, using a neutral stimulus to signal a reward or punishment, is called *classical conditioning*. What's relevant to our discussion of changing what people derive satisfaction from is that classical conditioning causes dogs and people to "like" or "hate" the bell. When we use a neutral stimulus to signal a strong positive or negative event, we nudge it off neutral.

Brian Wansink, a consumer behavior psychologist, shows how classical conditioning influences something as basic as food preferences. He surveyed World War II veterans who had served in the South Pacific. He discovered that about a third of them loved Chinese food, while another third hated it. What made the difference? They had all eaten Chinese food during the war—it was all they had to eat. The third who had experienced heavy combat during the periods where they ate Chinese food hated it. The third who had been away from the front lines loved it. The soldiers had been classically conditioned to love or hate Chinese food, and these preferences remained 50 years later. In short, the preference was both learned and durable.

While Pavlov's experiments linked bells to something positive (food), other researchers used cues to signal something less desirable—say an electric shock. To no one's surprise, it turns out that fear and pain create even more dramatic changes in preferences. Remember the book A *Clockwork Orange*? Alex, a particularly nasty hoodlum, is given "aversive therapy." Prison doctors play images of violence choreographed to Beethoven's Ninth Symphony while giving Alex drugs that make him severely nauseous. The aversive therapy worked so well that Alex could no longer defend himself—or enjoy Beethoven.

But, alas, this is all more of a curiosity than a helpful tool. Although negative associations can indeed cause profound change in preferences, you won't find effective influencers using aversive or other aggressively manipulative methods. Shock collars all around, right? Wrong. They avoid painful techniques because they are ethical, principled, and nice people.

So, if we shouldn't poke people with sharp sticks as a way of propelling them away from their inappropriate behavior, what's left? Actually, there are two very powerful and ethical ways of helping humans change their reaction to a previously neutral or noxious behavior: creating *new experiences* and creating *new motives*.

CREATE NEW EXPERIENCES

A little knowledge is a dangerous thing. Sometimes people loathe the very thought of a new behavior because they lack adequate information to judge it correctly. They imagine what a new behavior will feel like, and their predictions come up negative. Unfortunately, they're often wrong.

Get People to Try It

This problem of guessing incorrectly about how an activity might make one feel is neither odd nor inconsequential. The average human being is actually quite bad at predicting what he or she should do in order to be happier, and this inability to predict keeps people from, well, being happier. In fact, psychologist Daniel Gilbert has made a career out of demonstrating that human beings are downright awful at predicting their own likes and dislikes. For example, most research subjects strongly believe that another $30,000 a year in income would make them much happier. And they feel equally strongly that adding a 30-minute walk to their daily routine would be of trivial import. And yet Dr. Gilbert's research suggests that the added income is far less likely to produce an increase in happiness than the addition of a regular walk.

Dr. Silbert confronts this inability to predict happiness every single day. It's her job to ask new residents at Delancey Street to do things that, to them, sound painful, boring, or both. For example, lifetime criminals have no idea what a law-abiding life might be like. When they do try to imagine it, they make some very predictable errors. They assume that it will be very much like their present life—minus the fun. You know, cleaning toilets while giving up the excitement of crime or the stimulation of drugs. They're unable to imagine the pleasure associated with getting a raise, owning a home, or any of a thousand other parts of a law-abiding life they've never experienced.

Silbert could spend a lot of time painting a picture of the Delancey vision. "Trust me," she could say, "you're gonna love it. By the time you're out of here, you'll have a high school diploma. You'll be literate. You'll have gone to concerts and museums. You'll have mastered three different trades and tried a dozen others. You'll have a whole new set of friends. Just sign here."

Right.

These arguments are easy to make but hard to sell because they involve verbal persuasion and the people you're talking to don't understand the language. You're describing activities and outcomes for which they have no frame of reference, and you're then asking them to make enormous immediate sacrifices (no gang, no drugs, no freedom) in order to achieve them. It won't work. It can't work.

Silbert realizes that it'll take a while before new residents *personally experience* the benefits of a new life. She explains, "After they get their high school equivalent, we offer two-year degrees through San Francisco State. Some even get a BA. But early on, residents hate the discipline that it takes to study. We also go with them to museums, operas, plays. Oh, believe me, they whine like crazy. They don't want to go. But I just keep saying, 'You can hate Chinese food, but not until after you've *had* Chinese food.' Coming in, our residents hate everything. But of course they've never done *anything!*"

So Dr. Silbert simply plods forward, demanding that residents try studying for a class, attending the opera, mentoring another student, and so forth. Experience has taught her that if residents try new behaviors, they end up liking many if not most of them. Okay, perhaps few become opera fans. Nevertheless, over 90 percent come to enjoy dozens of behaviors they never would have imagined they'd one day enjoy.

Silbert sticks with it until that Tuesday at 3:17 (Terri's experience) finally hits. She says it happens to virtually everyone at Delancey. There comes a day when residents become a person they've never met—and they like it. They care. They take satisfaction in accomplishment. They've discovered the intrinsic satisfaction that comes with living a law-abiding life.

The "try it, you'll like it" strategy can be further aided by the use of models. Many of our influence masters have found that vicarious experience can work in situations where they can't get people to try a vital behavior based on faith alone. For example, as you recall from an earlier chapter, Miguel Sabido inspired hundreds of thousands of illiterate Mexicans to sign up for literacy programs by engaging them in the story of a man *just like them*—someone who was "too old to learn." Someone who was initially unwilling to bear the shame of sitting in a class with much younger people and admitting his "defect."

Week after week as Sabido's audiences experienced the journey to literacy and *vicariously* experienced what it would be like to be able to read, it began to mean something. They imagined just how entertaining life would be with access to fascinating books. They saw the effect a grandparent could have on grandchildren. They felt what it would be like to have the sense of pride that comes from graduating from literacy class. And eventually they shut down the streets of Mexico City with their deluge of requests for literacy information that was advertised on the series.

What do you think happened when all these new people arrived at their first reading class? They quickly found that learning to read was difficult and not always a whole lot of fun. They couldn't go home that night and read to their grandchildren. Fortunately, the characters in the television show had demonstrated the difficult side of the learning process, so it wasn't a huge surprise. People understood the pleasures of reading, but knew they'd have to work to become proficient before these pleasures would be theirs.

Make It a Game

Let's look at another way of transforming neutral or detestable behavior into something enjoyable. Let's say an individual tries the new behavior but still doesn't like it all that much. Now what? Take hope from the fact that humans invest themselves in a wide variety of pursuits that on the surface don't look particularly engaging or rewarding, and yet somehow they extract enjoyment. So, what's the trick?

It turns out that one of the keys to motivation lies in a force just barely outside the activity itself. It lies in the mastery of ever-more challenging goals. Mihalyi Csikszentmihalyi, a researcher at the University of Chicago, has devoted his career to what he has come to call "flow" or the feeling of enjoyment that comes from losing yourself in an engrossing activity. He has discovered that almost any activity can be made engaging if it involves reasonably challenging goals and clear, frequent feedback. These are the elements that turn a chore into something that feels more like a game.

For example, imagine that you removed the scoreboard from a basketball court. How long would you expect fans to stick around without knowing the score? How long do you think the players would run breathlessly up and down the court destroying their knees with every step? Much of what we do to transform intrinsically unpleasant behavior into something enjoyable is merely to turn it into a game.

Keeping score produces clear, frequent feedback that can transform tasks into accomplishments that, in turn, can generate intense satisfaction. The designers of many of today's video games have an intuitive feel for Dr. Csikszentmihalyi's research and have used it to create games that call for highly repetitive activities that end up being amazingly addictive as individuals strive for that next level of achievement.

CREATE NEW MOTIVES

The "try it, you'll like it" strategy assumes that people will find a new activity rewarding if they just give it a chance. But many activities produce few natural rewards. They're also very difficult to transform into a game through constant feedback. What can you do when neither the activity itself nor the natural feedback the activity produces are inherently pleasant or motivating?

This is an important question because many important human endeavors fall into this "not inherently pleasant" category. For example, if you're a villager with five Guinea worms burning their way out of your body, your sole focus will be on finding relief. You're in pain, and you want it to stop. "Try gutting it out, and you'll like it" won't work here. Adding a scoreboard (how long can you stay away from the water?) is equally unlikely to change your experience. So what's left? How can you help people *not want* to run and plunge their body into the pain-relieving water supply when they crave relief right now?

Connect to a Person's Sense of Self

Unpleasant endeavors require a whole different sort of motivation that can come only from within. People stimulate this internal motivation by investing themselves in an activity. That is, they make the activity an issue of personal significance. Succeeding becomes more than the challenge of reaching the next level on a video game—it becomes a measure of who they are. They set high standards of who they'll be, high enough to create a worthy challenge, and then they work hard to become that very person.

For example, meet Grigori Perelman. Grigori worked his head off for years in his dingy apartment in St. Petersburg,

Russia. A few years ago the grizzled and gawky math wiz did the formerly impossible. He solved the Poincare Conjecture—a problem no other mathematician had been able to solve despite a century of intense worldwide effort. It's a problem so arcane that most of us wouldn't even understand the question.

Here's what's interesting about Perelman. He did it just for fun. The only way the world discovered that Grigori had solved the problem was that he went to the minimal trouble of posting the solution on a Web site. After spending years of his life in intense concentration, with no compensation or reward, Perelman celebrated his dramatic accomplishment with a Web posting.

What kept Perelman going for all those years? It certainly wasn't the fame or fortune. His obscure Web posting caught the attention of the judges of mathematics' version of the Nobel Prize. And for that reason alone he was offered the Field Medal for Mathematics—and a $1 million prize. Perelman refused both. He was on to his next task and wanted only to be left alone. He sits today in his cramped St. Petersburg apartment working on another problem.

Perelman is unique in his mathematical skills, but his source of motivation is so common and so profound that every influence genius needs to master its use. The most powerful incentive known to humankind is our own evaluation of our behavior and accomplishments. When people are able to meet their personal standards, they feel validated and fulfilled. They also feel as if they're living up to the image of who they want to be.

In this particular case, Perelman probably exacted pleasure from all three of the intrinsic sources we just discussed. He reveled in the accomplishment, loved the challenge of the game, and took pleasure in acting true to the vision of who he wanted to be. When Perelman conquered the Poincare Conjecture, he felt a satisfaction so deep and pure that the million-dollar prize would have only spoiled it for him.

Engage in Moral Thinking

Most of us aren't Perelman or anything like him. In addition to the fact that we're not math savants, we also don't pursue a passion the way he does. Many of us spend much of our days going through the motions without associating what we're doing with a sense of greater purpose. Consequently, these intrinsic sources of motivation are almost never brought into play. Why is this?

Often humans react to their immediate environments as if they were on autopilot. They don't pause to consider how their immediate choices reflect their ideals, values, or moral codes. The connections between their actions and personal standards are rarely "top of mind." Michael Davis calls this failure to connect values to action, "microscopic vision." Ellen Langer calls it "mindlessness." Patricia Werhane prefers to refer to it as a lack of "moral imagination."

No matter their terms, each of the scholars was referring to the human tendency to burrow into mundane details while failing to consider how they connect to our values, morals, and personal standards. This means that when we make horrific and costly mistakes, more often than not we're not purposely choosing to do bad things. It's almost as if we're not choosing at all. It's the *lack* of thought, not the *presence* of thought, that enables our bad behavior.

As disconnected and unreflective as we may be during our daily activities, it only gets worse when we feel threatened or challenged. Under stress, when our emotions kick in, our time horizons become even shorter, and we give less weight to our abstract values. For instance, Robert Lund, vice president of engineering at Morton Thiokol, sat in a meeting in January of 1986 where a group of very smart people deliberated about whether or not to allow the space shuttle Challenger to launch.

Lund is a good guy. He's a family man. He's a good neighbor. He's an upstanding citizen. He rose to his rank as a senior engineer at Thiokol because of his professionalism, dedication, and attention to detail. Yet in the January meeting, Lund behaved in a way that begs understanding. Days earlier Lund's engineering staff had warned him that no one knew how O-rings would perform at very low temperatures. The previous lowest launch temperature had been 54 degrees Fahrenheit. Expectations were for a 26-degree launch. If the O-rings failed, the consequences could be disastrous.

Now Lund is sitting in a launch meeting. NASA is asking for hard data showing that O-rings would fail at the low temperature. Lund has to make a decision. As he's trying to decide what to say—what stand to take—his supervisor says to him, "Take off your engineering hat and put on your management hat." And that did it. Suddenly the moment transformed into management decision making. No longer was it about protecting lives. With a modest verbal shift, Lund's feelings about what he needed to do changed. Unproven O-ring risks were just a management uncertainty—of which there are many. Saving lives was no longer the top priority. Lund assented to the launch. The rest is history.

Robert Lund moved from torturing over moral issues to managing uncertainty as he buried himself in the details of the risk analysis. When Lund needed to be at his best with his most moral behavior, he was at his worst. And we all do it. When facing the harsh demands of the moment, instead of acting on our values and principles, we react to our emotions by shortening our vision and focusing on detail. We act against our own values in a way that we ourselves would otherwise abhor. If only we could step away from the moment and take a look at the big picture.

So, here is the challenge influencers must master. They must help individuals see their choices as moral quests or as personally defining moments, and they must keep this perspective despite distractions and emotional stress.

To learn how to link people's actions to their values—in gracious and effective ways—we return to our reliable guide, Dr.

Albert Bandura. Bandura has repeatedly looked at the question, How can we stimulate people to connect their actions to their values or beliefs? and has turned it on its head by asking, How is it that people are able to maintain *moral disengagement*? That is, how do people find ways to enact behaviors that appear so clearly at odds with their espoused values?

Bandura's research has uncovered four processes that allow individuals to act in ways that are clearly disconnected from their moral compass. These strategies that transform us into amoral agents include moral justification, dehumanization, minimizing, and displacing responsibility.

Let's turn to a real-life case to see how these four processes work in combination to keep people morally disengaged. When Dennis Gioia, Ford recall director, looked at "graphic, detailed photos of the remains of a burned out Ford Pinto in which several people had died," you would think he would have immediately issued a recall of the car. And yet he didn't. Data showed that a 30-mile-per-hour rear-end collision would cause the fuel tank to rupture, causing unspeakable injury or death to the passengers. And now Gioia was staring at the devastating result. The good news was that a fix would cost a mere $11 per vehicle.

But Gioia didn't issue a recall because he had been trained to use cost-benefit analysis when reviewing equipment, and that's what he did. The National Highway Traffic Association set the value of a human life at $200,000, so a simple calculation of the cost of the recall revealed that the greatest dollar benefit would come from keeping the vehicle cheap and settling inevitable claims. Perhaps there would be a hundred or so such claims.

Gioia's training established a moral framework that justified what others would call manslaughter. And lest we judge him too harshly, take note that we all do something similar every day. When we accept lower prices rather than demand stiffer pollution standards, we are, in essence, making life harder for some number of individuals who have weak respiratory systems.

And yet we don't think of the issue in those terms. Like Gioia, who thought of *claims*, not *lives*, we think of *costs*, not *health*.

As Bandura suggested, we're able to justify our behavior by focusing on other moral outcomes—e.g., we're making the product affordable to the masses. In so doing, we dehumanize those who may be affected by our choices. Then we attempt to minimize and justify our actions. "It's only 100 lives. Compare that to the hundreds of thousands of people who will benefit from this vehicle." Finally, we displace responsibility: "I didn't set the rules for cost-benefit analysis. This is just the way it's done."

The only way out of the nasty practice of disconnecting ourselves from our moral grounding is to reconnect. This means that we must take our eyes off the demands of the moment and cast our view on the larger moral issues by reframing reality in moral terms. And we have to do it in a way that is both vibrant and compelling. Simple lectures, homilies, and guilt trips—verbal persuasion at its worst—won't work. If we don't reconnect possible behavior to the larger moral issues, we'll continue to allow the emotional demands of the moment to drive our actions, and, in so doing, we'll make short-term, myopic choices.

Connect Behavior to Moral Values

When we inspect our actions from a moral perspective, we're able to see consequences and connections that otherwise remain blocked from our view. Renowned psychologist Dr. Stanton Peele reports that taking a broader moral perspective enables humans to face and overcome some of their toughest life challenges. In fact, Peele has been able to systematically demonstrate that this ability to connect to broader values predicts better than any other variable who will be able to give up addictive and long-lasting habits and who won't. Peele has found that individuals who learn how to reconnect their distant but real values to their current behavior can overcome the most addictive of habits—cocaine, heroine, pornography, gambling, you name it.

At Delancey, Mimi Silbert follows Peele's advice by helping residents connect behaviors to values every single day. As we suggest earlier, when residents first arrive at Delancey, they're told that everyone must challenge everyone. New residents view this action as "ratting out their buddy." Ratting is morally despicable. It's disloyal. No decent person would do it. So no one does it—certainly no one from their previous life. Should a friend head out Delancey's front gate in search of a fix, residents' old credo would tell them to be loyal and clam up. And they'll continue to act this way unless they can recast the behavior of "ratting" into more positive moral terms. Then residents will challenge every wrong action according to the code.

Sure enough, Silbert helps them do just that. She reframes the habit of reporting violations to the authorities as a vital behavior, even a mission, that carries with it profoundly moral meaning. She doesn't merely hint at the morality of the code; she fully embraces it. In her own words:

> Our approach here is kind of an odd one. We talk morals all the time. Although I studied criminology and psychology, I approach these issues as if I have no idea what causes criminal behavior. We just say, "This is our family and this is our home. And in our home, here's what we believe. Here's what we do. Here's why. If you turn others in, it helps them. We do it because we must help each other if we want to succeed." We develop a community based on simple moral ideas and then make the norms so strong that the community sustains them.

Silbert believes that if people can make their behavior part of a broader and more important moral mission, they can do almost anything, including giving up crime, drugs, and violence.

Listen to her argument. She's working with a population that walks in the gate with zero self-esteem, so she teaches residents how to regain their sense of worth by connecting to a broad moral mission. She explains, "I don't like the word *self-esteem*. Ultimately if you don't *earn* your own self-respect, you'll tear yourself apart. No one else can give it to you. It doesn't come from sitting in a group and having someone say, 'I feel very good about you.' . . . *You* convince *yourself* over time that you're good, and it takes hard work.

"But you can't do it alone. You don't get it by someone helping you. You get it by you helping someone else. It's being the helper that makes you like yourself. So will you confront people who screw up? Yes, you will. Will you take responsibility for someone else's problems? Yes, you will. And when you do, you'll respect yourself. Because you matter when you matter to someone else."

So there you have it. Dr. Silbert connects behavior—in this case behavior that is originally cast in ugly terms ("ratting")—to consequences, values, and an overall sense of morality. Does it work? Can this kind of old-fashioned moral motivation help residents reengage their sense of responsibility and self-control? Delancey has no guards, no locks, no restraints. Just thousands of success stories.

Spotlight Human Consequences

Let's see where we are. We're trying to find a way to make good behaviors intrinsically pleasurable and bad ones objectionable. To do so, we're looking at how to tap into people's overall values and moral framework as a means of transforming unpleasant behavior into pleasant activities.

Now let's turn our attention to the other side of the coin. People are doing bad things—let's say they're abusing other people—but without feeling bad about themselves or what they are doing. And when we say *abuse*, let's define it in the broadest sense. In addition to crimes against humanity, let's include ignoring the legitimate needs of a customer, eliminating jobs with no consideration for the human toll, setting up another department to fail, or parking in a handicapped spot for a quick dash into the grocery store.

How can humans so easily disconnect their behavior from the negative outcomes they're causing? What can influence masters do to help people connect their behavior to their results and in so doing reconnect people to their espoused values of treating others with dignity and respect?

First, we must understand how people can abuse others without feeling bad. The mechanism that allows people to act viciously, but with impunity, is actually quite simple. When we see less of the humanity of another person or when we disrespect people, it becomes easy for us to dismiss our actions toward them. We're nice to good people, but bad people, well, they deserve whatever we give them.

Albert Bandura tested this proposition in a way that shows just how insidious dehumanization can be. He asked, "Can a *one-word label* that minimizes a victim's humanity turn good people into perpetrators?" Here is how the study worked.

Bandura told subjects that they'd be helping to train students from a nearby college by shocking them when they erred on a task. Their shock box had 10 levels of intensity that they could deliver over 10 trials. Just as the study was about to begin, the subjects were allowed to "overhear" an assistant talking to the experimenter. The assistant uttered one of three phrases:

Neutral: "The subjects from the other school are here."

Humanizing: "The subjects from the other school are here. They seem *nice*."

Dehumanizing: "The subjects from the other school are here. They seem like *animals*."

From this point on Bandura did not pressure subjects to use the shock box. The decision was completely up to them. And here's what Bandura found: The subjects who imagined their victims seemed like animals shocked them at increasing levels over each trial, giving them significantly more punishment than those who had heard the neutral phrase. The subjects who had heard the humanizing phrase shocked their victims at significantly lower levels.

The one-word label was enough to cause good people to become perpetrators.

Dr. Don Berwick, head of IHI's 100,000 Lives Campaign, identifies still another way we routinely dehumanize people and their circumstances by transforming them from people into cold, hard data. In this case, Berwick explains how safety problems can be unwittingly minimized by some health-care executives as they dehumanize the problem.

"Executives aren't ignoble, but they can become insulated—a little out of touch." And it's no wonder. These executives are routinely overwhelmed with streams of data that demand immediate responses. Information overload plays a role in this problem, but more important is the abstract quality of the information that transforms human disaster into facts and figures.

Most executives get their information in the form of cold numbers that don't carry much emotional weight. "Abstraction poisons the type of energy I need," Berwick continues to explain. "When raw personal trauma is boiled down into the same kind of spreadsheet or graph used to track laundry, too much of its essence is lost. When an executive sees a number in a spreadsheet, not a patient with a gaping wound, it's easy to imagine the negative outcome isn't quite as bad as it really is."

As a result of this dehumanization, executives can easily view patient safety data with detachment. Instead of giving them special treatment or priority, the executive considers them alongside every other spreadsheet number on the desk.

The way Berwick helps executives reconnect to the human elements of every safety problem is by creating powerful vicarious and direct experiences. As we explained earlier, Berwick relies on stories and significant emotional events to increase his ability to create change. Were he to use the much-abused tool of verbal persuasion, particularly facts and figures, he'd lose both credibility and power. Ironically, when you want an individual disaster—one with a name and a face—to seem even more important, you're tempted to bundle it with dozens of other individual disasters into a one-lump "impressive" number. In so doing, you drop the names, the faces, and the humanity; eventually you also drop your ability to exert influence.

Dr. Berwick never makes this mistake. Instead he helps hospital CEOs create vicarious experiences by asking them to, "Find an injured patient in your system and investigate the injury. Don't delegate it. Do it yourself. Then return and share your story." The CEOs Berwick is working with already know the statistics about hospital injuries and accidental deaths. But what makes them "zealots for quality improvement" from that experience forward is the dramatic experience they have firsthand with human consequences. They can no longer remain morally disengaged through the use of dehumanizing statistics because they now know a *name*.

Now for a corporate application. If you're a leader attempting to break down silos, encourage collaboration, and engage teamwork across your organization, take note. Moral disengagement *always* accompanies political, combative, and self-centered behavior. You'll see this kind of routine moral disengagement in the form of narrow labels ("bean counters," "gear heads," "corporate," "the field," "them," and "they") used to dehumanize other individuals or groups. To reengage people morally—and to rehumanize targets that people readily and easily abuse—drop labels and substitute names. Confront self-serving and judgmental descriptions of other people and groups. Finally, demonstrate by example the need to refer to individuals by name and with respect for their needs.

Win Hearts by Honoring Choice

Let's get tactical for a minute. As you do your best to help others take more pleasure from healthy activities and less pleasure from unhealthy activities, you'll need to choose your tactics carefully. When you attempt to help others reconnect their behaviors to their long-term values or moral anchors, you often come off as preachy or controlling and generate a great deal of resistance. Of course, the more you try to control others, the less control you gain. This is particularly true with individuals who are addicted to their wrong behavior. They have already suffered through the impassioned speeches of their loved ones, listened to the clever audio CDs from the experts, and squirmed in their pew as their minister has harangued them for their self- and other-defeating actions.

Nevertheless, these offenders have been able to withstand the shrill cry to return to the right path because they aren't accidentally disengaged from their moral compass; they're purposefully disengaged. The lack of a connection between their actions and their values is so obvious and the resultant dissonance so painful that they openly and aggressively resist anyone who has the nerve to shine a light on the humiliating discrepancy. Verbal persuasion and other control techniques aren't going to work with these folks.

William Miller is the influence expert who has found a way to help addicts connect to their moral compass and thus greatly improve their life habits. He started his impressive research by asking the simple question, "What's better—more therapy or less?" and found that the length of time therapy lasted was irrelevant. This finding, of course, made him extremely unpopular with the vast majority of people who worked in the field. Next he asked, "Is there one therapeutic technique that works better than others?" and found that the method didn't matter much either.

After offending almost everyone in his field by undermining the apparently irrelevant distinctions upon which people build careers, he stumbled onto an interesting finding. He found a distinction that *did* matter. It had to do less with what the counselor *did* than with what the counselor *didn't do*.

A reigning but inaccurate assumption in counseling is that confrontation motivates change. But despite all the hoopla about family interventions and counselor-led confrontations, Miller learned that forcing people to face their demons along with their friends, colleagues, and therapists who hated those demons also didn't work. In fact, in one study, he found that confrontation actually increased alcoholic binging. This led Miller in a different direction. He began to explore the opposite. What if the counselor merely helped patients figure out what *they* wanted rather than what their fed-up friends wanted?

With the new question, Miller discovered that the best way to help individuals reconnect their existing unhealthy behaviors to their long-term values was to stop trying to control their thoughts and behaviors. You must replace judgment with empathy, and lectures with questions. If you do so, you gain influence. The instant you stop trying to impose your agenda on others, you eliminate the fight for control. You sidestep irrelevant battles over whose view of the world is correct.

This discovery led Miller to develop an influence method called *motivational interviewing*. Through a skillful use of open and nondirective questions, the counselor helps others examine what is most important to them and what changes in their life might be required in order for them to live according to their values. When you listen and they talk, they discover on their own what they must do. Then they make the necessary changes.

Dozens of studies have shown Miller's approach to be effective in helping people overcome alcoholism, smoking, drug addiction, HIV risk behaviors, and diet failures, and to improve things like psychiatric treatment adherence and exercise commitments. And the additional good news is that the power of motivational interviewing isn't limited to therapeutic settings. Smart leaders accomplish the same results when they replace dictates with dialogue.

For example, Ralph Heath, now president of Lockheed Martin Aeronautics, was tasked by the company to move the fifth generation F-22 fighter jet from drawing board to production floor in 18 months. To do so, he had to engage 4,500 engineers and technicians who had developed a decade-long culture of invention. Heath had to convince them that results mattered more than ideas and that engineering needed to bow to production. Tough sell.

So Heath didn't sell; he listened. He spent weeks interviewing employees at all levels. He tried to understand their needs, frustrations, and aspirations. When he finally began issuing orders, he framed them in ways that honored the needs, concerns, and goals of his colleagues. His influence didn't result from merely confronting problems, but from listening to people.

What William Miller teaches us is that a change of heart can't be imposed; it can only be chosen. People are capable of making enormous sacrifices when their actions are anchored in their own values. On the other hand, they'll resist compulsion on pain of death. The difference between sacrifice and punishment is not the amount of pain but the amount of choice.

Ginger Graham, the CEO of the medical devices company Guidant, learned this in a crisis. After the company introduced a new cardiovascular stent, sales went through the roof. Graham wrote of this in her April 2002 article for the *Harvard Business Review* titled, "If You Want Honesty, Break Some Rules." Almost overnight, demand for the stent far outstretched supply. And all this hit as the holidays were approaching. Executives figured that just meeting demand until new sources of production could come online would require three full shifts and seven-day weeks. Graham could have simply mandated the work and required people to fill their obligations. But she knew that wouldn't work. Not only was it unfair to the employees to force this on them when they deserved time off, but it would also provoke resentment and hurt productivity.

So instead, Graham asked. At an all-company meeting, she praised the work that had brought about the wonderful success. She shared the sales data. She read success stories from doctors who were using the stent to avoid bypass surgery and save patients' lives. She extrapolated the sales data and showed how many unmet needs would result if supply couldn't be stepped up substantially. And then she made a request: "We have the chance to do something [for patients and for ourselves] that no company has ever done in the history of our industry. We have an obligation to rise to the challenge. And if you'll rise to the challenge, we'll do all we can to make your lives easier during the tough times."

Within half an hour, employees had made a list of all the things management could do to help them through the holidays — including shop for their presents, wrap them, supply late-night taxis, bring in pizza, and so on. And with that, employees made a pact with management. Production hit new records, and the product was available on time for all patients who needed it. Total sales almost tripled in one quarter. Employees earned nice bonuses. But more importantly, all those who went through this experience felt they were part of something special. Something important. A moral quest. All because they were allowed to choose.

What Miller, Heath, and Graham learned is that you can influence even a resistant group of people if you're willing to surrender control. When you surrender control, you win the possibility of influencing even addictive and highly entrenched behaviors. And you gain access to one of the most powerful human motivations — the power of a committed heart.

SUMMARY: INTRINSIC SATISFACTION

Helping people extract intrinsic satisfaction from the right behavior or feel displeasure with the wrong behavior often calls for several influence strategies. With individuals who believe that the required behaviors won't be pleasurable, simply immerse them in the activity. With our out-of-shape and overweight friend Henry, for example, he'll learn to like certain healthier foods and take pleasure in certain means of exercise only when he gives them a fair chance.

As you experiment with new actions, focus on the sense of accomplishment associated with the result. Revel in achieving for the sake of achieving. Tap into people's sense of pride and competition. And when it comes to long-term achievement, link into people's view of who they want to be. For instance, Henry sees himself as a healthy and fit person—despite his current condition—and needs to stop and consider the pleasure associated with his new healthy behaviors as well as celebrate new levels of accomplishment.

When dealing with activities that are rarely satisfying or unhealthy activities that are very satisfying, take the focus off the activity itself and reconnect the vital behavior to the person's sense of values. Don't be afraid to talk openly about the long-term values individuals are currently either supporting or violating.

For instance, during the first few weeks of his exercise regimen, Henry may need to focus on his value of living a fit life, not on the discomfort he's experiencing. Later, as exercising becomes less painful, even enjoyable, he'll be able to take satisfaction from enacting the vital behaviors themselves.

As people slip further into inappropriate behavior—even causing severe damage to themselves or others—help them reconnect their actions to their sense of morality by fighting moral disengagement. Don't let people minimize or justify their behavior by transforming humans into statistics.

Finally, when facing highly resistant people, don't try to gain control over them by wowing them with logic and argument. Instead, talk with them about what they want. Allow them to discover on their own the links between their current behavior and what they really want.

In short, as you think about the problems you're trying to resolve, don't be afraid to draw on the power of intrinsic satisfiers. As Don Berwick so aptly stated: "The biggest motivators of excellence are intrinsic. They have to do with people's accountability to themselves. It's wanting to do well, to be proud, to go home happy having accomplished something." Berwick recognizes that people have a powerful desire to do what's right. Harnessing that intrinsic desire is a far more powerful influence tool than using extrinsic rewards or exacting punishments.

5
Surpass Your Limits
PERSONAL ABILITY

It's a funny thing, the more I practice the luckier I get.
—Arnold Palmer

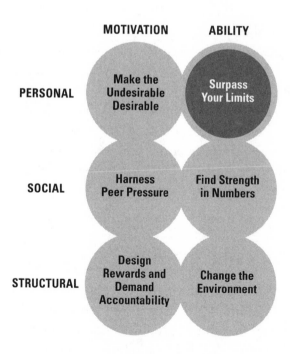

In Chapter 4 we examined ways to tap into personal passions as a way of influencing vital behaviors. To that we add that we can limit our success when we assume that any influence failure is exclusively a motivation problem. We commit what psychologist Lee Ross calls the *fundamental attribution error.*" We assume that when people don't change, it's simply because they don't *want* to change. In making this simplistic assumption, we lose an enormous lever for change.

Even when we do realize that people may lack the *ability* required to enact a vital behavior, we often underestimate the need to learn and actually *practice* that behavior. Corporate leaders make this mistake when they send employees to an intensive day of leadership training that consists of flipping through a binder or listening to engaging stories—but not actually trying any of the skills being taught. Participants mistakenly assume that *knowing* the leadership content and *doing* it are one and the same. Of course, they aren't the same at all, so participants usually return to the office and apply only a fraction of what they studied.

When leaders and training designers combine too much motivation with too few opportunities to improve ability, they don't produce change; they create resentment and depression. Influence masters take the opposite tack. They overinvest in strategies that help increase ability. They avoid trying to solve ability problems with stronger motivational techniques.

To see how easy it is to confuse motivation and ability problems, let's return to Henry—our friend who is trying to lose weight.

THERE'S HOPE FOR EVERYONE

One of Henry's vital behaviors—snacking on mini carrots rather than chocolate—is at risk. At this very moment, Henry is pulling the foil back on a partially eaten, two-pound chocolate bar. In Henry's defense, he didn't buy it. A colleague who knew of his deep affection for chocolate gave it to him. The tempting bar sat on his desk for over a week.

Moments ago Henry decided to heft the plank-sized confection merely to see what two pounds felt like. When he did, he noticed that the adhesive holding the wrapper around the inner foil lining had failed. It appeared as if it was about to fall away, seductively revealing the beautiful red, shiny foil beneath it—the last defense before the chocolate itself.

Henry tugged at the wrapper playfully, and with almost no effort it came free. The next few seconds were almost a blur. Without thinking, Henry's hands peeled back the top flap of the foil and exposed the rich chocolate. In a rush, chocolate-filled childhood memories poured through his head as his fingers pried loose a single dark brown section—a modest, harmlessly small packet of pleasure. He brought the treat to his lips—and then it was over. The chocolate began its inexorable transformation from cocoa, fat, and sugar to cellulite.

Here's the problem. At the moment when Henry should be enjoying one of his secret pleasures, he's depressed. As he now gobbles down the chocolate, with each bite he's convinced that he strayed from his diet because he lacks the proper strength of character. It's clear that he doesn't have moxie or willpower. In short, he's a weak person. Up until this sad indulgence, he had valiantly cut back on calories while sincerely promising himself to start an exercise regime. This new, iron-willed Henry ruled for eight full days. And then the mere touch of the red foil lining brought him to ruin.

Henry wonders if he can overcome the genetic hand that he's been dealt. He has neither self-discipline to diet nor the athletic prowess to exercise effectively. Surely he's doomed to a life of huffing and puffing. But then again, unbeknownst to Henry, a long line of research suggests that maybe he isn't doomed at all. There's a good chance that he can actually learn what it takes to withstand the temptations of chocolate as well as how to improve his ability to exercise properly.

In fact, many of the stories Henry has been carrying in his head since he was a young man may be equally wrong. When his mother once told him that he wasn't exactly a gifted speaker and later when his father suggested that leadership "wasn't his thing," Henry believed that he hadn't been born with "the right stuff." He wasn't born to be an elite athlete; that's for certain. Later he learned that music wasn't his thing, and his interpersonal skills weren't all that strong. Later still he discovered that spending in excess, getting hooked on video games, and gorging on Swiss chocolate *were* his thing. But none of this is going to change because Henry, like all humans, can't fight genetics.

Fortunately, Henry is dead wrong. Henry is trapped in what Carol Dweck, a researcher at Stanford, calls a "fixed mindset." If he believes he can't improve, then he won't even try, and he'll create a self-fulfilling prophecy. But Henry is in luck. Genes don't play the fatalistic role scholars once assumed they played in determining physical prowess, mental agility, and yes, even self-discipline. Characteristics that had long been described by scholars and philosophers alike as genetic gifts or lifelong personality traits appear to be learned, much the same way one learns to walk, talk, or whistle. That means that Henry doesn't need to accept his current status. He can adopt what Dweck refers to as a "growth mindset." Henry simply needs to learn how to develop a set of high-level learning skills and techniques that influence masters use all the time. He needs to learn how to learn. Henry, like most of us, was actually born with the right stuff; he just hasn't figured out how to get it to work for him yet.

To illustrate, let's consider the lengthy hunt researchers conducted in a quest to find the all-important trait of self-discipline. Here was a personality trait worth studying. If the ability to withstand the alluring smell of chocolate or the siren call of buying shiny new products before you have the cash to pay for them—the ability to delay gratification—isn't a reflection of one's underlying character, then what is?

Professor Walter Mischel of Stanford University, curious about people's inability to withstand temptations, set out to explore this issue. Did certain humans have the right stuff while others didn't? And if so, did the right stuff affect lifelong performance? What Mischel eventually came to understand altered the psychological landscape forever.

MUCH OF WILL IS SKILL

When "Timmy," age four, sat down at the gray metal table in an experimental room in the basement of Stanford's psychology department, the child saw something that caught his interest. On the table was a marshmallow—the kind Timmy's mom put into his cup of hot chocolate. Timmy *really* wanted to eat the marshmallow.

The kindly man who brought Timmy into the room told him that he had two options. The man was going to step out for a moment. If Timmy wanted to eat the marshmallow, he could eat away. But if Timmy chose to wait a few minutes until the man returned, then Timmy could eat *two* marshmallows.

Then the man exited. Timmy stared at the tempting sugar treat, squirmed in his chair, kicked his feet, and in general tried to exercise self-control. If he could wait, he'd get two marshmallows! But the temptation proved too strong for little Timmy, so he finally reached across the table, grabbed the marshmallow, looked around nervously, and then shoved the spongy treat in his mouth. Apparently Timmy and Henry are kindred spirits.

Actually, Timmy was one of dozens of subjects Dr. Mischel and his colleagues studied for more than four decades. Mischel was interested in learning what percentage of his young subjects could delay gratification and what impact, if any, this character trait would have on their adult lives. Mischel's hypothesis was that children who were able to demonstrate self-control at a young age would enjoy greater success later in life because of that trait.

In this and many similar studies, Mischel followed the children into adulthood. He discovered that the ability to delay gratification had a more profound effect than many had originally predicted. Notwithstanding the fact that the researchers had watched the kids for only a few minutes, what they learned from the experiment was enormously telling. Children who had been able to wait for that second marshmallow matured into adults who were seen as more socially competent, self-assertive, dependable, and capable of dealing with frustrations; and they scored an average of 210 points higher on their SATs than people who gulped down the one marshmallow. The predictive power was truly remarkable.

Companion studies conducted over the next decade with people of varying ages (including adults) confirmed that individuals who exercise self-control achieve better outcomes than people who don't. For example, if high schoolers are good at self-control, they experience fewer eating and drinking problems. University students with more self-control earn better grades, and married and working people have more fulfilling relationships and better careers. And as you might suspect, people who demonstrate low levels of self-control show higher levels of aggression, delinquency, health problems, and so forth.

Apparently, Mischel had stumbled onto the mother lode of personality traits. Kids who had been blessed with the innate capacity to withstand short-term temptations fared better throughout their entire lives. The fact that a four-year-old's one-time response to a sugary confection predicts lifelong results is at once exciting and depressing—depending on whether you are a "grabber" or a "delayer." You're either well fitted to take on the temptations of the world or doomed to a lifelong fate of enjoy now, pay later—as might well be the lot of our friend Henry.

But is this what's really going on in these studies? Are some people wired to succeed and others to fail?

One thing was clear from these studies: The ability to delay gratification did predict a large number of long-term results. That part of the marshmallow research nobody was arguing about. However, for years scientists continued to debate the cause of this strong effect. Did self-control stem from an intractable personality characteristic or something more malleable and thus learnable?

In 1965, Dr. Mischel collaborated on a study with Albert Bandura who openly challenged the assumption that *will* was a fixed trait. Always a student of human learning, Bandura worked with Mischel to design an experiment to test the stability of subjects who had delayed gratification. In an experiment similar to the marshmallow studies, the two scholars observed fourth- and fifth-graders in similar circumstances. They placed children who had not demonstrated that they could delay gratification into contact with adult role models who knew how to delay. The greedy kids observed adults who put their heads down for a nap or who got up from the chair and engaged in some distracting activity. The original "grabbers" saw techniques for delaying gratification. And to everyone's delight, they followed suit.

After a single exposure to an adult model, children who previously hadn't delayed suddenly became stars at delaying. Even more interesting, in follow-up studies conducted months later, the children who had learned to delay *retained* much of what they'd learned during the brief modeling session. So what about those hardwired genetic characteristics or traits that had predicted so much?

The answer to this important question is good news to all of us and most certainly offers hope to Henry. When Mischel took a closer look at individuals who routinely held out for the greater reward, he concluded that delayers are simply more *skilled* at avoiding short-term temptations. They didn't merely avoid the temptation; they employed specific, learnable techniques that kept their attention off what would be merely short-term gratification and on their long-term goal of earning that second marshmallow.

So maybe Henry *can* learn how to delay gratification—if he learns tactics that will help him do so. But will that be enough to transform him into the physically fit person he'd like to become? After all, he's not good at jogging or weight lifting either. In fact, he's horrible at all things athletic. Surely factors as hardwired as body type, lung capacity, and musculature are predictors of good athletic performance. Henry has no hope of ever becoming one of those chiseled hunks you see hanging out at health clubs. Or does he?

MUCH OF PROWESS IS PRACTICE

Psychologist Anders Ericsson offers an interesting interpretation of how those at the top of their game get there. He doesn't believe for a second that elite-level performance stems from zodiacal forces or, for that matter, from enhanced mental or physical properties. After devoting his academic life to learning why some individuals are better at certain tasks than others, Ericsson has been able to systematically demonstrate that people who climb to the top of just about any field eclipse their peers through something as basic as *deliberate practice*.

We've all heard the old saw that practice doesn't make perfect, *perfect* practice makes perfect. Ericsson has spent his life proving this to be true. While most people believe that they are born with inherent limits to their athletic ability, Ericsson argues that there is little evidence that people who achieve exceptional performance ever get there through any means other than carefully guided practice—*perfect* practice. His research demonstrates that prowess, excellence, elite status—call it what you like—is not a matter of genetic gifts; it's a matter of knowing how to enhance your skills through *deliberate practice*.

For instance, Ericsson describes how dedicated figure skaters practice differently on the ice: Olympic hopefuls work on skills they have yet to master. Club skaters, in contrast, work on skills they've already mastered. Amateurs tend to spend *half* of their time at the rink chatting with friends and not practicing at all. Put simply, skaters who spend the same number of hours on the ice achieve very different results because they practice in very different ways. In Ericsson's research, this finding has held true for every skill imaginable, including memorizing complex lists, playing chess, excelling at the violin, and conquering every extant sporting skill. It also applies to more complex interactions such as giving speeches, getting along with others, and holding emotional, sensitive, or high-stakes conversations.

Before we move on, let's take care to avoid a very large and dangerous trap. The fact that improvements in performance come through deliberate practice makes all the sense in the world when it comes to activities such as figure skating, playing chess, and mastering the violin. However, few people, if any, would think of practicing with a coach to learn how to get along with coworkers, motivate team members to improve their quality measures, emotionally connect with a troubled teen, or talk to a physician about a medical error. Most of us don't even think that soft and gushy interpersonal skills are something you need to study at all, let alone something you'd study and practice with a coach.

But that's precisely what should be going on. Consider a common problem at hospitals. A surgeon has just committed a medical error. While performing a mastectomy, she's accidentally ripped a tiny muscle guarding the patient's chest cavity. The anesthesiologist sees a gauge jump, so it appears as if one lung is no longer taking in air. Two of the nurses assisting the operation see similar signs of distress. If the medical team doesn't start corrective action soon, the patient could die. But before this happens, either the surgeon needs to take responsibility or one of the other professionals needs to raise an alarm.

Let's focus on staff members who are assisting and predict what they might do. Most would certainly hesitate for a few seconds before suggesting that the surgeon has just made a mistake. They'll hesitate because if they don't handle the situation well, they'll come off as flippant or even insubordinate. There are legal issues at play, and that only makes the discussion that much more delicate. Worse still, they've seen colleagues who've expressed a concern, turned out to be wrong, and then received a tongue-lashing. Better to let someone else take the risk. Precious seconds continue to pass.

This and tens of thousands of similar medical errors continue to happen because individuals who may have practiced drawing blood or moving a patient or reading a gauge dozens of times haven't studied and practiced how to confront a colleague—or even more frightening—a physician. They aren't exactly sure what to say and how to say it. They certainly lack the confidence that comes from having practiced.

Of course, health care isn't the only field in which a lack of interpersonal know-how has caused serious problems. Every time a boss expresses a half-baked, even dangerous, idea and subordinates bite their tongues for fear of being chastised, good ideas remain a secret and teams make bad decisions. Speaking up to an authority figure requires skill, and skill requires practice. The same is true for confronting a mentally abusive spouse or dealing with a bully at school or—here's a hot one—just saying no to drugs. Try that without getting ridiculed or beat up. Interpersonal interactions can be extraordinarily complicated, and most will improve only after individuals receive instruction that includes deliberate practice.

Consider the problem Dr. Wiwat Rojanapithayakorn faced when attempting to encourage young, poor, shy, female sex workers to deny services to older, richer male customers if the customers refused to use a condom. At first the young girls mumbled their disapproval, only to be intimidated by their vocal clients. Not knowing what to say or how to say it, they'd quickly give in and put themselves and thousands of others at risk.

Eventually Wiwat asked more seasoned sex workers to train young girls on how to defend their health. They shared actual scripts that helped them avoid offending the customer while at the same time holding a firm line. Equally important, the young women actually practiced the conversation until they had gained confidence in what they were going to say and how they would say it. They continued to practice and receive feedback until they had mastered their scripts well enough to actually use them at work. In this particular case, providing detailed coaching and feedback helped compliance with the strict condom code rise from 14 percent to 90 percent in just a few years—saving millions of lives.

Many of the profound and persistent problems we face stem more from a lack of skill (which in turn stems from a lack of deliberate practice) than from a genetic curse, a lack of courage, or a character flaw. Self-discipline, long viewed as a character trait, and elite performance, similarly linked to genetic gifts, stem from the ability to engage in guided practice of clearly defined skills. Learn how to practice the right actions, and you can master everything from withstanding the temptations of chocolate to holding an awkward discussion with your boss.

PERFECT COMPLEX SKILLS

Let's return to a point we made earlier. Not all practice is good practice. That's why many of the tasks we perform at work and at home suffer from "arrested development." With simple tasks such as typing, driving, golf, and tennis, we reach our highest level of proficiency after about 50 hours of practice; then our performance skills become automated. We're able to execute them smoothly and with minimal effort, but further development stops. We assume we've reached our highest performance level and don't think to learn new and better methods.

With some tasks, we stop short of our highest level of proficiency on purpose. The calculus we perform in our heads suggests that the added effort it'll take to find and learn something new will probably yield a diminishing marginal return, so we stop learning. For instance, we learn how to make use of a word processor or Web server by mastering the most common moves, but we never learn many of the additional features that would dramatically improve our ability.

This same pattern of arresting our development applied over an entire career yields fairly unsatisfactory results. For example, most professionals progress until they reach an "acceptable" level, and then they plateau. Software engineers, for instance, usually reach their peak somewhere around five years after entering the workforce. Beyond this level of mediocrity, further improvements are not correlated to years of work in the field.

So what *does* create improvement? According to Dr. Anders Ericsson, improvement is related not just to practice, but to a particular kind of practice—something Ericsson calls *deliberate practice*. Ericsson has found that no matter the field of expertise, when it comes to elite status, there is no correlation whatsoever between time in the profession and performance levels.

The implications are stunning. A 20-year-veteran brain surgeon is not likely to be any more skilled than a 5-year rookie by virtue of time on the job. Any difference between the two would have nothing to do with experience and everything to do with deliberate practice. Time is required (most elite performers in fields such as music composition, dance, science, fiction writing, chess, and basketball have put in 10 or more years), but it is not the critical variable for mastery. The critical factor is using time wisely. It's the *skill* of practice that makes perfect.

Most of us already have all the evidence we need to confirm that deliberate practice can have an enormous effect on performance levels. Just look at what's happened to our capacity to teach everything from mathematics to high jumping. Roger Bacon once said that it would take a person 30 to 40 years to master calculus—the same calculus that is taught in most high schools today. Today's musicians routinely match and even surpass the technical virtuosity of legendary musicians of the past. And when it comes to sports, the records just keep falling. For example, when Johnny Weissmuller of Tarzan fame won his five Olympic gold medals in swimming in 1924, nobody expected that years later *high school* kids would post better times.

What, then, is deliberate practice? And how can we apply the techniques to our vital behaviors and thus strengthen our influence strategy?

Demand Full Attention for Brief Intervals

Deliberate practice requires complete attention. Deliberate practice doesn't allow for daydreaming, functioning on autopilot, or only partially putting one's mind into the routine. It requires steely-eyed concentration as students watch exactly what they're doing, what is working, what isn't, and why.

This ability to concentrate is often viewed by students as their most difficult challenge, enough so that elite musicians and athletes argue that maintaining their concentration is usually the limiting factor to deliberate practice. Most can maintain a heightened level of concentration for only an hour straight, usually during the morning when their minds are fresh. Across a wide range of disciplines, the total daily practice time of elite performers rarely exceeds five hours a day, and this only if students take naps and sleep longer than normal.

Provide Immediate Feedback Against a Clear Standard

The number of hours one spends practicing a skill is far less important than receiving clear and frequent feedback against a known standard. For example, serious chess players spend about four hours a day comparing their play to the published play of the world's best players. They make their best move, and then compare it to the move the expert made. When their move is different from the master's, they pause to determine what the expert saw and they missed. As a result of comparing themselves to the best, students improve their skills much faster than they would otherwise. This immediate feedback, coupled with complete concentration, accelerates learning. Players know quickly when they are off course, and they learn from their own poor moves.

As you might imagine, sports stars require rapid feedback to improve performance as well. They tend to focus on small but vital aspects of their play and scrupulously compare one round to the next. Swimming gold medalist Natalie Coughlin completes each leg of her races with fewer strokes than her opponents, giving her a tremendous advantage in stamina. Her practice is focused on the minute details of each stroke. She explains: "You're constantly manipulating the water. The slightest change in pitch in your hand makes the biggest difference." At the conclusion of each lap, Natalie is acutely aware of the number of strokes she took to complete it, and she adjusts her hand position for the next lap. This kind of focused, deliberate practice enhances performance more rapidly than does merely swimming laps.

This concept of rapid feedback stands traditional teaching methods on their heads. Many teachers believe that tests are painful experiences that should be given as infrequently as possible so as not to discourage students. Research reveals that the opposite is true. Ethna Reid taught us that one of the vital behaviors for effective teachers is extremely short intervals between teaching and testing. When testing comes frequently, it becomes familiar. It's no longer a dreaded, major event. It provides the chance for people to see how well they're doing against the standard.

Think about how deliberate practice with clear feedback compares with the way we currently train our leaders. Rarely do business school and management faculties think of leadership as a performance art. Faculty members typically teach leaders how to think, not how to act. So when would-be executives take MBA courses or graduate executives attend leadership training, they're routinely asked to read cases, apply algorithms, and the like, but there's a good chance that they'll never be asked to practice anything.

Granted, business schools typically offer a course in giving presentations and speeches where the performance components that students are asked to practice are so obvious. But this is not the case with other important leadership skills, such as addressing controversial topics, confronting bad behavior, building coalitions, running a meeting, disagreeing with authority figures, or influencing behavior change—all of which call for specific behaviors, and all of which can and must be learned through deliberate practice.

Break Mastery into Mini Goals

Let's add another dimension to deliberate practice. We start with a test. How would you motivate patients to take pills that one day might prevent them from experiencing a stroke? If they've already had one stroke, you'd think it would be easy to get them to take the lifesaving pills. But let's add a confounding factor. The pills often cause leg cramps, painful rashes, loss of energy, constipation, headaches, and sexual dysfunction. So patients take a pill, and they will most assuredly suffer short-term results, but maybe they won't have a stroke sometime way out in the future. This is going to be a hard sell. In fact, for years many stroke patients didn't take their pills because they didn't like the odds.

This all changed when researchers stopped focusing on long-term goals (avoiding another stroke) and created a regimen that helped patients set mini goals and then provided rapid feedback against them. Researchers gave patients packets of pills, a blood pressure monitor, and a log book. Every day they took the pills, monitored their blood pressure, and recorded changes in the log book along with other achievements. The change was dramatic and immediate. By setting small goals (daily monitoring and recording) and meeting them, patients now focused on something they could see and control. This enhanced their sense of efficacy, clarified the effect of the medicine, and motivated compliance. Now these patients take their pills.

Influence masters have long known the importance of setting clear and achievable goals. First, they understand the importance of setting specific goals. People say that they understand this concept, but few actually put the concept into practice. For example, *average* volleyball players set goals to improve their "concentration" (exactly what is that?), whereas top performers decide they need to practice tossing the ball correctly—and they understand each of the elements in the toss.

As part of this focus on specific levels of achievement, top performers set their goals to improve behaviors or processes rather than outcomes. For instance, top volleyball performers set process goals aimed at the set, the dig, the block, and so on. Mediocre performers set outcome goals such as winning so many points or garnering applause. In basketball, players who routinely hit 70 percent or more of their free throws tend to practice differently from those who hit 55 percent or less. How? Better shooters set technique-oriented goals such as, "Keep the elbow in," or, "Follow through." Players who shoot 55 percent and under tend to think more about results-oriented goals such as, "This time I'm going to make ten in a row."

This difference in focus is also borne out when players blow it. Researchers stopped players who missed two free throws in a row and asked them to explain their failure. Master shooters were able to cite the specific technique they got wrong. ("I didn't keep my elbow in.") Poorer shooters offered vague explanations such as, "I lost concentration."

The role of mini goals in maintaining motivation also deserves attention. With certain skills, people are deathly afraid that they won't succeed. And once they do fail, they fear that bad things will happen to them. As you might imagine, when people predict that their actions will lead to catastrophic results, these failure stories lead to self-defeating behavior. Individuals begin with the hypothesis that they will never succeed and that the failure will be costly, and then they look for every shred of proof that they're about to fail so they can bail out early before they suffer too much—which they do anyway.

When fear dominates people's expectations, not only do you have to improve their actual skill, but you have to take special care to ensure that their expectations of success grow right along with their actual ability. But how? As we learned earlier, simply using verbal persuasion isn't enough to convince them. ("Go ahead, the snake won't bite!") For example, in one line of research scholars learned that you can teach dating skills to shy sophomores, but the students need to see proof of constant progress before they're willing to admit that they've learned anything useful or before they put the new skills into practice.

And where do people find this proof of progress? From progress itself. Nothing succeeds like success. As people succeed, they learn through personal experience (the real deal for changing understanding, which can be a powerful tool for changing minds) that they actually can achieve their goals. Unfortunately, skeptical people aren't likely to attempt behaviors that they perceive to be risky, so they never succeed. Now what's a person to do?

Dr. Bandura points out that to encourage people to attempt something they fear, you must provide rapid positive feedback that builds self-confidence. You achieve this by providing short-term, specific, easy, and low-stakes goals that specify the exact steps a person should take. Take complex tasks and make them simple; long tasks and make them short; vague tasks and make them specific; and high-stakes tasks and make them risk free.

If you want to see how to put short-term, specific, easy, low-stakes goals into play on a much grander scale, take a look at our friends at Delancey Street. The entering criminals and societal castoffs that Dr. Silbert works with are typically illiterate and completely unskilled. Not only do they not have job expertise or academic talent, but they also lack interpersonal and social survival skills.

So what do you do when you have to teach residents dozens or even hundreds of skills? You eat the elephant one bite at a time. You select one domain, say a vocational skill such as working in a restaurant, then choose a small skill in that area. For example, on the very first night you teach the nervous newcomer how to set a table—maybe just the forks. Then, this novice who is very likely to be suffering from drug withdrawal along with culture shock and other physical and emotional problems practices placing the fork until he or she gets it right. Next comes the knife.

Prepare for Setbacks; Build In Resilience

As important as it is to use baby steps to ensure short-term success during the early phases of learning, if subjects experience only successes early on, then failures can quickly discourage them. A short history of easy successes can create a false expectation that not much effort is required. Then if subjects run into a problem, they become discouraged.

To deal with this problem, people need to learn that effort, persistence, and resiliency are eventually rewarded with success. Consequently, the practice regime should gradually introduce tasks that require increased effort and persistence. As learners overcome more difficult tasks and recover from intermittent defeats, they see that setbacks aren't permanent roadblocks, but signals that they need to keep learning.

This capacity to tell ourselves the right story about problems and setbacks is particularly important when we're already betting against ourselves. When faced with a setback, we need to learn to say, "Aha! I just discovered what doesn't work," and not, "Oh no! Once again I'm an utter failure." We need to interpret setbacks as *guides*, and not as brakes.

Initially, failure signals the need for greater effort or persistence. Sometimes failure signals the need to change strategies or tactics. But failure should rarely signal that we'll never be able to succeed and drive us to pray for serenity. For instance, you find yourself staring at a half-eaten ice cream cone in your hand. Should you conclude that you're unable to stick with your eating plan so you might as well give up? Or should you conclude that since it's hard to resist when you walk past the ice cream parlor on your way home from work, you should change your route? The first conclusion serves as a discouraging brake on performance, whereas the second provides a corrective guide that helps refine your strategy.

BUILD EMOTIONAL SKILLS

Let's end our exploration into self-mastery where we began. Henry is staring down at his half-opened chocolate bar. His eyes, lips, and taste buds are prodding his brain to satisfy their demands. He wants chocolate. To see if Henry is doomed—or if he can learn a skill to help him delay gratification—let's turn to research that helps us better understand the original marshmallow study.

Contemporary research reveals that human beings operate in two very different modalities, depending on the circumstances. However, as Mischel and Bandura informed us, these modalities or systems are viewed less as character traits or impulses and more as behaviors that can be regulated through skill. The first of these two operating modalities is referred to by contemporary theorists as our "hot" or "go" system. It helps us survive. We stumble upon something threatening—say a tiger—and as our "go" system takes over, our brain sends blood to our arms and legs, our heart rate and blood pressure increase, and, like it or not, we start producing cholesterol—just in case we face blunt trauma.

More intriguing still, as our "go" system kicks in and blood flows out of the brain and toward our arms and legs, we start relying on a much smaller part of our brain (the amygdala) to take over the job of "thinking." When the amygdala takes control, we no longer process information in a cool, calm, and collected way. Rather than cogitating, ruminating, and completing other high-level cognitive tasks, the amygdala or "reptilian brain" is made for speed. It's wired for quick, emotional processing that, when activated, triggers reflexive responses including fight and flight. The amygdala instinctively moves us to action. We see a tiger and bang, we're off and running. This hot/go system develops very early and is most dominant in the young infant.

The second system, known as the "cool" or "know" system, serves us well during more stable times. It's emotionally neutral, runs off the frontal lobe, and is designed for higher-level cognitive processing. Consequently, it helps us thrive, rather than survive. It's the part of the brain we're using as we're calmly picking blackberries while chatting with a friend. This system is very ill suited to dealing with the tiger that is just about to appear around the corner. Our "know" system is slow and contemplative and begins to develop at around age four—just about the time children are first able to delay gratification.

As terrific as it is to have two very different operating systems, each perfectly suited to its own unique tasks, when you have two of anything, you always run the risk of employing the wrong one given your circumstances. For instance, a tiger appears, and you remain emotionally neutral, marveling at the cat's amazing speed, while you carefully contemplate your options. "Let's see, if I climb that tree, there's a chance . . ."

Too late—you're tiger food. Too bad your "know" system had wrestled control away from your "go" system.

To be honest, calling up our "know" system when it's our "go" system that would serve us better isn't all that common. It's the "go" system we call into service every chance we get. After all, it's better to run at the first sign of danger than remain mired in the "know" too long. Consequently, the "go" system often turns on at the mere hint that you're about to fall under attack. Heaven forbid you think complexly and clearly in such a case.

For example, an accountant who works with you makes fun of an idea you offer up in a meeting. This ticks you off. How dare this knuckle-dragging bean counter mock your idea! Of course, this isn't exactly a life-threatening circumstance you face; it's an accountant, not a tiger. Nevertheless, better safe than sorry. So, like it or not, your "go" system kicks in. In fact, it does so without your even asking for help. As your blood starts rushing to your arms and legs where it can do some good, your brain will just have to run off the amygdala. You're hot, you're ready to go, you're not the least bit contemplative, and you verbally tear into the poor fellow from accounting like an early human on a fallen woolly mammoth. What were you thinking? More to the point, what part of your brain were you thinking with?

This inappropriate emotional reaction is exactly the same thing that happens whenever your appetites or cravings kick in at a moment you would prefer that they remain less active. Your "go" system isn't designed merely for fight or flight; it's also designed to take charge whenever a quick, reflexive, survival behavior might suit you. For example, you smell fresh donuts as you walk by the company cafeteria, and an urge from within whispers, "Eat now before it's too late."

So there you have it. Sometimes we switch into the wrong version of our two operating systems, and this change causes us huge problems. That's why in spite of the fact that we're committed to a vital behavior, we often crumble at stressful moments. If only we could learn how to wrestle control away from the amygdala when it's kicking in hard at the wrong time. Then perhaps we could be ruled by reason, and not let passion take charge. The good news is that this powerful self-management skill is *learnable*. And if you want to equip yourself or others to survive the tide of opposing emotions, this skill is pivotal.

KICK-START OUR BRAIN

To learn how to take charge of our "go" system, let's return to the marshmallow studies. Once Mischel and others had divided their research subjects into "grabbers" and "delayers," they turned their attention to transforming everyone into a delayer. What would it take to help people survive immediate temptations in order to achieve long-term benefits? More importantly, they wanted to avoid the mistake of relying on verbal persuasion by simply telling people to gut it out, or to "show some self-control!" Instead, they wanted to teach people the skills associated with emotional management. But what were these skills?

Mischel discovered through a series of experiments with varied age groups and rewards that if subjects didn't trust that the researcher would actually return and give them the longer-term reward, they wouldn't delay. Why hold out only to be disappointed? Similarly, if subjects believed that they wouldn't be able to do what it took to withstand the short-term temptation, they also wouldn't delay. In short, Mischel confirmed what Bandura taught us earlier. People won't attempt a behavior unless: (1) they think it's worth it, and (2) they think they can do what's required. If not, why try?

In his original experiments, Mischel had observed that children who were able to delay gratification were better at distracting themselves from thinking about either the short- or the long-term reward. Delayers managed their emotions by distracting themselves with other activities. They avoided looking at the marshmallows by covering their eyes, turning their chairs away, or resting their heads on their arms. Some even created their own diversions by talking to themselves, singing, and inventing games with their hands and feet. One clever kid stood and traced the mortar seams in the wall with her finger. In short, delayers invented clever ways of turning aversive and boring waiting time into something that was more like a game.

When Mischel taught other children these same tactics—and thus helped them take their minds off the rewards and place them on something else—subjects routinely increased their ability to delay gratification. In similar studies where subjects were given specific tasks that would help them earn their long-term rewards, subjects who focused on the tasks as opposed to the rewards delayed longer. In contrast, individuals who glanced at the reward the most often were the least persistent. Researchers also found that distracting individuals by having them focus on the cost of failure, or thinking bad thoughts, did not enhance delay.

Finally, asking subjects to employ "willpower" by directing their attention to tasks that were difficult, aversive, or boring didn't work. Despite the fact most people are convinced that individuals who show poor self-control merely need to exert a stronger will—demanding that subjects dig down, suck it up, or show strength of character—research found the opposite. Telling people to hunker down didn't improve performance.

The far better strategy was to transform the difficult into the easy, the aversive into the pleasant, and the boring into the interesting. We examine methods for doing exactly this in Chapter 9. Suffice it to say that when industrial engineers began to find ways to help employees and others make their tasks easier and more pleasant, leaders learned that they didn't have to continually harangue people to stick to their unpleasant or boring tasks. And when leaders began to learn how to measure and focus on short-term goals, it took the pressure off having to continually motivate people into hanging on until the end.

Another effective way to manage emotions is to argue with your feelings. Psychologists call this particular strategy *cognitive reappraisal*. When emotions come unbidden through the "go" system, they can be dragged into the light of the "know" system by activating skills only the "know" system can do. To do this, call out to your frontal lobe by asking it to solve a complex problem. That's right. If you ask your brain to work on a question that requires more brain power than the amygdala can muster, this mental probe can help kick in the know system and restore normal thought.

To start the reappraisal process, distance yourself from your need by labeling it. (I have a craving for a cream-cheese-covered bagel. Bad.) Debate with yourself about it by introducing competing thoughts or goals (What I *really* want is to be proud of myself after lunch when I write down what I ate). Distract yourself (conjure up a potent image of the feeling you have when your belt feels loose). Or delay. That's right—the "go" system can often be outwaited.

For example, as a strategy to help obsessive-compulsives cope with their tendencies, therapists teach them to wait 15 minutes before giving in to a maddening mental demand—such as washing their soap-worn hands for the hundredth time in eight hours. In the moment, we often believe that our emotions will not subside until they're satisfied. This turns out not to be true. If you delay your urge, within a fairly short period of time the brain returns control to the "know" system, and different choices become easier.

Active strategies such as classifying, debating, deliberating, and delaying can help change what you think. They do so by changing *where* you think. Your "know" system starts to kick in, and you transfer control from the amygdala to the frontal lobe. Once you change *where* you think, you change how you think, which in turn changes what you think. You're now able to carefully contemplate, ruminate, and take a longer-term view.

So, if, like Henry, you find yourself obsessing over the possibility of gorging yourself on chocolate—or maybe gambling or spending obsessively to the point where you can scarcely think straight—realize that there's a set of skills you can call into play if you want to take control of your urges.

SUMMARY: PERSONAL ABILITY

When it comes to complex tasks that matter a great deal to you in your quest to resolve persistent problems, don't suffer from arrested development. Demand more from yourself than the achievement levels you reach after minimal effort. Instead, set aside time to study and practice new and more vital behaviors. Devote attention to clear, specific, and repeatable actions. Ensure that the actions you're pursuing are both recognizable and replicable. Then seek outside help. Insist on immediate feedback against clear standards. Break tasks into discrete actions, set goals for each, practice within a low-risk environment, and build in recovery strategies. Finally, make sure that you apply the same deliberate practice tactics to physical, intellectual, and even complex social skills. Many of the vital behaviors required to solve profound and persistent problems demand advanced interpersonal problem-solving skills that can be mastered only through well-researched, deliberate practice.

With instinctive demands and quick emotional reactions, don't let the "go" system take control from your "know" system unless you're facing a legitimate risk to life and limb. To regain emotional control over your genetically wired responses, take the focus off your instinctive objective by carefully attending to distraction activities. Where possible, completely avoid the battle to delay gratification by making the difficult easy, the averse pleasant, and the boring interesting. When strong emotions take over because you've drawn harsh, negative conclusions about others, reappraise the situation by asking yourself complex questions that force your frontal lobe to wrest control away from the amygdala.

Remember the good news here. Overcoming habits or developing complex athletic, intellectual, and interpersonal skills are not merely functions of motivation, personality traits, or even character. They all tie back to ability. Develop greater proficiency at deliberate practice as well as the ability to manage your emotions, and you significantly increase the chances for turning vital behaviors into vital habits.

6

Harness Peer Pressure

SOCIAL MOTIVATION

*I was part of that strange race of people aptly
described as spending their lives doing things
they detest to make money they don't want to buy
things they don't need to impress people they dislike.*

—Emile Henry Gauvreau

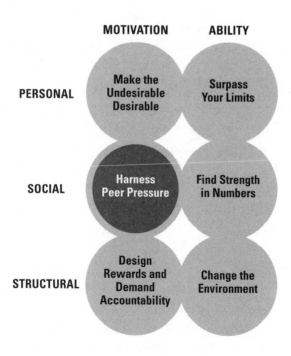

W hen seeking influence tools that have an impact on profound and persistent problems, no resource is more powerful and accessible than the persuasion of the people who make up our social networks. The ridicule and praise, acceptance and rejection, approval and disapproval of our fellow beings can do more to assist or destroy our change efforts than almost any other source. Smart influencers appreciate the amazing power humans hold over one another, and instead of denying it, lamenting it, or attacking it, influencers embrace and enlist it.

THE POWER

In 1961, when psychologist Stanley Milgram set out to find U.S. citizens similar in disposition to what society believed were the crazy misfits, blind fundamentalists, and psychological wrecks who had marched Jews, Poles, and Romanies into the gas chambers at Auschwitz, the world was surprised by what he discovered. In fact, Dr. Milgram's findings were so disturbing that he fell under attack from every corner. Nobody wanted to believe the data.

Mystified by what had happened in Hitler's Germany, Dr. Milgram was interested in what *type* of person could be compelled to annihilate his or her innocent friends and neighbors. Naturally, blind fundamentalists who followed unspeakable orders all in the name of political zealotry would be hard to locate in the suburbs of Connecticut. Nevertheless, Milgram was determined to track down a few of them and put them under his microscope.

Of course, as a respectable researcher, Milgram couldn't create circumstances under which his neighbors actually killed each other. But maybe he could trick subjects into thinking they were killing someone else, when in truth their victims would remain unharmed. To create these odd circumstances, Dr. Milgram ran an ad in the New Haven newspaper asking people to take part in an experiment that lasted one hour and for which they would be paid $4.50. Interested persons reported to the basement of Linsly-Chittenden Hall on the campus of Yale University where they were told that their job would be to take part in a study that examined the impact of negative reinforcement on learning.

While waiting for their turn to earn $4.50, subjects would chat with another participant about the upcoming job. This friendly stranger was actually a confederate of Dr. Milgram's who was working as part of the research team. Next, a scientist in a lab jacket would appear and ask each of the two subjects to reach into an urn and draw out a slip of paper to determine who would perform which of the two jobs that were available. One would be a "teacher," and one would be a "learner." In actuality, both slips said "teacher," guaranteeing that the actual research subject would take the role of the teacher.

The teacher would then accompany the learner and the researcher into a small booth where the learner was invited to sit down while the researcher applied special paste to his arms. "This," he explained, "is to ensure solid contact between your skin and the electrodes when we administer the shocks." At this point, the learner would matter-of-factly explain, "A few years ago in the veterans' hospital I was told I had a bit of a heart condition. Will that be a problem?" To which the researcher would confidently say, "No. While the shocks may be painful, they are not dangerous."

After strapping the electrodes to the learner, the researcher and teacher would close the booth door and move to the adjoining room. There the teacher would see a frightening piece of electrical machinery with which he or she would deliver shocks to the learner. To reassure subjects that the machine was pumping out real electrons, each "teacher" would be given a 45-volt burst from the machine as a sample of the initial shock the learner in the other room would receive during the experiment. It hurt.

The stated goal of the experiment was to measure the impact of negative reinforcement on learning. To test this, the teacher would read a list of paired words loud enough for the learner to hear in the adjoining room. The subject would then read the first word in each pair, and the learner would try to recall the second word. Should the learner get the word wrong, the subject would throw a switch that would shock the poor learner with the heart problems. With each subsequent missed word, the teacher would raise the voltage, flip the switch, and give the learner an even larger shock.

Despite the fact that the subject thought he was increasing the voltage with each new error, the "learner" received no electric shock whatsoever. Instead, with each throwing of the switch, the researchers would play prerecorded audio that the subject could hear through the wall. With the first shock came a grunt. The second shock produced a mild protest. Next, stronger protests. Then screaming and shouting. Then screaming and banging on the wall with a reminder that he had heart problems. Eventually, when the voltage levels exceeded 315 volts, the subject would hear nothing but silence as he read the words, raised the voltage, and cruelly flipped the switch.

Of course, Dr. Milgram knew he would have to experiment with a lot of subjects before he'd find anyone who would keep cranking up the volts. In fact, when Milgram asked a sample group of social psychologists to predict the results of this chilling study, they suggested that only 1.2 percent of the population, only a "sadistic few," would give the maximum voltage.

When you watch black-and-white film clips of Milgram's actual subjects taking part in the study, the hair stands up on the back of your neck. At first these everyday folks off the streets of Connecticut chuckle nervously as they hear the learner grunt in protest after being given a 45-volt shock. Some show signs of stress as they increase the voltage and the learner starts to shout. Many pause at around 135 volts and question the purpose of the experiment.

If at any time the subject called for a halt, he was told by the scientist in the white lab jacket that the experiment required him to continue—up to four times. If the subject requested to stop a fifth time, the experiment stopped. Otherwise the experiment came to an end only after the subject had given the maximum 450 volts—to a learner who was no longer protesting, but who had gone completely silent—giving the teacher the distinct impression that the learner had either passed out or died.

Clearly the subjects who continued to send more and more volts to their protesting, screaming, and begging cohort took no pleasure in what they were doing. It's unnerving to watch clips as anguished subjects suggest that they should stop the torture. After offering their suggestion, they are immediately told that the experiment calls for them to continue.

Researchers watched and recorded the subjects, taking comfort in knowing that only a few subjects would administer much of a shock. As it turned out, "only" 65 percent of subjects would.

That's the finding that got Milgram in trouble. He hadn't discovered a tiny handful of Connecticut zealots and sociopaths who would gladly give their souls over to the totalitarian cause. He had found the vulnerable target within all of us. He had looked for the freak and found himself—and you and me. And nobody liked it.

What was going on? Why do human beings place such a high premium on the approval of others—often strangers? Certainly that's what you'd ask if you were a social scientist. If you were a student of influence, you'd ask how this amazing social force might work either for or against you as you do your best to orchestrate change. You'd want to co-opt the awesome power of social pressure for your own purposes.

Savvy people know how to tap into this enormous source of influence in hundreds of different ways. They do so by following one simple principle. They ensure that people feel praised, emotionally supported, and encouraged by those around them—every time they enact vital behaviors. Similarly, they take steps to ensure that people feel discouraged or even socially sanctioned when choosing unhealthy behaviors.

The actual methods that influence masters use to exploit the enormous power of "the fellow in the lab jacket" deserve a much closer look. Whole literatures are built upon the foundation of social influence. Topics ranging from leadership to interpersonal influence to group dynamics draw from this same source of social power.

This being the case, we take care to narrow our search by first examining how social support can be harnessed for good. Then we look at three best practices that help magnify the power of social support. First, we explore how to make use of that unique group of people who routinely exert more influence than anyone else—the much-vaunted opinion leaders. Next, we examine how influence geniuses routinely assail not *people* per se, but their shared norms. We'll see how brilliant leaders directly attack norms that would otherwise impede vital behaviors. Finally, we look at what it takes to create an entire culture of social support.

THE POWER OF ONE

Stanley Milgram clearly demonstrated that one respected individual can create conditions that compel ordinary citizens to act in curious, if not unhealthy, ways. But he also found the opposite to be true. After discovering that he could propel people to act against their own consciences, he began exploring which variable had the largest impact on compliance. Was it the size of the room, the look and feel of the electronic machine, or the distance to the subject? After conducting tests with over a thousand subjects of every ilk and under every imaginable condition, Milgram concluded that one variable more than any other affected how people behaved: the presence of one more person.

Dr. Milgram learned that if a confederate either shocked the person all the way to 450 volts or stood up to the authority figure, it dramatically affected how the research subjects acted. He could increase the already stunning 65 percent of all-the-wayers to 90 percent if only one other person (a confederate) gave a full dose of power just before the subject had a turn at the machine. Equally important, he discovered that the number who would administer the full shock dropped to a mere 10 percent if one person before him or her *refused* to do so. Either way, it just took one person to turn the tide of compliance.

This finding paints a much brighter picture of humanity and offers us a wonderful influence tool. To harness the immense power of social support, sometimes you need to find only one respected individual who will fly in the face of history and model the new and healthier vital behaviors.

Here's how this works. We (the authors) once watched the power of stepping out against the norm at a large defense contracting firm. At this company the CEO was trying to transform a rather timid culture into one where individuals openly stated their differing opinions as a means of resolving long-standing problems. After months of lecturing, he faced a moment of truth. In a meeting of his top 200 managers, the CEO extended an invitation. "I've been told that I'm unapproachable," he began. "I am trying to work on it. But to be honest, I don't know what it means entirely. I'd appreciate feedback from any of you who would be willing to help me."

For a few seconds, the auditorium felt like a morgue. As the CEO scanned the audience for any takers, he was about to break the awkward silence and move on when a fellow by the name of Ken raised his hand. "Sure, Bill. I've got some suggestions."

With that announcement, the CEO set an appointment to talk one-on-one with Ken. As you might guess, from that moment on most of the water-cooler chatter was about the foolish risk Ken had just taken. Pay-per-view could have made a fortune selling access to the private meeting between Ken and the CEO. But in the end, the entire story came out—from the CEO.

After meeting with Ken, the CEO sent out an e-mail detailing the feedback he'd gotten. He made commitments to a couple of changes that he hoped would make him more approachable, and he was as good as his word. Equally important, the CEO sincerely thanked Ken for his candor. The CEO showed his genuine support of the behavior of being candid by not becoming defensive and by rewarding the person who had taken the risk to be honest—even when it hurt—and he then made personal changes to demonstrate his commitment.

The results were far-reaching. The CEO's and Ken's living examples of seeking and giving feedback emboldened the other 199 managers. Within months candor among employees increased dramatically across the entire organization. Employees began to open up and successfully solve problems.

Although it's true that neither Ken nor the CEO wore white lab jackets, they did exert social influence. Both were respected individuals, and both demonstrated how to break from tradition and speak frankly. Had the CEO only given lip service to the proposed vital behavior, he would have doomed the change effort. Had he simply used verbal persuasion, his influence would have been equally limited. Instead, the big boss encouraged candor, embraced it, celebrated it, and rewarded the first person who had the guts to speak his mind.

When a respected individual attempts a vital behavior and succeeds, this one act alone can go further in motivating others to change than almost any other source of influence. But take note, the living examples of other humans exert power only to the extent that the person who is modeling the vital behaviors is truly respected. For example, when an HR manager at a midsized plywood mill we (the authors) consulted with tried to put teeth into a training program she was touting, she videotaped the president of the company singing the praises of the new training. The president ended his short, energetic speech with, "I encourage each of you to take to heart the concepts taught in today's training."

When the HR manager showed the video clip at the beginning of the first training session, participants jeered, hooted, and mocked the president. It turns out that members of the audience despised anything coming out of headquarters. They thought the president was a raging hypocrite, and his ringing endorsement only served to harm the training's credibility.

Some individuals can exert a great deal of influence on one another; others can't. So how do you know who's who?

THE POWER OF *THE RIGHT* ONE

We've seen that one person can have an enormous effect on motivating others to enact vital behaviors. We've also seen that the influence of formal leaders (like the CEO and the guy in the white lab coat) can have a remarkable influence on the behavior of those in their sphere of influence. So if you want to influence change, it's essential that you engage the chain of command. Smart influencers spend a disproportionate amount of time with formal leaders to ensure that the leaders are using their social influence to encourage vital behaviors.

But the bosses are only half of what you'll need. It turns out that there's a second and often overlooked group of people whose social support or resistance will make or break your influence efforts. To find out who this group is and how to enlist it, let's take a look at the work of Dr. Everett Rogers. His contribution to influence theory remains one of the greatest in history and has important implications to how all parents, coaches, and leaders can best make use of social support.

After graduating with a Ph.D. in sociology and statistics, Dr. Rogers took an intriguing job with the local university extension service. It was his responsibility to encourage Iowa farmers to use new and improved strains of corn. What could be easier? The new strains of corn Rogers was touting produced greater yields and were dramatically more disease resistant, and therefore, far more profitable than current strains.

As Dr. Rogers talked with local farmers about the terrific new seeds he was recommending, he quickly learned that his education and connection to the university didn't impress them. He wasn't exactly one of them. Farmers dressed differently; their hands were rough from physical labor; they read different magazines and watched different TV programs. Other than speaking the English language, they scarcely had a thing in common with Rogers.

At first, Dr. Rogers figured that this difference would actually work to his advantage. The reason the farmers should listen to his advice was because he *hadn't* done what they had done. He had made a careful study of the crops they should grow. He was now working for the experts in agronomy. In fact, Rogers figured that when he talked, farmers would be taking notes and thanking him for helping them increase their yields.

But it didn't work that way. It turns out that Rogers wasn't just different. In the farmers' view, he was the wrong kind of different. He was naive. He was a city slicker. He had never plowed a field. Sure, he said he read books, but what if he was wrong? Who would dare put their annual harvest at risk by listening to a young fellow just out of college? None of the farmers. That's who.

After being summarily rejected by his target population, Rogers grew increasingly confused and desperate. What good is it, Rogers wondered, to invent better methods—in fact, *far* better methods—if no one will put them into practice? The very advance of civilization relies on citizens letting go of old, inefficient ways and embracing new, efficient ones. And Rogers just happened to know what those better ways were—at least for the farmers.

What could Dr. Rogers do if people didn't respect him (which they most certainly didn't)? The very fact that he was the one suggesting the new idea prevented people from listening to it. Perhaps Dr. Rogers could get a farmer to embrace the new strains of corn. Then a person from within the farming community could point to the better results, and everyone would be jumping on the bandwagon. If Dr. Rogers could find a person who would be interested in trying the latest strains, he would be halfway home.

Eventually he enticed a farmer into giving the most current strains of corn a try. He wasn't much like the other farmers. He was a rather hip fellow who actually wore Bermuda shorts and drove a Cadillac. He had a proclivity for embracing innovation, so he tried the new strains of corn and enjoyed a bumper crop. Now his neighbors would see the better results and be motivated to change.

Only they weren't.

The farmers didn't adopt the new corn because they didn't like the weirdo in Bermuda shorts who spurned their lifestyle any more than they liked the pretentious academic who had the nerve to tell them what to do.

This unvarnished failure changed the course of Rogers's life. He spent the rest of his career learning what happens to innovations as they move through a social system. He wanted to learn why some ideas are adopted and others aren't. He also wanted to uncover why certain individuals are far more influential in encouraging people to embrace an innovation than others.

As Rogers set to work, he examined every known study of change. He reviewed how new drugs catch on among doctors. He looked at how new technologies, such as VCRs, become popular. He studied the latest gadgets and discoveries. As he pored over the data, he was startled at how many great ideas simply die. For example, when Vasco de Gama made his triumphant voyage around the Cape of Good Hope, he took 160 men with him. Only 60 returned because the rest died of scurvy. Fortunately, in 1601, an English sea captain named

John Lancaster discovered a cure for scurvy. He gave a little bit of lime juice to his sailors every day, and *no one* died of scurvy. And yet it took almost 200 years for the practice to catch on. Initially the British were actually mocked for their curious practice, and the derisive term *limey* was born.

Rogers was shocked to discover that the merit of an idea did not predict its adoption rate. What predicted whether an innovation was widely accepted or not was whether a specific group of people embraced it. Period. Rogers learned that the first people to latch onto a new idea are unlike the masses in many ways. He called these people *innovators*. They're the guys and gals in the Bermuda shorts. They tend to be open to new ideas and smarter than average. But here's the important point. The key to getting the majority of any population to adopt a vital behavior is to find out who these innovators are *and avoid them like the plague*. If they embrace your new idea, it will surely die.

The second group to try an innovation is made up of what Rogers termed "early adopters." Many early adopters are what are commonly known as opinion leaders. These important people represent about 13.5 percent of the population. They are smarter than average, and tend to be open to new ideas. But they are different from innovators in one critical respect: They are socially *connected* and *respected*. And here's the real influence key. The rest of the population—over 85 percent—will not adopt the new practices *until opinion leaders do*.

So it turns out that when the fellow with the Bermuda shorts used the new seeds, he didn't do Rogers a favor. As far as farming methods were concerned, Cadillac man was an *innovator*. He was the first to adopt new ideas in his community, and like many innovators, he cast suspicion on the "new ways" he endorsed. Since he was different from the majority of his peers in visible ways, and since much of what he did appeared to disrespect traditional methods, this made him a threat. He was neither respected nor connected.

As Rogers later explained, he learned that his recommendations would have fared better if he had carefully sought out opinion leaders to tout his strains of corn.

Given the boost opinion leaders can offer an influence strategy, it is no surprise to learn that the influencers we studied routinely use this powerful source of influence. For example, when Dr. Don Berwick and IHI try to influence the behavior of hundreds of thousands of physicians across the United States, they first engage the *guilds,* as they call them. These are the associations and research groups other physicians look to as credible sources. When the guilds talk, physicians listen.

Similarly, when Dr. Howard Markman tries to influence the communication behavior of couples across the country, he also looks for opinion leaders. He has found that if he trains members of the clergy to teach couples how to solve problems, the results are better than if an unknown outsider in Bermuda shorts swoops into town and offers training.

And how about the Guinea worm disease? Donald Hopkins and his team don't consider going into a village without first working with the village chief or drawing on the power of a respected official. From there, the local official or chief identifies respected village members from different groups or clans who will be listened to when they teach people the vital behaviors required to eradicate the Guinea worm disease. Imagine what would happen if Hopkins recruited a person of no social standing to carry a lifesaving message that challenges old beliefs and norms. Such a person would probably be discounted in a heartbeat.

"The message," Hopkins reports, "is no more important than the messenger."

Interestingly, the power of opinion leaders is available even when you don't have *real* opinion leaders. The TV and radio heroes we referred to earlier *become* opinion leaders. For example, in the village of Lutsaan, India, a community action group made a solemn covenant to educate their daughters after listening to the wildly popular show *Tinka, Tinka Sukh* ("Happiness Lies in Small Things"). In this poignant TV drama, a beloved young girl dies in childbirth after being forced into an early marriage. After vicariously experiencing her death, audience members wrote over 150,000 letters in reaction to the episode. Listeners were so affected by what happened to the young girl that 184 Lutsaan villagers placed their thumbprints on a large public poster in honor of their fallen heroine in a gesture of solidarity and support.

"Of course I will not marry off my daughter before she turns 18," one listener told Dr. Arvind Singhal, who was commissioned to study the effects of the serial drama. "Prior to listening to *Tinka, Tinka Sukh*, I had it in my mind that I need to marry off my daughter soon. Now I won't, and I tell others as well."

Since *Tinka, Tinka Sukh* always featured an epilogue during which a respected person from the community asked questions, made a call to action, and encouraged public discourse, the show made double use of opinion leaders. The comments from the respected figure combined with the actions of the beloved characters made excellent use of social support as a means of promoting change.

To see how to work with opinion leaders, independent of other influence strategies, let's take a look at what Mao Zedong did some 40 years ago. A terrible human being in most respects, Mao understood a thing or two about leveraging social influence to accomplish a bit of good.

On June 26, 1965, Mao lit a fire under the Chinese Ministry of Health, citing its poor record in improving health practices in the far-flung rural regions of China. Rather than wait for the stodgy ministry and medical institutions to solve the problem, Chairman Mao engaged 1.8 million change agents in the cause.

When deciding who would make up his population of change agents, he didn't go with existing health specialists.

Instead, Mao zeroed in on locals who came from the villages they were to serve, who were recommended by their peers, who were committed to serve the people, and who had a basic level of formal schooling, which put them close to their fellow villagers but slightly above them in education. In short, Mao chose opinion leaders.

These "barefoot doctors," as they were later called, were given just a few months of medical training that covered basic preventive practices that could quickly and significantly improve public health in rural areas. They also learned how to treat the most common maladies. And to reduce risk, they were taught to refer more difficult cases to commune hospitals.

The results were immediate and dramatic. Health-related habits in rural villages improved overnight. Villagers adopted practices such as observing basic hygiene and boiling water; and they adopted these practices much faster than predicted. Mao broke from his traditional methods and didn't issue unilateral commands or create harsh policies because he knew they wouldn't have had much effect in rural China. Instead, he coupled support from the top with the actions of on-the-ground opinion leaders.

ENLIST SOCIAL SUPPORT

Rogers's discovery offers enormous leverage to leaders, parents, and the general population alike. When it comes to creating change, you no longer have to worry about influencing everyone at once. If you preside over a company with 10,000 employees, your job is to find the 500 or so opinion leaders who are the key to everyone else. Spend disproportionate time with them. Listen to their concerns. Build trust with them. Be open to their ideas. Rely on them to share your ideas, and you'll gain a source of influence unlike any other.

You don't get to decide whether or not you engage the help of opinion leaders. By definition, they will always be engaged.

They always observe and judge your influence strategy—that's what they do. Then they will give your ideas either a thumbs-up or a thumbs-down. And since they're respected and connected, they will exert their widely felt influence and decide the destiny of your influence strategy—whether you like it or not.

If you're interested in engaging opinion leaders in your own change efforts, the good news is that finding them is quite easy. Since opinion leaders are employees who are most admired and connected to others in the organization, simply ask people to make a list of the employees who they believe are the most influential and respected. Then gather the lists and identify those who are named most frequently (typically ten or more times). These are the opinion leaders. Once you know who they are, enlist them and partner with them in your efforts to institute change.

Enlist Social Support to Influence *You*

On a more personal note, if you're trying to change something within your own life, co-opt the power of those who have an influence on you. If it's true that we'll electrocute a stranger because a guy in a lab coat says, "The experiment requires that you continue," what could we get ourselves to do if we could only find a way to marshal the social support of our actual loved ones and friends?

It turns out, quite a lot. For instance, research demonstrates that those who simply receive e-mails from a friend checking on their progress with smoking cessation, dieting, or exercise do a much better job of sticking with their plans than those who receive no inquiries. (This means that our friend Henry needs to enlist the emotional support and encouragement of his wife, coworkers, and loved ones if he expects to live a healthy lifestyle.) When diabetics involve a loved one in their disease maintenance, compliance soars. Social psychologists learned long ago that if you make a commitment and then share it with friends, you're far more likely to follow through than if you simply make your commitment to yourself.

Better still, team up with someone who is attempting to make the same changes you are. Exercise together. Diet together. Work on your explosive tempers together. Encourage each other, keep each other in the loop, and hold each other accountable. We crave the acceptance and admiration of those we admire. So co-opt the power of social support for your own benefit.

Become an Opinion Leader Yourself

If you aspire to become an effective influencer, you should also aspire to become an opinion leader within your own work and family circle. Parents, in particular, do well when they remain a respected voice with their children throughout the developmental years, and not just until their kids turn 13. Despite the stereotype of all teenagers eventually dismissing their parents' opinions, there are many parents who remain an important source of influence, even during their children's most trying years. This doesn't mean that their offspring eagerly embrace every parental opinion or admonition, but that their parents' opinions still carry weight, even when they go against the wishes of their children.

Here's what it takes to become and remain an opinion leader. People, including children, pay attention to individuals who possess two important qualities. First, these people are viewed as knowledgeable about the issue at hand. They tend to stay connected to their area of expertise, often through a variety of sources. Second, opinion leaders are viewed as trustworthy. They don't merely know a great deal about a certain area, but they also have other people's best interest in mind. This means that they aren't seen as using their knowledge to manipulate or harm, but rather to help. If others believe that you're missing either of these two qualities, you won't be very influential.

But being respected and trusted isn't enough. Opinion leaders are also generous with their time. They frequently rub shoulders with the people who look up to them, and when doing so, they speak their minds in a direct, healthy way. For instance, when we (the authors) examined the factors that contribute to employees' satisfaction in their relationship with their boss, we found that the best predictor was frequency of interaction. Long periods of absence don't help. Bosses who are accessible, talk openly, and spend informal time chatting with their direct reports are far more likely to be influential than those who maintain their distance. The same is true with parents.

So when it comes to drawing on the power of social influence, think opinion leader. Identify opinion leaders, partner with opinion leaders, and become an opinion leader in your own right. If you want to be an opinion leader with your coworkers, direct reports, friends, and family members, you have to be both *respected* and *connected*. More often than not, that calls for face-to-face dialogue where you jointly discuss issues, work through differences, and come to shared agreements.

THE POWER OF *EVERYONE*

Occasionally the problem you're dealing with stems from long-held and widely shared norms. Virtually everyone has done the same thing for years—even generations. As these norms begin to change, everyone needs to talk about the changes before anyone can successfully act in new ways without facing ridicule and eventual isolation. Changes in behavior must be preceded by changes in the public discourse.

However, openly discussing certain norms is often considered taboo or at least politically incorrect. The chances for creating change in such cases are especially dim—unless, of course, an effective influencer finds a way to partner with opinion leaders in making the undiscussable discussable. Learn how to transform taboo subjects into a routine part of the public discourse, and you possess an enormously powerful tool for dealing with some of the toughest cases imaginable.

Make Undiscussables Discussable

In the early 1980s, the authors were invited to help a management team revive a dying manufacturing plant that labored in the very center of the industrial rust belt. The task was to increase profits in the facility by reducing costs and increasing productivity. This manufacturing facility posted a productivity level significantly below that of the average offshore competitor. If this embarrassing benchmark continued to drag bottom, the place was doomed.

To find out what it would take to turn the productivity problems around, the authors met with key personnel and asked one question: "If you could fix one thing around here, what would it be?" The very first person we posed this question to was a superintendent who had worked in the plant for over 20 years. When answering the question, he leaned forward, lowered his voice, looked around twice to see if anyone was listening in, and stated, "All we need to do is one thing. If we could get a good six hours a day out of our skilled labor force, we could make a profit."

The nervous fellow went on to explain that while it was true that many employees were giving the job an honest effort, many weren't. In fact, most had developed a lifestyle that depended on overtime pay, and, to ensure this overtime, they had slowed down. The majority of these free-effort employees were on the clock for an average of ten hours a day, but they were actually working only about four. So if they could just get six hours . . .

We couldn't help but notice that the superintendent was talking to us in much the same tone and style of an FBI informant. He didn't want anyone to know he was making this horrible indictment. People weren't very productive, but this just wasn't something you said aloud. He even swore us to secrecy.

Over the next few years we interviewed hundreds more people at the facility and surfaced dozens of other issues, but the first fellow had it right. He was dead on when he suggested that if you stated aloud that people weren't working hard, it would put you in an awkward position. People would accuse you of being bitter, unfair, and insensitive. People would accuse you of being disrespectful of American workers. They might even threaten you.

To make matters worse, the public discourse at this time was very different. Every voting year, politicians would actually stand in front of cameras and brag about the American workforce and its unparalleled work ethic. The people we worked with would roll their eyes in disgust with each pronouncement, but they wouldn't openly disagree. Nobody could actually say such heresies aloud. When we suggested to the leadership team that the influence strategy we had in mind would directly deal with low productivity, they told us that we had to couch the problem in different terms: We would teach leaders "how to hold people accountable." So we did. Of course, when leaders held people accountable, they only dealt with safety, cost, and quality problems because they couldn't talk about productivity. This issue was still totally undiscussable.

The next year when the labor contract came up for renewal, we begged the HR professionals who were going to sit at the big table during negotiations to bring up the productivity issue. They did, repeatedly, but to no avail. Eventually they were told by the union and company leaders to drop the subject. It was just too divisive, too volatile. They couldn't talk about productivity anymore.

In a place where productivity was the elephant in the living room, nobody on the change team could talk about it. So we didn't. We worked on dozens of different problems, teaching a variety of skills, and making dozens of changes, but we never dealt directly with productivity. Was that a smart move? Take a look at what has happened with the vast majority of America's skilled trade jobs over the past couple of decades, and you'll probably conclude that remaining silent about the issue was a huge mistake.

To see what we should have done to solve the productivity problem, let's return to the Indian village of Lutsaan and revisit the mechanism through which the radio drama *Tinka, Tinka Sukh* affected public opinion. And although it's true that the villagers didn't face a productivity challenge, they did run into a powerful social norm that caused many of them great pain, and their problem was also completely undiscussable.

In one of the *Tinka, Tinka Sukh* story lines a beloved character was not allowed an education, forced to marry young, and died in child birth. As a result of the poignant episodes, the listeners in the village of Lutsaan were propelled to find a way to change the long-held practice of marrying young. But what actually brought about this tremendous change in norms? According to Dr. Arvind Singhal, the power of the show stemmed from its ability to force an undiscussable topic into the public discourse. Long-settled beliefs were suddenly opened to question and discussed at every corner, workstation, and shop—and eventually reshaped.

Before the airing of the episodes, millions of people had placed pressure on their friends, children, and coworkers to continue to honor the traditions of their past. This was peer pressure at its strongest. Some people had already changed their views on the treatment of young girls, but it was difficult for them to share their differing views openly without falling victim to public ridicule for not honoring their past. Many people were uncertain about the tradition and wanted to be able to talk it through, but once again, it just wasn't done.

Entertainment education specialists applied the power of vicarious stories to the issue. They didn't preach the evils of the traditional treatment of girls because, as we all know, verbal persuasion typically leads to resistance. But the practitioners didn't back away either. Instead, they created a serial drama containing likable characters who talked about the social problem in the privacy of their home—while thousands listened in. The beloved family discussed the pros and cons of the tradition, and each show ended with the words of a respected narrator who merely asked questions.

As the radio family experienced its tragedy, family members modeled healthy dialogue. They helped others first think about the issues and then talk about them with their friends, coworkers, neighbors, and family. As a result, the topic moved from the dark into the light. An undiscussable became a discussable, and what had remained underground for centuries wilted in the light of public discourse.

This particular example may sound a bit far removed from the world you experience, so let's bring it a little closer to home. Obviously the tongue-tied manufacturing leaders who weren't allowed to discuss productivity fell victim to this same code of silence. We also found the same norm of silence in a year-long study of health care where we were trying to discover why many hospital patients contract unnecessary infections.[*]

When we asked neonatology nurses and doctors how infections find their way into the pristine environment of a neonatal unit, people would lower their voices, look both ways, and then relate very similar stories. First was the story of the physician who would periodically fail to gown up, glove up, or wash up as he or she should. The second story was of a nurse who, when starting an IV on a very tiny baby, would clip a finger out of his or her sterile glove to expose his or her finger tip. The nurse had a good reason for doing this; it's extremely hard to find a vein on a baby who can fit in the palm of your hand. Nevertheless, exposing the finger was an egregious violation of safety practices—a violation that helped spread infections to babies.

[*]For a full report of the health-care study, visit www.silencekills.com.

Let's not lose the point here. The problem in this particular hospital was not merely that a doctor or nurse broke rules. The problem was that there was a conspiracy of silence held in place by powerful norms that kept people from speaking when colleagues violated hygiene, safety, or any other protocol. The existing social norm called for silence. If someone screws up, you must circle the wagons against lawsuits and infamy. Never speak to outsiders about the real cause. And now for the bigger point: It is silence about the norm of silence that sustains the norm. If you can't talk about it, it will never go away.

If you're reading these examples but not wearing hospital greens, then you're not off the hook. We've also poked around in every type of organization imaginable and have found this same code of silence that sustains unhealthy behavior. For instance, we conducted a year-long study of project management titled "Silence Fails."* In it we explored the colossal failure rates of most high-stakes projects, programs, and initiatives. For example, the vast majority of product launches, reorganizations, mergers, and improvement initiatives either fail or grossly disappoint. In all, roughly 90 percent of major projects violate their own schedule, budget, or quality standards.

So we went in search of the cause behind these embarrassing results. At first we learned that 88 percent of those we surveyed were currently working on projects or initiatives which they predicted would eventually fail—and yet they continued to plod along. Most agreed that the expression that best described the state of their current project was "a slow-motion train wreck."

Then we learned the reason behind the reason: *Fewer than one in ten respondents said that it was politically acceptable to speak openly about what was going wrong.* Most suggested that problems such as weak sponsorship, unreasonable constraints,

*For a full report, visit www.silencefails.com.

or unmotivated team members were eventually going to kill their efforts, but that no one — including the project managers themselves — could bring the issues out into the open.

So, what could the project managers, health-care professionals, or the rust-belt change agents have done to solve their pressing problems? When it came to productivity, we had been routinely told that speaking about the issue in public would make people angry. We were told that talking about the problem would cast us in a bad light and only make the problem worse. And we listened.

Here's what we should have done. First, we should never have accepted the argument that it's wrong to talk openly and publicly about a problem. Critics often do their best to shut people up by labeling a topic as "undiscussable." To confront this attack on open dialogue, we should have gathered data that shined light on the problem. Then we should have presented these data to the leaders of the organization as well as to the opinion leaders of the workforce. Next we should have discussed the inevitable consequences of not changing.

We should have insisted on a frank discussion of the pros and cons of the existing productivity levels — along with the underlying causes. The productivity norms had to change. That's a given. But, more importantly, the norm that mandated silence had to change *first*. The same is true in all the examples we've shared — from hospital-transmitted diseases to project management failures. When you make the undiscussable discussable, you openly embrace rather than fight the power of social influence.

Create a Village

Now for our final use of social support. Some problems will never wilt at the mere glance of a stranger in a white lab jacket. These challenges are so large that they require opinion leaders to step up and lead the way. Other problems will go away only after opinion leaders take previously undiscussable topics and interject them into public discourse.

But there's more. Still other problems are so profound that they won't vanish, even if everyone talks openly and new norms are formed. For instance, some personal changes are so significant that asking people to embrace many new behaviors requires that you shape them into entirely new people; this level of transformation calls for the work of an entire village. You have to draw on the social support of virtually everyone. And when it comes to creating an entire village, Dr. Silbert once again leads the way.

It's semester break at Delancey Street. All 500 residents in the San Francisco location have gathered in the family room where they quietly jostle and joke with one another. There's an air of excitement. After all, it's graduation day. This means that some of the residents are about to advance to more responsible positions. Others will move to a new job, and some will earn their GED. Even greenies may be ready to graduate from maintenance, where the requirements are pretty basic. But the accomplishment will be no less celebrated than the person who is about to receive a college degree—as a number will.

So here the residents sit, waiting for graduation to begin. Those who haven't been through the ceremony before look terribly uncomfortable. They know they will be singled out in front of 499 of their peers, and they have no clue how to deal with the moment. Then before you know it, their name is called. They stand up and are told that they have graduated from maintenance. They have done good work and are now assigned to food services. Congratulations!

All of a sudden new residents hear a sound that has never before been directed at them. They stumble forward to be acknowledged as they experience the most pleasurable wave of discomfort they've ever felt. Everyone is clapping for them.

"It's the most wonderful time," says Silbert. "They're crying. Huge clapping. You'll see this huge guy who doesn't know what to do with his arms because he's so uncomfortable. And it's the best thing in the world."

So what's going on here? Silbert knows how to gain an upper hand over her number-one enemy. Previously enacted illegal, immoral, and antisocial behavior required a strong social system to support it. Criminals run in packs. The distinctly different and healthy behavior that Delancey will demand of each new resident will require an equally strong social system. So that's precisely what Silbert serves up. Delancey immerses residents in nothing short of a whole new culture composed of healthy expectations.

This means that from day one residents are hit by an unrelenting wave of praise and punishment. Remember, one of Delancey's vital behaviors calls for everyone to challenge everyone—and residents do. Silbert has gone to great pains to structure positive and negative peer feedback into everyday life. And since frequent and crystal-clear feedback comes from people who have lived the same life, it's hard for new residents to dismiss the data.

Part of Delancey's enormous force for change stems from the fact that there are 20–30 formal and informal leaders who know everything that's going on with each resident. "If your mom died," says Delancey resident James, "others learn about it and all are saying, 'Are you okay?' We're all checking on each other all the time. If we don't watch out for each other in all regards, we'll go down."

Powered by an incessant wave of positive and negative feedback from people who matter a great deal to them, Delancey residents find that change is the path of least resistance. That's why 90 percent of those who graduate from Silbert's community stick with the changes they've made for the rest of their lives.

And yet it would be easy to escape the tendrils of the new culture. All the ex-cons need to do is walk out the door. There's nothing to stop anyone from exiting; the locks keep people out, not in. But a strange, new, and powerfully magnetic pull draws residents into their new social network. For the first time in their lives these former drug dealers, hookers, and thieves belong to a group of people who care about their long-term well being. Sure residents receive more direction than they're used to, and it's often served up with the bark on, but it always comes with their best interest in mind. And when residents hit their daily and weekly goals, they're embraced and praised.

Best of all, for the first time in their lives Delancey residents belong to a social unit that promotes pro-social behavior. Previous colleagues (usually gang members) wanted something *from* them, not *for* them, and they continually propelled them away from everyday society and into the hostile confines of state and federal prisons. Their new friends are *real* friends, rather than accomplices. They're hell-bent on shaping their coresidents into healthy people who can make it on the outside.

So here's the key to still another source of social influence—one that works for Delancey. Create an environment where formal and informal leaders relentlessly encourage vital behaviors and skillfully confront negative behaviors. When this happens, people make personal transformations that are hard to believe.

Of course, not everyone is about the business of creating an entire new social network, but there are social elements from Silbert's work that apply to any influence effort. Reformed criminals aren't the only ones who respond to praise. The need to belong—to be accepted and admired—is deeply human and affects everyone from riveters to royalty.

For example, Dr. Don Berwick and his team routinely influence one of the most sophisticated populations imaginable—doctors and health-care executives. Yet despite their sophistication, he generously offers praise. He constantly talks up what's working. For instance, when he appears on *Dateline*, it's always with a doctor or health-care leader who's enacting vital behaviors and saving lives. "I learned a long time ago," Berwick tells us, "that credit is infinitely divisible. Give it away every chance you get, and there's always plenty left for you."

SUMMARY: SOCIAL SUPPORT

People who are respected and connected can exert an enormous amount of influence over any change effort. Under stressful and ambiguous circumstances, the mere glance from what appears to be a respected official can be enough to propel people to act in ways that are hard to imagine. Fortunately, this "power of one" can also be used to encourage pro-social behavior.

When a required behavior is difficult or unpopular or possibly even questionable, it often takes the support of "the right one"—an opinion leader—to propel people to embrace an innovation. Learn how to identify and co-opt these important people. Ignore opinion leaders at your own peril.

Sometimes change efforts call for changes in widely shared norms. Almost everyone in a community has to talk openly about a proposed change in behavior before it can be safely embraced by anyone. This calls for public discourse. Detractors will often suggest that it's inappropriate to hold such an open discourse, and they may even go so far as to suggest that the topic is undiscussable. Ignore those who seek silence instead of healthy dialogue. Make it safe to talk about high-stakes and controversial topics.

Finally, some change efforts are so profound that they require the help of everyone involved to enable people to make the change. When breaking away from habits that are continually reinforced by a person's existing social network, people must be plucked from their support structure and placed in a new network, one where virtually everyone in their new social circle supports and rewards the right behaviors while punishing the wrong ones. Dr. Silbert shows us how to do such an amazing thing. No influence strategy that is less socially disruptive offers as much promise.

As it turns out, it's the desire to be accepted, respected, and connected that really pulls at human heart strings. And as far as the rest of us are concerned—managers, parents, and coaches—learn how to co-opt this awesome power, and you can change just about anything.

7
Find Strength in Numbers

SOCIAL ABILITY

*Never run after your hat—others will be
delighted to do it; why spoil their fun?*

—Mark Twain

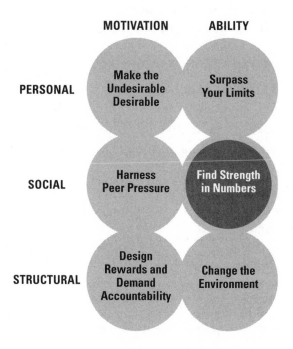

W
e start this chapter with an example of how individuals help each other solve problems and reach new goals and objectives. It's based on a social interaction that, thanks to an important and powerful influencer, takes place in tens of thousands of places around the world.

Seated in a tight circle in a neat, tin-roofed building located in a small village in central India, we find five housewives—Tanika, Kamara, Damini, Payal, and Sankul. They're in the middle of the most important meeting they'll ever attend. They're selecting the first of five businesses they'll start (one each) through small loans from SKS, a local microcredit firm that has set up shop in the region.

Despite the fact that none of these women has ever held a job outside the home or taken a single course in business—and despite the fact that all are caring for families of their own with little or no help from their husbands or ex-husbands—nobody will tell these five women what businesses to start. They will invent businesses on their own as a team.

Today Tanika plans to propose that she be the first of the five women to start her own business. She is desperate to get started because, like many women within a radius of several hundred miles, she lives in gut-wrenching poverty.

"Maybe I can start an egg business like my friend Chatri," Payal suggests with a shy smile.

"You can't start there," Sankul explains. "It takes three or four loans to work your way up to such a large investment. We have to think smaller."

"My cousin Mitali has enjoyed great success with the mini-van she rents," Kamara enthuses.

Once again Sankul sets her friends straight. "That requires an even larger investment. It has taken your cousin over five years to work her way up to a vehicle. We're beginners and have to start much smaller."

"I've got it!" Damini suggests. "I would like to make puffed rice. It takes very little money, and I've heard that many women in nearby villages are now doing well with similar ventures."

"That's the problem," Tanika says. "Too many people are in that business, and profits could drop."

"Then what do you think will work?" Damini asks Tanika.

Tanika makes her move. "I think I have a plan that will make money, even for a beginning person like me. You all know that I have earned money in the past by collecting hair from the local barber shops and making wigs."

"Yes, and they're beautiful," Sankul responds. "But you haven't been able to live off of that."

Tanika remains undeterred. The circumstances she faces are far too desperate for her to back away at the first sign of discouragement. Three months earlier when her husband sold his rice crop for far less than he expected, he came home one evening screaming obscenities, beat her, accused her of dragging him into poverty, called her ugly, and threw her and their three daughters into the street. Under normal circumstances in her village, a divorce such as this would have been a death sentence for Tanika and her children.

But these weren't normal circumstances. One day as Tanika sat in her tiny hut, worrying about her family's next meal, her neighbor Sankul approached her with wonderful news. A group of people from the city was starting to loan money to women such as her as a means of helping them start new businesses.

"It's our turn!" Sankul had said. "It's our turn to help lift ourselves out of poverty." Tanika liked the idea but had to admit that the radical words sounded like something Sankul must have heard from one of the strangers from the city. What did they know that she didn't?

"Who would loan money to a nearly starved woman of no means?" Tanika had wondered. *"How will I be able to come up with an idea for a successful business?"*

As a gentle but unrelenting rain starts to beat its tattoo on the tin roof over the five Indian women, Tanika continues to articulate her partially formed idea.

"You're right; I can't count on wig making. But I know of a place that will buy hair and use the oil from the hair follicles to make health products. I was thinking that if I could find new ways to gather hair, I could sell it to that company and make enough money to feed and clothe my family."

"How do you propose to do that?" asked Payal, the shiest of the five would-be entrepreneurs.

"I'll gladly give you the hair from my hair brushes. It does me no good," said Damini, offering her support.

"So will I," Kamara chimed in. "And I bet we could get all of our neighbors to do the same."

Tanika had thought about asking her neighbors for the hair from their brushes and was encouraged to hear that her friends would support her.

"I was thinking that maybe I could hire people to gather hair from surrounding neighborhoods," she explained.

"Yes," Sankul agreed, "but how would you pay them?"

"Hire children," Kamara proposed. "You wouldn't have to pay them much, and surely children can gather hair."

"Toys!" Damini shouted. "Buy a batch of small plastic toys and offer them to any child who brings you hair. That way you'll get hair for almost nothing, and the money from your sales will be nearly all profit."

And with that final addition to her original idea, Tanika had all the elements of a business plan. Tanika secured a loan of $20 and immediately bought a bag full of inexpensive plastic toys. Then, much like an entrepreneurial Santa Claus, Tanika trudged with her sack of trinkets from village to village.

"I'll let you pick any toy you'd like from the bag if you'll bring me all the hair in your mother and sisters' hairbrushes," Tanika explained to the first group of waifs she encountered.

When the word got out that hair earned toys, our unlikely entrepreneur was inundated. Eventually Tanika sold the hair, repaid her loan, and had capital left over to expand.

A year has passed, and Tanika now has hundreds of women working for her. They gather hair in the villages using toys and sell the hair to Tanika, who then sells it again for a profit. She no longer worries about her family's next meal. And not only has she raised her family to a position far above the poverty line, but Tanika is no longer the same shy, frightened person she was a year ago.

LESSONS FROM A NOBEL LAUREATE

This example raises an interesting question. Why was Tanika able to succeed despite the fact that hundreds of millions of people just like her have failed to fight their way out of poverty? To answer this question, we need to spend time with a recent Nobel Prize winner who just happens to be the genius behind Tanika's success. Meet the soft-spoken and brilliant Muhammad Yunus. He's the man who figured out how to help Tanika and another hundred million people out of poverty.

Here's the part of his amazing story that provides the central theme to this chapter. After leaving the United States with a doctorate in economics, Dr. Yunus decided to return to his homeland of Bangladesh to become a university professor. As he assumed his comfortable teaching position, he was horrified to discover that just outside the academic compound hundreds of thousands of people were dying of starvation.

As Dr. Yunus investigated, it didn't take him long to discover that the root cause of Bangladesh's acute and chronic poverty was not the indolence of the poor. Everywhere he looked in neighboring villages he saw people who worked hard but who were still unable to earn a decent wage. After interviewing 42 people in one village, he was shocked to discover that the biggest barrier was not energy, but capital. Few in these villages had traditional jobs. Most were self-employed. If they weren't supported by their own small plot of land, they were the sole proprietor of a small craft or service business.

To finance their businesses, they needed capital. Usually it was just a few pennies. Since none had even this small amount, they were forced to turn to local loan sharks who charged over 1,000 percent interest. The interest rate was set at just the point to guarantee that each entrepreneur would exhaust his or her income repaying the loan and forever be locked in a cycle of indebtedness. Yunus was dumbfounded when he discovered that a woman who made beautiful handcrafted stools was held in poverty because she lacked the five cents she would need to buy supplies each day. Five cents!

Yunus ended his research with the conclusion that if he could enable one vital behavior (villagers successfully securing and repaying a business loan), he could improve the financial fortunes of the 42 people he interviewed. In total, the 42 people he interviewed needed a paltry $27 to finance their businesses.

Yunus next turned to local banks and suggested that they offer loans to these 42 laborers at market rates. No takers. In fact, bank executives laughed him out of their offices. As far as they were concerned, no collateral, no loans! This harsh policy caused Dr. Yunus grave distress. In his own words:

> *Usually when my head touches the pillow, I fall asleep within seconds, but that night I lay in bed ashamed that I was part of a society which could not provide $27 to forty-two able-bodied, hard-working, skilled persons to make a living for themselves.*

Thirty years have passed since that tortured day, and Dr. Yunus now runs a multibillion-dollar banking and business conglomerate, known as Grameen Bank, that has started a revolution that has helped more than 100 million people like Tanika out of poverty. The microcredit group that loaned

Tanika the starting cash she needed in neighboring India was formed as a direct result of Dr. Yunus's work.

What makes this story even more remarkable is that Dr. Yunus's methods not only helped Tanika, but her four friends also opened small businesses and succeeded—as do 39 out of every 40 people that Dr. Yunus helps. That's correct—98 percent of the people to whom Yunus loans money enact the second vital behavior for moving themselves out of abject poverty: They pay back their loans with full interest.

The majority of these successful business owners move their families out of poverty. They educate their children, and by now many of these children have earned advanced degrees. Once-starving villagers who at one time earned two cents for a day's hard labor now run profitable businesses while their children attend universities.

As inspiring as this story is, the key takeaway lies in learning how Yunus was able to ensure that his poverty-stricken clients were able to enact the vital behaviors that led to success. What influence magic does he work to ensure that non-collateralized loans are paid back over 98 percent of the time? Equally important, which strategies can you and I put into place as still another powerful tool in our influence repertoire?

As is the case with any complex intervention that claims to change people with long histories of painful failures, Dr. Yunus makes use of virtually every method we mention in this book. His task is too large to rely on a single influence tool, so he uses them all. Nevertheless, by watching Tanika and her colleagues in action, we can focus on yet another high-leverage influence tool—the power of *social capital*.

Dr. Yunus didn't merely ask Tanika to submit a business plan that he would review. He demanded that she form a team with four of her neighbors, each of whom would submit plans of their own. Each person from the team would eventually be granted a loan. And with the granting of a loan, each of the other four people would cosign for the debt! That meant that Tanika had to convince her four friends that her business idea would work. More likely, she would have to work with them to create a plan that they would first coinvent and then support.

What do you suppose happens when people who have never worked a job, who are currently inches away from the jaws of the grim reaper, and who are being asked to cosign their new teammate's note in case the business fails? They don't put up with any half-baked ideas. They create smart and workable plans by uniting the intellectual capital of all five people in the group.

ENLIST THE POWER OF SOCIAL CAPITAL

In Chapter 6, we learned that other people can motivate us in profound ways. Now we add the second of the two social sources of influence—social ability. As the Beatles suggested, we're most likely to succeed when we have "a little help from our friends." These friends provide us with access to their brains, give us the strength of their hands, and even allow us to make use of their many other personal resources. In effect they provide us with social capital. In fact, with a little help from our friends, we can produce a force greater than the sum of our individual efforts. But we can do this only when we know how to make use of social capital—*the profound enabling power of an essential network of relationships.* And Dr. Yunus has made use of this power as well as anyone alive.

Popular author James Surowiecki explains why Tanika was able to come up with her successful business plan. Surowiecki would be the first to suggest that the idea he proposes in his book *The Wisdom of Crowds* has been around for a long time. In his very first sentence, Surowiecki points to British scientist Francis Galton, who applied statistical methods to demonstrate that groups—made up of people at all intellectual levels—often perform better than any one individual.

When 787 local residents who visited a regional livestock fair guessed the weight of a slaughtered and dressed ox, Galton calculated the average score of the locals who predicted the weight to be 1,197 pounds. The ox eventually weighed in at 1,198 pounds. The group average hadn't merely come close to the correct weight, it had been almost exactly correct. The point Surowiecki makes about crowds is: "Under the right circumstances, groups are remarkably intelligent, and are often smarter than the smartest people in them."

Long before Surowiecki popularized the idea that groups can do better than the smartest individuals, Dr. Yunus put this notion to work in his microcredit enterprises. Consider the five housewives who had never held jobs as they were brainstorming ways to leverage Tanika's scheme. No one person came up with the final plan, but, by playing off each other's suggestions, they jointly came up with a method that succeeded. They were able to do so because they weren't merely pooling ignorance; they were inventing products and services that would sell in their own village, and they all knew their village.

WHEN AND HOW TO INVEST IN SOCIAL CAPITAL

Sometimes it's obvious that a profound change in behavior will require help from others. For example, if Dr. Don Berwick and his team want to save 100,000 patients from accidental death in U.S. hospitals, it's clear that they'll need to involve doctors, nurses, administrators, housekeepers, and others. The same is true with Dr. Silbert's work with ex-cons. She doesn't merely rely on a village to help her; she actually *creates* a village.

Sometimes it's not so obvious that your change strategy requires anyone other than yourself. For example, you might think that sticking with a diet is a matter of individual will. In the solitary moments when you're deciding between a deep-fried apple turnover and an apple, it's all up to you. But you'd be wrong to make the assumption that you're alone. While all vital behaviors are enacted by individuals and often done in private, an enabling group of individuals can make an enormous difference in influencing change.

For example, Dr. Wiwat succeeded at influencing vulnerable sex workers who can feel quite intimidated when facing a liquored-up client who demands sex with no condom. As we'll see shortly, although the sex worker is flying solo in these moments, scores of other people will find a way to help her succeed. Clever influencers always consider ways to ensure that individuals have sufficient social support to step up and succeed in crucial moments.

So, when exactly should you build social capital to bring about challenging changes?

When Others Are Part of the Problem

Consider the following common business problem. It highlights exactly when people need to rely on the help of others in order to succeed at work.

Meet "Jess." At this very moment he's sweating like an Olympic boxer. That's because he's about to tell a lie, and he's afraid he'll get caught. Jess fears that he'll get caught because, unlike a good poker player who can bluff without giving off a clue, Jess has "tells" that he's powerless to mask. Right now in addition to sweating profusely, his left eye is twitching so violently that he's sure it must be visible from across the room. As Jess starts to speak, his throat constricts to the size of a straw—still another tell. After faking a coughing seizure, Jess eventually squeaks out the big, fat lie that's sure to get him in trouble.

"No problem," Jess mutters. "We're right on target."

Jess isn't the only fibber at the table. Everyone in this product development meeting is stretching the truth. In fact, at the 1,500-person software development group where Jess works, telling your coworkers and bosses that your work is on schedule when it actually isn't is deeply rooted in the culture. Lying about readiness is so common that Jess and his colleagues have given it a special name. It's called "project chicken."

Here's how the game is played. You say you're ready with your part of a project when you aren't in the hope that someone else will admit that he or she will need to extend the deadline. The first person to lose nerve and say, "I need more time" is the chicken. And like the vehicular version of the same game, once someone swerves, everyone else is safe. All the others are off the hook because they'll benefit from the new extended deadline, only they didn't have to admit that they messed up. In this particular meeting, most of the team leaders at the table, just like Jess, are dangerously behind. And yet none of them will admit it. Nobody swerves, the deadline isn't extended, and, as a result of their combined lying, a major product release will soon end in disaster.

When we (the authors) first started working with this particular software company, it was on the brink of bankruptcy. It had not met a product release date in years. And when the company finally did release products, they typically cost twice as much as they should have. Morale was at an all-time low, so in addition to product problems, the company was losing far too many of its most talented players.

Mike, the newly appointed VP of development, was tasked with turning this situation around. He had already identified the vital behavior he had to influence. He knew that if he could find a way to both motivate and enable employees up and down the organization to speak up early and honestly about problems, the company would improve morale, reduce costs, and gain control of the schedule. But that was a big order.

When we first met Mike, he had already tried several strategies. He'd implemented communication training. He'd identified opinion leaders and asked them to help solve the problem. He had even created an anonymous survey to measure whether or not behavior was changing. Still, the organization was stuck.

In fact, Mike told us that all he had to show for his effort was good solid data that they were failing.

What Mike didn't realize until late in the game was that Jess and his colleagues were not isolated actors making independent decisions about how to talk about deadlines in meetings. Lying in order to look good had been reinforced by managers, directors, and vice presidents. Even Mike had unwittingly played a role in encouraging people to bring only good news to the table. And since the behavior was created by the group, the group would have to be involved in changing it. So how could he make use of this social capital?

To answer this, let's see how someone else dealt with a similar problem. We travel 9,000 miles to South Africa to study Garth Japhet. No one has thought longer, harder, or more carefully about how to build social capital than Garth Japhet. He's a master at turning a *me* problem into a *we* problem.

Dr. Japhet began his career as a medical doctor, but he wound a circuitous path to his current position as CEO of Soul City, a South African media brain trust that has led successful efforts to fight AIDS, infant mortality, and malnutrition. More recently, Japhet has turned his attention to preventing violence against women. Dr. Japhet directed his attention to this particular problem because, within the borders of South Africa, the scourge of violence against women is nothing short of horrendous. One in nine women will be raped at least once in her lifetime. One in five will be physically or emotionally abused by her partner.

Dr. Japhet realized that he wasn't about to solve this deeply entrenched problem by teaching women individually to stand up on their own two feet and eventually overthrow the insensitive men who obviously deserved a comeuppance. Instead, Japhet realized that he'd have to find a way to include everyone who was *creating* the problem in *solving* the problem.

Japhet also understood that there were many in South African society who disapproved of the abuse—both women and men. And yet these people felt unable to exert sufficient influence to change the behavior they despised. So Japhet gave them a way. In his own words:

"On the TV program *Soul City*, we purposefully created a well-respected teacher, Thabang, who repeatedly abused his likable wife Matlakala. Viewers—both male and female—quickly concluded that Matlakala didn't deserve the abuse as tradition had often spoken. She was pleasant, easy to get along with, and nothing more than an innocent victim. Equally curious, Thabang was mostly a reasonable and good person—much like themselves."

Then the writers showed how interested friends and neighbors could be part of the solution. Dr. Arvind Singhal, who served as a research adviser to *Soul City*, reports, "On one episode the neighbors hear Thabang beating poor Matlakala and they can take it no longer, so they decide to let Thabang know that his actions aren't going unobserved. But how? How could they let Thabang know without being too intrusive? How could they do it without putting themselves at physical risk? Saying something directly would be unacceptable and dangerous."

Dr. Singhal explains. "To send their violent neighbor the message that his behavior is neither private nor acceptable, the neighbors gather outside Thabang's front door and bang pots and pans. They don't say a word; they just bang pots and pans." In the program, Thabang becomes embarrassed and begins to change his behavior.

What happened after that was totally unexpected. People in several townships across South Africa, upon hearing the sounds of spousal abuse next door, began to stand in front of their neighbor's homes and bang pots and pans.

The power of vicarious modeling had worked its magic. The message was out. Men would no longer be allowed to abuse their wives with impunity. Violent behavior, and the collective silence that supported it, were not part of the new norm.

Here's the influence takeaway. Japhet realized that if bad behavior is reinforced by a web of players, all the players have to be engaged in influencing change. In this particular case, the neighbors had to help lead the change for good because neighbors who stood by and allowed obvious abuse to continue were a big part of the problem.

And that's also how Mike finally eliminated "project chicken." He had first tried to solve the problem by confronting employees like Jess without addressing the role his managers, directors, and a host of others played in the problem. When he realized what was missing, he took a completely different tack. He asked the training department to teach people how to hold high-stakes conversations about project problems. Then he charged every one of his organization's leaders to be the teachers. It was a stroke of brilliance that changed everything.

Every two weeks the very manager who had previously sent subtle signals about suppressing candor taught a two-hour session on how to speak up about risky problems. In the first two sessions Jess listened passively and cynically. By the third session he raised a concern with his manager. In the context of the class, the manager felt a special responsibility to respond appropriately. By the sixth session many of Jess's peers had begun to open up. Within a matter of months powerful new norms emerged, and Mike's vital behavior of candor under pressure flourished. Within a year the organization had launched two product releases on time and on budget, and morale was at an all-time high.*

To see how the power of social capital can apply at home, let's return to our friend Henry as he continues his lifelong quest to eat healthily and keep his weight down. He's learned that when it comes to coworkers, friends, and family members,

*For more information on this and other case studies, visit www.vitalsmarts.com/corporatecasestudies.aspx.

most are full-out disablers, not enablers. Instead of acting like friends, they act like accomplices in the crimes against his body. They take Henry out to fancy restaurants, eat fatty and delicious food in front of him at work, give him gifts of the very food he loves but shouldn't eat, stock the pantry chock full of all the wrong ingredients, and so on.

In fact, when it comes to losing weight, Henry can't think of anyone who is enabling him in any way. One day when he asked his wife to stop buying bags of chocolate candy, she actually laughed out loud. She loves candy, buys candy, eats candy, and never gains a pound, so why shouldn't she buy candy?

But Henry knows it's hard to go it alone. "Hey, look at me. I live here in the apartment with you. I smell all that delicious chocolate, and it drives me crazy!"

And it wasn't just his olfactory powers that clued Henry in about the importance of enlisting others' help. He had recently read a study (conducted by our friend Albert Bandura) about research subjects who were trying to lower their cholesterol. As both Henry and Albert suspected, participants routinely achieved greater reductions in their cholesterol when their spouses took part in the program.

So Henry has to find a way to step up to his disablers and ask them to become enablers. This means that Henry will have to talk to others in a way that creates genuine dialogue rather than resistance and recrimination.

When You Can't Succeed on Your Own

The poet John Donne was right: No man is an island. When the people surrounding you are causing or contributing to the problems—playing the role of disabler rather than enabler— fight the urge to attack your detractors for their contribution to your pain. Instead, co-opt them. Turn a *me* problem into a *we* problem. Build social capital in order to resolve persistent and resistant behaviors.

Interdependence. When a vital behavior requires several people to work in concert—where no one person can succeed on his or her own—you have to develop people's ability to work as a team. There was a time when highly skilled craftspeople worked alone producing pots, candles, jewelry, and the like. But today corporate success often depends on experts who are at least as specialized as their predecessors, but who rely on one another to complete their tasks.

For instance, a typical software development team consists not only of code writers but also of designers, marketers, writers, and salespeople. At various stages in the development, all have to connect, bring their piece of the project online, and, at the interpersonal level, find a way to collaborate. Leaders who fail to appreciate this concept are regularly disappointed when their influence efforts bear no fruit.

We (the authors) once worked with a production team that had decided to lower costs by shifting to just-in-time inventory. This meant that no longer would the company maintain a stock of parts and work-in-progress as the product made its way through the production line. One expert would hand his or her finished work to the next expert instead of placing it in a stack that the next person would get to at his or her leisure. This new design, of course, called for impeccable timing (each person's job needed to take the same amount of time as the person's before and after him or her). It also called for genuine collaboration. Any one person could slow down, speed up, take an unscheduled break, or fail to meet a quality standard, causing the previous and next person fits.

When we arrived to help with the project, the company had learned that the old style of stacking expensive inventory between employees had masked the workforce's inability to cooperate. Now that employees were immediately dependent on the person before and after them, they were constantly bickering, complaining, and asking to change positions in the line. Supervisors would routinely intervene to help their direct reports work through problems, but they ended up spending most of their time refereeing heated arguments.

It turns out that the company wasn't prepared to shift to a just-in-time system because it didn't possess the social capital to collaborate. When executives purposefully built interdependence into the work design, it quickly revealed that employees lacked interpersonal problem-solving skills along with the ability to hold one other accountable. Working in isolation had atrophied their ability to interact effectively. No longer did employees "work and play well" with their friends.

The company was unable to implement the new inventory system until each employee had been trained in interpersonal problem solving. Interdependence calls for individuals to share ideas, provide materials, lend a hand, subordinate one's personal needs to the needs of the group, and otherwise willingly and ably collaborate. Leaders who don't continually help interdependent employees learn new and better ways to work in tandem tend to routinely suffer from rivalry, and are never able to make full use of their valuable social capital.

Novelty. Tanika's group demonstrates another circumstance that calls for the power of social capital. Tanika and the other members of her borrower group were certainly not specialists, and they faced problems that were completely new to them. Fortunately, the toys-for-hair plan the five came up with grew out of the best thinking of the group. No one person had exactly the right idea, but as one partial idea was added upon and then changed again, each person helped create a strategy that, if left to her own devices, none would have invented.

When facing changing, turbulent, or novel times—calling for novel solutions—multiple heads can be better than one. By demanding that no budding entrepreneur work alone, Dr. Yunus ensures that his microcredit clients always work in teams, think in teams, and meet every single week and brainstorm as teams. Grameen Bank counts on synergy through forced interaction.

Risk. As you might expect, among all the influencers we have studied, those who faced the biggest risks also drew most heavily from the power of social capital as a means of reducing that risk. Toward the top of this list, of course, would be Dr. Silbert, whose job it is to transform hardened criminals into productive citizens. Think of what Silbert's wards do as a matter of their daily work, and you'll appreciate just how much risk she and her organization face.

Every day about a hundred of Silbert's San Francisco residents invade people's residences across the Bay Area and remove their valuables. This is something many of them did before joining Delancey. The difference now is that they are doing so as part of the Delancey Moving Company. That's right, people who had once made a living moving furniture and other goods illegally are now doing so legally. You'd think that this business strategy was far too risky, given the employees' job histories. Nevertheless, every single valuable Delancey movers remove shows up at the new residence. Delancey is the largest privately owned moving company in the Bay Area for a good reason. The company has never had a loss or theft. Imagine what would happen if even one pearl necklace came up missing? Delancey's reputation would be lost, and the moving company along with its 100 jobs would simply disappear. In spite of huge risk, Delancey has *no* problems.

Equally astounding is the fact that in the Delancey restaurant, residents still reeling from alcohol or drug withdrawal serve alcohol to customers as part of their daily job. Hearing about this obvious incongruity for the first time, we asked Silbert how she deals with "relapses." Without hesitation, she answered, "We don't have relapse." When we pressed her, she thought back to the last instance of abuse and acknowledged that a year earlier one person had "gotten dirty." To fully appreciate what this means, we need to consider that the average rehab program has a very low success rate.

Silbert sends criminals into people's homes, and she asks alcoholics to serve drinks—with almost *no* problems. When you ask her why her influence strategy succeeds, she explains that a key lies in the complex, pervasive, and powerful social system of Delancey. The organization does not have a single in-house professional, but it does have a great deal of social capital. Delancey relies on a web of helping relationships that Silbert has constructed for over 30 years.

Here's how she draws on the power of social capital as a means of supporting vital behaviors. Silbert structures the entire Delancey experience around residents giving each other instruction, mentoring, and guidance. That means that a resident who has been onboard for a single day is likely to be asked to assist someone who has just arrived. And despite the fact that a resident may have shown up at the front door hung over, uneducated, and skilled only in criminal behavior, he or she will eventually earn the equivalent of a Ph.D. in mentoring, coaching, and teaching—or nobody would make it out alive.

In Silbert's words, "You learn a little and then teach it to someone else—'Each one teach one.' For example, you're at Delancey a hot minute and someone newer than you comes in. So someone says to you, 'Do me a favor, take him under your wing.' From that point on people talk with you more about how you're doing with the guys under you than about yourself."

To ensure that individuals assist one another, Delancey is structured with one goal in mind. From the moment a resident arrives at Delancey—frightened and suspicious—he or she is immersed in a culture and language system designed to maximize peer support. If you were a resident, here's how you'd be enriched with social capital.

When you first show up, you're assigned to a dorm of nine individuals of different races. Next, you're placed in what is known as a "minyan." A *minyan* is made up of ten people from different dorms. The word minyan originates from Jewish tradition and refers to a congregation consisting of 10 adults. A full minyan is required to be present before public services can be held. So, the Delancey version of a minyan is a self-support-ing group that's able to do what residents would be unable to do on their own. At Delancey, minyans practically print social capital.

Minyan leaders take primary responsibility for residents' growth, needs, and supervision. Minyans, in turn, are super-vised by a "barber." (A good bawling out on the street is some-times referred to as a "haircut." Hence, the title *barber* goes to those whose job it is to ensure that everyone in the minyan is challenging everyone else.)

The use of social capital takes on still more forms. For example, residents work for crews with crew bosses who are also peers. The average person arrives with a seventh-grade educa-tion, and each is required to leave Delancey with at least a high school equivalency certificate. And Delancey achieves this amazing result without hiring a single professional teacher. They build social capital by tutoring each other.

To see how all this coaching, teaching, modeling, and tutor-ing plays itself out, consider the field of romance.

"We're not healthy," our Delancey resident James admits. "We shouldn't be in relationships until we can see the thing is more than sex. We tend to just say, 'The hell with it!' when the relationship gets tough."

So to prepare to go on dates (something they're not allowed to do for at least six months), residents attend couples' groups which, as you've probably guessed, are taught by resident cou-ples who have been dating slightly longer than the new students. The more seasoned couples teach others how to behave on dates as well as how to talk about what's working and what isn't. And guess who will be going along with each new couple on their first few dates. A chaperone who is assigned by the barber to keep the two on the straight and narrow.

This is but a small sampling of how an organization that has virtually no professional resources invests in social capital as the primary asset for changing people's behavior—and lives. Now, if a philanthropist left a billion dollars to Delancey so that the institution could afford to hire professional teachers, counselors, and coaches, do you think Dr. Silbert would allow it? Of course not. By helping others, residents help themselves even more. Teachers learn more than students, mentors more than mentees, and trainers more trainees, so why restrict all this important learning to outside professionals who have already been to school?

At the business level, more than one organization is beginning to understand how to reduce risk by making better use of social capital. For example, venture capitalists in Silicon Valley create "business incubators" as a way of helping new businesses survive the risky start-up phase. These are a system through which specialists of all types freely offer expertise to companies when it's most needed.

From a personal career standpoint, the need to build social capital by connecting with others has never been greater. Tom Boyle of British Telecom coined the expression NQ, or network quotient, to highlight the importance of a person's ability to form connections with others. He argues that from a career standpoint a person's NQ is now more important than his or her IQ. Since you can't know everything, it's essential that you find people who can make up for your blind spots. A whole host of recent studies reveals that today's most successful employees have networks of people they can go to for expertise, as well as networks of people they can trust with sensitive requests. Successful people not only refuse to see themselves as islands, but they carefully reduce their personal vulnerability by ensuring that they're valued members of hyperconnected networks.

All these examples deal with the same problem. Changing, complex, turbulent, and risky times require multiple heads to come up with creative solutions that no one person could ever invent. So take your lead from Dr. Yunus. When problems call for creativity and multiple views, place people in teams. To make the best use of your existing human resources and dramatically lower your risks, take your lead from Delancey by turning your more experienced employees into coaches, trainers, instructors, and mentors.

Blind Spots. Perhaps the most obvious condition that demands social support as a means of influencing vital behaviors comes with the need for feedback that can be offered only by a pair of outside eyes. Anyone who has ever tried to learn tennis on his or her own and then gone head-on with someone who has spent a similar amount of time practicing with the aid of a coach quickly learns that real-time feedback from an expert beats solo practice any day. This being the case, you'd think that most people would turn to coaches to help in key areas of their lives, but they don't. Only a few ask for feedback outside of sports arenas.

But there are exceptions. For example, in health care, where doctors are required to insert tubes in people's hearts and perform other such high-stakes practices, professionals long ago learned the power of real-time coaching. In many instances, physicians aren't allowed to merely watch others perform a detailed and dangerous procedure before they try it on their own. Instead, they must attempt the delicate procedure while a coach provides immediate feedback on what's working and what isn't.

When it comes to business and other lower-risk settings, leaders rarely think of using real-time coaches. Some of today's companies provide their leaders with call-in advisers who discuss what happened yesterday when the leader faced a challenge and didn't do all that well. But few provide real-time coaching. This should change.

For example, when we (the authors) worked with Lauren—a rather vibrant executive who was a terrible speaker—we provided her with a speech coach. It was amazing to watch someone once described as having "the uncanny ability to whip a crowd into a nap" be transformed into a solid speaker in a matter of a few hours. Lauren didn't take a course or read a book; she merely practiced giving a speech while receiving immediate feedback: "Pick up the speed by 10 percent." "Pause after the word 'successful.'" After four hours of guided instruction, Lauren learned what might have taken months without feedback.

Since you're on the wrong side of your eyeballs, you can't always see exactly what it is that you're doing that works or doesn't work. So invest in still another form of social capital: Seek real-time feedback from an expert.

Group Solidarity. In a parable by William Forster Lloyd published in 1833, we first hear of a problem that is now known as the "tragedy of the commons." The parable describes how a town allowed farmers to graze livestock at will on common soil—soil often owned by nobility. This well-intentioned practice eventually led to a public disaster. The more successful a farmer became, the more sheep he grazed, until eventually there were so many sheep grazing on the land that "the common" was destroyed. What was good for the individual farmer was bad for the collective whole.

You might have faced a similarly constructed scenario. For instance, after plodding along for an hour in stop-and-go traffic, you come across the cause of the hold-up. You discover that a large box lies in one lane, causing the snarl. On the one hand what's good for you—zooming off immediately—is bad for everyone who follows. On the other hand, if you were to sacrifice your own interest and step out of the car and remove the box, everyone else would benefit.

Under these conditions, individuals have to learn how to invest in one of the most powerful forms of social capital—solidarity. We must give ourselves up to the larger cause and act for the good of everyone else, or the plan will fail. For instance, we (the authors) were once charged with creating a leadership class that taught newly appointed frontline supervisors how to hold their direct reports accountable. To create the course, we looked for positive deviance. We watched those who succeeded where others failed in action, learned what they did, and then included their unique skills in an accountability class.

After completing the course, all the graduates were asked to put into practice what they had just learned by talking to people who broke rules, violated procedures, or otherwise behaved badly. But a few didn't put their new skills into practice. These "late adopters" waited to see if their colleagues were going to step up to the challenge before they gave their new tools a trial run. The majority who did confront their direct reports about deviations were soon ridiculed for being too tough. Hourly folks pointed to the supervisors who weren't setting the same standards for their employees and concluded that their own bosses were unfair or hard-nosed. Eventually everyone stopped applying what he or she had studied.

We learned from this incident the power of solidarity. From that point on we secured the promise of every supervisor that he or she would step up to problems before we sent anyone into action. With that particular change project, asking employees to toe the line turned out to be an all-or-nothing deal.

To see the importance of solidarity on a much larger scale, let's look at how our friend Dr. Wiwat from Thailand exploited social capital to help stop the spread of HIV/AIDS. After failing to make a dent in the problem using traditional influence methods, Wiwat took a much more direct approach. Shutting down the sex industry in Thailand was the ideal, but leaders were unable to do so, and the vicious virus was spreading at unprecedented rates. So leaders turned their attention to stopping the spread of HIV/AIDS. Since almost all the new cases were coming from sex workers who weren't protecting themselves or their clients, Wiwat started a campaign of solidarity.

In Wiwat's view, one group of people—sex workers—could bring the spread of HIV/AIDS to a halt, but it would have to be done as a group. When a client offered money for sex and the sex worker demanded protection (a solution to the spread of AIDS), more often than not the client would simply go elsewhere.

But what if *every* worker demanded protection and always refused the financial incentive? Then there would be no place where clients could find sex workers who offered unprotected sex and eventually every client would practice safe sex, thereby stopping the spread of AIDS. But once again, this plan called for an all-or-nothing deal. If one sex worker broke ranks or one brothel eased its demands, the game would be off.

To ensure that everyone complied, Wiwat held a meeting to which he invited all sex business owners. Then he held a meeting for all their workers. In both forums he explained the economics of why every single person had to participate in the plan or AIDS would eventually kill them all along with their businesses. He then informed them of HIV growth rates and detailed what would happen if any individual or establishment refused to sign up for the program.

Eventually, when every worker bought into the plan and the entire population banded together by demanding protection, compliance rates increased from around 14 percent to over 90 percent. As a result of demanding solidarity and providing needed social support, an estimated 5 million people have been spared the horrific consequences of contracting HIV/AIDS in Thailand.

What role might solidarity play closer to home? When studying parenting, it doesn't take long to uncover the simple yet important notion that, with effective parents, no means no. Effective parents help bring predictability into a child's turbulent life by letting him or her know that parents' word is their bond. If a child hits her sister, she'll pay a consequence. If a teenager comes home after curfew, it'll come with a cost. With two parents in the home, the expectation that *no* actually means *no* can of course be achieved only when both parents stand unified, shoulder to shoulder. Otherwise, the child plays one parent off the other, and anarchy prevails. When it comes to disciplining children—as is the case with many profound and pervasive problems—solidarity rules.

SUMMARY: SOCIAL ABILITY

In an interdependent, turbulent world, our biggest opponents—the mortal enemy of all families, companies, and communities—may well be our inability to work in concert. Since
rarely does any one of us have all that's required to succeed with
the complex tasks we face every day, we desperately need to
build social capital.

However, that's certainly not the message we've been fed
for years. The movie and TV heroes of the last half century
have fought the enemy within—the big bosses, the establishment, "the man." This constant celebration of the rugged indi-
vidualist has had an enormous dampening effect on people's
willingness to draw on others to enable change.

Savvy influencers know better than to turn their backs on
social capital. They're quick to consider what help, authority,
consent, or cooperation individuals may need when facing risky
or daunting new behaviors. Then they develop an influence
strategy that offers the social capital required to help make
change inevitable.

8

Design Rewards and Demand Accountability

STRUCTURAL MOTIVATION

I can take any amount of criticism,
so long as it is unqualified praise.

—*Attributed to Noel Coward*

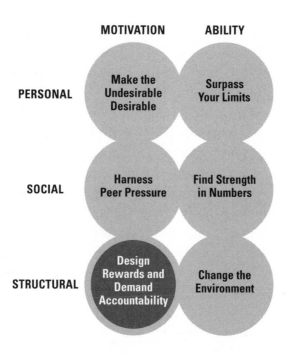

So far we've explored both personal and social influence. Now we step away from human factors and examine how to optimize the power of *things* such as rewards, perks, bonuses, salaries, and the occasional boot in the rear.

CHOOSE EXTRINSIC REWARDS THIRD

We're about to step on dangerous ground. Stories of well-intended rewards that inadvertently backfire are legion. The primary cause of most of these debacles is that individuals attempt to influence behaviors by using rewards as their *first* motivational strategy. In a well-balanced change effort, rewards come *third*. Influence masters first ensure that vital behaviors connect to intrinsic satisfaction. Next, they line up social support. They double check both of these areas before they finally choose extrinsic rewards to motivate behavior. If you don't follow this careful order, you're likely to be disappointed.

This particular concept came to the world's attention with a nursery school study that sent out a warning that won't soon be forgotten. In fact, in 1973 when Dr. Mark Lepper and his colleagues examined the effects of rewarding children (giving them their favorite snack) for engaging in activities that they already enjoyed (playing with their favorite toy), change agents, coaches, parents, and leaders all took note.

Dr. Lepper revealed that rewarding people for engaging in an activity that is already satisfying may work against you. Instead of increasing the frequency of the activity, once the reward is taken away, subjects may do less of it. At least, once the favorite treat was taken away from the Bing Nursery School kids that Lepper studied, they played with their favorite toy less often than they played with it before they were rewarded for doing so.

Think of the implications. You want your daughter to learn to love reading with the same joy and fervor you and your spouse have. You notice that she's starting to pick up the habit on her own, so you decide to reinforce it. To encourage her, you create an incentive program. Every time she picks out a book on her own and reads it, you give her five dollars. She loves the plan, starts reading more, and after a while spends her earnings on a new video game for her latest game system. In fact, it's not long until she's able to buy several games, for which she thanks you profusely.

After a while you think that you've rewarded reading enough and that the pure pleasure of soaking in the words of some of the world's best authors has become its own reward. So you pull away the incentive. Surely your encouragement has helped your daughter learn to love reading good books even more. Most certainly she'll now snuggle up with her favorite author's latest work without any encouragement from you.

But your plan backfires. The minute you stop paying your daughter for reading, she turns to her video game system and reads less than she did before you started the incentive program. Apparently she has learned to earn money to purchase video games, and the incentive you tried didn't leave the impression you wanted. She's just like those nursery school kids. Where did you and Dr. Lepper go wrong?

The explanation for this phenomenon, known as "the overjustification hypothesis," suggests that if people receive rewards for doing something they initially enjoy, they conclude the same thing an outsider watching them in action might conclude. When thinking about what's happening, humans recognize that they're doing something *and* getting paid a special bonus for doing it. They conclude that since they're being rewarded for the task, it must not be all that satisfying (why else would someone offer a reward?), and therefore they're doing it for the bonus. And now for the dangerous part. Once the reward is removed, the person believes that the activity isn't as much fun as he or she judged earlier, so he or she does it less often.

Generally people are perfectly happy getting rewarded for something they already enjoy. For example, imagine that you absolutely love playing the harp (a hobby you picked up in your forties) and your next-door neighbor asks you to play at his son's wedding reception—for a nice fee. You love playing, you love the attention, and you are really psyched about getting paid for doing something you already love doing. You can't believe your luck. For you, getting paid to do what you love doing doesn't diminish your affection one tiny bit.

Sometimes, however, making use of extrinsic rewards can be complicated. As Dr. Lepper learned, not every reward has its desired effect. Sometimes extrinsic programs can completely backfire and serve as a punishment. For example, a company's "Employee of the Month Program" is supposed to give special attention to people who have done something, well, special. They're singled out at an all-hands meeting and are given a plaque.

Comedian Demetri Martin summed up the way a lot of employees feel about such programs when he said, "I think employee-of-the-month is a good example of when a person can be a winner and a loser at the same time."

To many employees, being singled out in front of and compared to peers might not be all that rewarding. It could be just the equivalent of saying, "Congratulations! Here's a hundred dollars, a beautiful plaque with your name engraved on it—and four weeks of unrelenting ridicule from your coworkers!"

Organizational scholars have long found that many employees leave corporate award ceremonies not motivated and excited as intended, but with exactly the opposite reaction. They exit demotivated and upset because they themselves weren't honored. In fact, many see the whole ceremony as a sham. Interviews reveal that typically half of those who attend corporate awards programs believe that they were far better qualified than the person who was honored but that they didn't get picked for political reasons.

And it's not just token awards that can go amiss. You could fill volumes with stories of how carefully considered incentive schemes have run amok. One hospital, for example, found that anesthesiologists who were paid based on personal production were less willing to jump in and help one another when someone else's patient was reacting badly.

Consider a couple of the former Soviet Union's attempts to dabble in incentive schemes. In the energy sector, rubles were literally being thrown away in the search for oil reserves because Soviet workers received bonuses according to the number of feet they drilled. It turns out that it's far easier to drill many shallow holes than to drill a few deeper ones—which is exactly what happened. Instead of following the geological advisories to drill deep to find existing reserves, workers were happy merely poking the surface over and over—turning up very little oil. After all, it's what they were rewarded for doing. Similarly, in a Soviet nail factory, leaders who paid bonuses based on the total weight of nails produced did see weight production shoot up. Unfortunately, it climbed as workers produced exactly the same number of nails as they had before—the nails were just bigger. Not pleased with the increase in the size of the nails, leaders began offering rewards based on the number of nails produced. Once again, the incentive worked and production shot up, but the factory produced only very small nails.

One woman we worked with—a manager at an internationally renowned company—decided that her employees weren't as innovative as they needed to be, so she instituted a simple suggestion program. What could be more innocent? To encourage creativity, she asked each work group to meet for at least a half hour per week to brainstorm new work methods, solutions to long-standing problems, and possible new products. To put teeth into the new program, she put together a committee that reviewed submissions and then awarded cash prizes to employees who came up with ideas that were judged as "real moneymakers."

Within a few months the cash-for-ideas program had completely broken down. In fact, members of one work group ended up beating up one of their own team members as a result of the program. It turns out the team came up with a really good idea, and Charlie, the aforementioned team member, promised that he'd take care of the paperwork. He then submitted the suggestion under his own name and kept the $5,000 bonus for himself. When his teammates found out about the deception, first they confronted him, then someone shoved him, then a melee broke out, and Charlie ended up in the emergency room.

To avoid further injuries, the owner did away with the incentive program. Of course, she still invited suggestions, but none came in. Employees now believed that she was shorting them by asking for ideas without offering incremental pay. She had hoped to use the suggestion program to stimulate innovation, but found that by paying people for their thoughts, she had inadvertently sent the message that making suggestions was outside a person's normal job requirements. Now employees believed that if they came up with a good idea, they deserved to be paid a bonus. Otherwise, they were being exploited.

What's a leader to do?

USE INCENTIVES WISELY

Remember the principle we started with. Don't use incentives to compensate for your failure to engage personal and social motivation. Nevertheless, let's be clear. Influence masters eventually use rewards and punishments. For instance, if you don't repay a loan to Muhammad Yunus's Grameen Bank, your borrower group has to pay it back for you. And remember, people there know where you live! If a person in a rural African village discovers that his neighbor is hiding a Guinea worm infection—and if that person brings it to the attention of village leaders—the good citizen is given an attractive T-shirt (emblazoned with a Guinea worm logo).

So, the question is, how do you use incentives wisely?

Take care to ensure that the rewards come soon, are gratifying, and are clearly tied to vital behaviors. When you do so, even small rewards can be used to help people overcome some of the most profound and persistent problems. For example, Johns Hopkins Hospital completed a study of alcoholics who had been admitted to the hospital to, of all things, drink alcohol — but only in moderate quantities. The idea of the project wasn't to encourage the subjects to climb on the wagon or to go cold turkey, but to learn how to drink in moderation.

To influence patients' behavior, each day staff members determined privileges on the basis of how much alcohol the patients consumed. If they drank too much, they were given pureed food instead of the normal offering. Their amount of consumption also affected phone privileges, visiting hours, and so on. When compared to control patients who were simply told how much to drink with no incentives, experimental subjects were 60 percent more likely to reach their target consumption level.

When you first hear that a simple incentive such as phone privileges can help patients break free from something as powerful as the steel grip of alcoholism, it's a bit hard to believe. Nevertheless, this example pales in comparison to the work of Dr. Stephen Higgins, who routinely uses vouchers to help direct the behavior of cocaine addicts. Cocaine addicts typically fail to make progress in recovery programs because they quit before the program starts to take effect. With Dr. Higgins's voucher system, outpatients are required to submit a urine sample three times a week. If all three samples test negative, the subjects receive a bonus voucher that they can exchange for goods and services provided by the research staff.

With something as tremendously addictive as cocaine, you'd expect that a simple voucher that could be traded only for a rather small prize wouldn't have much of an effect. In Dr. Higgins's own words: "It surprises many people that a stack of paper can outweigh the powerful urge to use cocaine, but it makes sense in terms of what we know about why people use drugs."

Obviously, vouchers alone wouldn't be enough to keep cocaine addicts clean. However, when used with subjects who are already morally and socially invested in giving up cocaine, and when they're combined with traditional methods, those who were given incentives benefited from the motivational boost. Of the patients who were given vouchers, 90 percent finished the 12-week treatment program, whereas only 65 percent of non-voucher subjects completed the program. The long-term effects were similarly impressive.

To show how small incentives can be powerful motivators for almost anyone, take a look at your luggage. If you're like millions of other travelers around the world, you're sporting a plastic tag that touts your status in your favorite frequent-flier program. It's almost embarrassing to acknowledge the way these programs have reshaped our behavior.

For example, a friend of ours recently took a trip from Salt Lake City to Singapore. If you were to take out a globe and draw a route from Salt Lake to Singapore, you'd pass through places such as San Francisco and Hawaii. But neither destination appeared on our friend's itinerary. Instead he first flew two hours east to Minneapolis, Minnesota, before flying back west to Anchorage, Alaska, and Seoul, Korea, on his way to Singapore.

Our friend added hours to his flight because it maximized his frequent-flier miles. This enormous inconvenience probably earned him a whopping $30 worth of benefits. But he wanted those miles. He needed those miles. In fact, flyers have become so obsessed with maximizing their miles that the dollar value of unused frequent-flier miles on the planet now exceeds all the cash circulating in the U.S. economy.

If you're still not convinced that small rewards can affect behavior, consider the following example. In a group home for troubled teenage girls, administrators noted an alarming trend. Suicide attempts among residents had increased dramatically. After administrators tried everything from giving emotional speeches, to holding group sessions, to enlisting the help of friends and family—all to no avail—they came up with, of all things, an incentive. They came up with an incentive that could be invoked on the spot, that was immediately motivating, and that was clearly tied to the desired behavior. This wasn't any old incentive, but one that on its face sounded crazy. Here was the incentive. If a teenage resident attempted suicide, she would be denied TV privileges for the next week. Suicide attempts dropped to zero.

Without going into the complex psychology of suicide attempts versus suicide gestures and then missing the point of the example, suffice it to say that small incentives that are immediately linked to vital behaviors can yield amazing results with some of the world's most difficult problems.

If You're Doing It Right, Less Is More

From the examples we've provided, it should be clear that when it comes to offering extrinsic rewards, the rewards typically don't need to be very large—at least if you've laid the groundwork with the previous sources of motivation. Nobody's suggesting that corporate executives should ask employees to come to work without any compensation or that children should never get paid for helping out around the house. However, when you do want to provide a supplemental reward to help shape behavior, as the much maligned adage goes, it's often the thought, not the gift, that counts. That's because the thought behind an incentive often carries symbolic significance and taps into a variety of social forces that carry a lot of weight, much more so than the face value of the incentive itself. So, as you think of awards, don't be afraid to let the thought behind the award carry the burden for you.

Consider the work of Muhammad Yunus, "banker to the poor." When Dr. Yunus began to create a financial institution to administer loans to the working poor of Bangladesh, he discovered that some of the best young bank officers (who were often required to go door to door and meet with people living in the humblest of conditions) were former revolutionaries who had once fought to overthrow the government. Many put down their guns and picked up clipboards as they learned that they were able to effect more change through administering microloans than they could ever hope to achieve through violent means.

If you've ever visited any of the settings where these young people have worked their magic, you can't help but be impressed with the nobility of their work. Villagers who had once lived on the edge of starvation—whose children were often born with severe handicaps resulting from the arsenic found in the unfiltered water, and who often died at a young age—now run small businesses. They also rear healthy children who, for the first time in their family's history, attend school.

Given the enormous intrinsic and social benefits associated with their jobs, what could possibly provide additional incentive to these erstwhile revolutionaries? Earning a gold star. An executive discovered this surprising fact almost by accident. To ensure that local branches were focusing on the right goals, one of the regional managers instituted a program where branches of Dr. Yunus's bank earned different-colored stars for achieving mission-central results—one color for hitting a certain number of loans, another for registering all the borrower's children in school, another for hitting profit goals, and so forth.

Soon it became the goal of every manager to become a five-star branch. Individuals who were doing some of the most socially important work on the planet—and already working diligently and with focus—kicked their efforts to a new level when faced with the opportunity of earning colored stars. Of course, there was nothing of tangible value in these ten-a-penny stars, but symbolically and socially they provided more incentive than anyone had ever imagined.

Once again, if you've done your work with both personal and social motives, symbolic awards take on enormous value. If you haven't, extrinsic rewards can become a source of ridicule and cynicism. Fortunately, in this case, bank employees' deep regard for Dr. Yunus, along with their commitment to serving the poor, made gold stars more valuable than money. In fact, if Yunus had offered large cash rewards, it might have undercut the moral and social motivation that already drove these employees every day.

Hundreds of executives showed this same high-energy response to a symbolic incentive when a large consulting firm in the United States decided to offer awards for completing training assignments. The plan was simple. Senior leaders would meet weekly in a world-acclaimed training program where they would be given specific behavioral goals to ensure that they put their learnings into practice. The leaders would then report back to their trainer when they had fulfilled their commitment.

Soon leaders were going to great lengths to not only complete their assignments, but, in the event that they were called out of town, they'd e-mail their trainer to report on their progress. Senior executives jumped through these administrative hoops because, competitive souls that they were, they all wanted to earn the top award—an inexpensive brass statuette of a goose. Once again, it wasn't the cash value of the reward that mattered. It was the symbolic message that motivated behavior. It was the moral and social motivation that gave the token award supreme value.

Mimi Silbert, as you would guess, is a veritable master when it comes to making use of small rewards—one heaped upon another. Delancey residents quickly learn that with each new accomplishment they receive new privileges. Residents move from grunt work to increasingly complicated and interesting jobs. They move from a nine-person dorm, to a five-person room, through several steps to the Brannon building where they are awarded their own room. Eventually they arrive at Nirvana—an apartment of their own. Ultimately, probably at the top of the value chain, residents are given "WAM"—walk-around money—and the privilege to use it.

Finally, when it comes to demonstrating the power of small rewards administered quickly and tied to vital behaviors, consider what happened at Cedars-Sinai Medical Center when Leon Bender, a urologist from Los Angeles decided to pit a best practice he had observed on a cruise ship against one of the finest hospitals in the world.

Dr. Bender had noticed that each time passengers returned to the waiting cruise ship, someone squirted a shot of Purell on their hands. Crew members also distributed the disinfectant to passengers as they stood in the buffet lines. The good doctor began to wonder if it was possible that the cruise ship staff was more diligent with hand hygiene than the hospital staff he had worked with for nearly four decades.

The problems associated with poor hand hygiene, Dr. Bender realized, weren't restricted to remote islands or developing-world shopping bazaars. The acclaimed hospital he worked at (similar to all health-care institutions) constantly fought the battle of hospital-transmitted diseases that are a product of poor hand hygiene. A health-care professional picks up bugs from one patient and then passes them on to another. It happens all the time. Consequently, hospitals remain one of the most dangerous places in any community, causing tens of thousands of deaths annually. Find a way to get people to wash their hands thoroughly between patients, and you'd go a long way toward eliminating hospital-transmitted diseases.

When Dr. Bender returned home, he started a hand-hygiene campaign. He quickly learned that most doctors believed that they washed often and thoroughly enough. One study even found that while 73 percent of doctors said they washed effectively, only 9 percent actually met the industry standard.

According to Paul Silka, an emergency room physician at Cedars-Sinai, doctors often believe, "Hey, I couldn't be carrying the bad bugs. It's the other hospital personnel." Nobody believes that he or she is part of the offending majority.

To help set the record straight as well as propel doctors to wash effectively, administrators tried several techniques. First they deluged doctors with e-mails, posters, and faxes. That didn't work. It's likely that most physicians continued to believe that the problem was someone else's, not theirs. In fact, nothing worked until administrators stumbled on a simple incentive scheme. Staff members met doctors in the parking lot and handed them a bottle of hand disinfectant. Then Dr. Silka assigned a group of staff members to see if they could catch doctors in the act of using the disinfectant (choosing a positive over a negative approach).

Now here's where incentives came into play. When administrators "caught" physicians using the disinfectant, they gave them a $10 Starbucks card. That's it. They gave a $10 coupon to the highest-paid professionals in the hospital as an enticement for not passing on deadly diseases. With this incentive alone, compliance in that particular facility moved from 65 to 80 percent.

Reward Vital Behaviors, Not Just Results

Earlier we learned that it's best to take complex tasks and turn them into small, achievable goals. Now we're adding another concept. Reward small improvements in behavior along the way. Don't wait until people achieve phenomenal results, but reward small improvements in behavior.

As simple as this sounds, we're bad at it, especially at work. When polled, employees reveal that their number-one complaint is that they aren't recognized for their notable performances. Apparently people hand out praise as if it were being rationed, and usually only for outstanding work. Make a small improvement, and it's highly unlikely that anyone will say or do anything. Each year a new survey publishes the fact that employees would appreciate more praise, and each year we apparently do nothing different.

This is odd in light of the fact that humans are actually quite good at rewarding incremental achievement with their small children. A child makes a sound that approximates "mama," and members of the immediate family screech in joy, call every single living relative with the breaking news, ask the kid to perform on cue, and then celebrate each new pronouncement with the same enthusiasm you expect they'd display had they trained a newborn to recite "If" by Rudyard Kipling.

However, this ability to see and enthusiastically reward small improvements wanes over time until one day it takes a call from the Nobel committee to raise an eyebrow. Eventually kids grow up and go to work where apparently the words *good* and *job* aren't allowed to be used in combination, or so suggest employee surveys. There seems to be a permanent divide between researchers and scholars who heartily argue that performance is best improved by rewarding incremental improvements, and the rest of the world where people wait for a profound achievement before working up any enthusiasm.

Reward Right Results *and* Right Behaviors

Perhaps people are stingy with their praise because they fear that rewarding incremental improvement in performance means rewarding mediocrity or worse.

"So you're telling me that every time a screwup finally does something everyone else is already doing, you're supposed to hold some kind of celebration?"

Actually, no. If employees' current performance level is unacceptable and you can't wait for them to come up to standard, then either terminate them or move them to a task that they can complete. On the other hand, if an individual is excelling in some areas, while lagging in others—but overall is up to snuff—then set performance goals in the lagging areas, and don't be afraid to reward small improvements. This means that you shouldn't wait for big results but should reward improvement in vital behaviors along the way.

For example, while working on a change project in a massive production facility in Texas, a member of the change steering committee abruptly informed the leaders that the culture was too negative. Apparently he had read the surveys. His exact words were: "Do something right around here, and you never hear about it. But do something wrong, and it can haunt you for your entire career."

With this in mind, the CEO asked all the leaders to keep an eye open for a notable accomplishment—something they could celebrate. For about a week nothing happened. Then one of the assembly areas set a performance record. The crew had assembled more units in one day than ever before. The CEO immediately called for a celebration.

While it seemed like a victory, the details the leaders uncovered as they researched this record revealed something quite different. It turned out that in order to set a record in production, the afternoon shift had reduced quality standards on the product. They had also focused only on producing, and not on replacing the stock they used up, which left the morning shift with a lot of extra work. Finally, the workers had purposely underperformed the previous day in order to set themselves up to hit record numbers on the day in question.

In short, leaders were horrified to discover that they were inadvertently rewarding behaviors that ultimately hurt the company and morale. They had rewarded results without giving any thought to the behaviors that drove them.

Reward Vital Behaviors Alone

In addition to the fact that rewarding results can be unwise if you're unable to observe people's actions, it's important to remember that behavior is the one thing people have under their control. Results often vary with changes in the market and other external variables. Consequently, influence masters continually observe and reward behaviors that support valued processes.

For example, the book *Kaizen*, by Masaaki Imai, highlights the Japanese appreciation for the importance of rewarding effort and not outcome. Imai tells the intriguing story of a group of waitresses whose job it was to serve tea during lunch at one of Matsushita's plants. They noted that the employees sat in predictable locations and drank a predictable amount of tea. Rather than put a full container at each place, they calculated the optimum amount of tea to be poured at each table, thus reducing tea-leaf consumption by half.

How much did the suggestion save? Only a small sum. Yet the group was given the company's presidential gold medal. Other suggestions saved more money (by an astronomical amount), but the more modest proposal was given the highest recognition because it captured what the judges thought was the best implementation of Kaizen principles. They rewarded the process, knowing that if you reward the actual steps people follow, eventually results take care of themselves.

Watch for Divisive Incentives

People are so often out of touch with the message they're sending that they inadvertently reward exactly the wrong behavior. Just watch coaches as they speak about the importance of teamwork and then celebrate individual accomplishment. Kids quickly learn that it's the score that counts, not the assist, and it turns many of them into selfish prima donnas.

Or consider the family whose son has a serious drug addiction. In their effort to express love and support, family members unintentionally enable his addiction. With their words they say, "You should really stop taking drugs." But with their actions they say, "As long as you're taking them, we'll give you free rent, use of our cars, and bail whenever you need it." They are, in fact, rewarding the very behavior they claim to want to change.

For years U.S. politicians have wrung their hands over the fact that Americans save so little money. For a time they looked jealously across the ocean at Japanese citizens, who save money at many times the rate of Americans. Some analysts speculated that there was just something different about Japanese character. Perhaps they were more willing to sacrifice. But then again, maybe the difference could be attributed in part to incentives. For example, in the United States interest earned on savings is taxable. For many years in Japan it wasn't. In the United States during that same time period, interest on consumer debt, like that from credit cards and home loans, was tax deductible. In Japan it wasn't. Maybe we were more alike than we thought.

Many organizations set up an entire reward system that, by design, motivates the wrong behavior. Dr. Steve Kerr first drew attention to this problem in his now classic piece, "On the Folly of Rewarding A, While Hoping for B." For example, some veterans and scholars were concerned at a phenomenon that had occurred in previous wars, but increased significantly during the U.S. war in Vietnam. While still not the norm, U.S. soldiers in Vietnam were more likely to avoid conflict—even "fragging" their own officers to do so—than soldiers in previous wars had been. And instead of going on search-and-destroy missions, as had their predecessors, some learned to "search and escape." How could this happen?

Clearly soldiers in Vietnam labored under a set of conflicted emotions that had no corollary in World War II. It's hard to imagine how U.S. soldiers in Vietnam functioned at all, knowing how hostile many of their fellow citizens were to their mission. And yet, according to Kerr, there was more going on that influenced this behavior than a fuzzy mission and a hostile citizenry.

Examine the reward structure. Both generations of soldiers wanted to go home. That was a given. Nobody liked putting his or her life at risk. The typical GI from WWII knew that in order to go home, he and his comrades had to win the war. They'd never go home until the enemy was defeated. Avoiding a mission simply put off the inevitable and might well give the enemy more time to gain ground.

Contrast their circumstances to that of their own children—the Vietnam soldiers. They went home when their tour was over, not when the war was over. And if they disobeyed orders, avoiding immediate danger, Vietnam war soliders were less likely to be held accountable. So, rational beings that they were, in a morally confusing environment, with less accountability and greater incentive to lay low—it's no surprise that "search and escape" was a more common phenomenon than it was a generation earlier.

So take heed. When behaviors are out of whack, look closely at your rewards. Who knows? Your own incentive system may be causing the problem.

PUNISHMENT SENDS A MESSAGE, AND SO DOES ITS ABSENCE—SO CHOOSE WISELY

Sometimes you don't have the luxury of rewarding positive performance because the person you'd like to reward never actually does the right thing. In fact, he or she does only the wrong thing—and often. In these cases, if you want to make use of extrinsic reinforcers, you're left with the prospect of punishing this person. Fortunately, since punishment is from the same family as positive reinforcement (half empty/half full), it should have a similar effect. Right?

Maybe not. Punishment far from guarantees the mirror effect of positive reinforcement. In virtually hundreds of experiments with laboratory animals and humans, punishment decreases the likelihood of a previously reinforced response, but only temporarily. And it can produce a whole host of other undesired effects. When you reward performance, you typically know that the reward will help propel behavior in the desired direction, but with punishment you don't know what you're going to get. You might gain compliance, but only over the short term. Then again the person in question may actually push back or purposely rebel. And there's a good chance that this person is not going to appreciate you for what you've done, thereby putting your relationship at risk.

Actually, punishment can create all sorts of serious and harmful emotional effects, particularly if it is only loosely administered. For instance, Martin Seligman, in his book *Learned Helplessness*, reports that if you place a dog on a metal grid and then shock the animal—randomly electrifying one part of the grid, then another, then another—eventually the poor animal cowers in one spot, and doesn't even bother to move when the shock is randomly administered. When exposed to random pain, the unfortunate subject becomes helpless, broken, and neurotic. So take heed. When it comes to punishment, you must be very careful.

Before Punishing, Place a Shot across the Bow

One way to make use of punishment without actually having to administer it is to "place a shot across the bow" of those you're trying to influence. That is, provide a clear warning to let them know exactly what negative things *will* happen to them should they continue down their current path, but don't actually administer discipline yet. Then if they stay clear of the wrong behavior, they enjoy the benefit of the threat without having to actually suffer its consequences. This method may sound manipulative, but before you pass too harsh a judgment, consider a novel and effective police tactic that is currently being used with drug dealers and other perpetual criminals in North Carolina and other communities. Here's how the method used by authorities makes use of warnings as opposed to merely tracking down offenders and throwing them in jail.

Traditionally, cops tried to put a dent in crime by implementing aggressive search-and-arrest strategies that focused on a targeted area. This blitz strategy tended to provoke public outrage and mobilize a community against the policing efforts, and rarely created effects that lasted very long. As soon as the cops moved to the next area, new faces came in to fill the old positions, and the bad guys were once again in charge.

With the new strategy, authorities take a different approach. Police invite individuals whom they are about to arrest to attend an offender notification forum. The district attorney's office promises that attendees won't be arrested during a 90-minute meeting where authorities then make use of every source of influence imaginable.

For example, along with the offenders, authorities bring in the attendees' friends, family, and other community opinion leaders who ask the criminals to give up their ways and seek normal employment. Next, public officials clarify existing laws and likely consequences: If you get caught, here's the likely penalty. Following this formal approach, ex-offenders (usually former gang members and drug dealers) talk about what they're currently doing to stay straight. Finally, heads of public agencies explain choices the offenders can make in order to avoid falling back into their old habits, including job programs and what it takes to get signed up.

Then comes the fun part. What makes these second-chance meetings so effective is not merely that they employ so many sources of influence, but that the meetings do such a terrific job in making it crystal clear that the offenders *will* be convicted and *will* serve long sentences. Nobody does a better job of providing a warning. Unlike the *Scared Straight* program that focused on how bad jail is—leaving room for subjects to conclude that only saps get caught and sent to jail—with this program, police make it abundantly clear that the offenders will indeed be caught and prosecuted.

After the first part of the meeting concludes, authorities invite the participants (who are often a bit bored with the sermon at this point) to a different room where they see posters tacked to the walls. Under each poster they find a small table with a binder on it. During previous weeks police have gathered evidence, including video footage of each of the attendees making at least one illicit drug sale.

As the drug dealers enter the new room, each is told, "Find your poster." When they do, they discover that the poster sports a high-resolution photo of them doing a drug deal. In the adjacent binder, they see all the case evidence the police intend to use to prosecute them. Next the invitees are asked to take a seat and watch a video. At this point the local prosecutor states: "Raise your hand when you see yourself committing a felony." One by one, they do. Next, authorities tell the offenders that they've been put on a special list and will be aggressively prosecuted when caught.

Combine this tactic with support from family and friends as well as job programs, and the results have been terrific. Small crimes have dropped by 35 percent in certain neighborhoods in North Carolina, and in the three neighborhoods where the initiative was implemented, 24 of 40 alleged dealers have stayed clear of the law. More importantly, community members have become far more active at reporting crimes and partnering with law enforcement officials.

All this is done without having to haul nearly as many people off to jail in order to catch their attention. Poignant, real, and immediate, threats of punishment help keep potential hardened criminals on the straight and narrow.

And to enhance the credibility of their efforts, the authorities never bluff. They invite drug dealers to the open forum, and those who don't come are immediately arrested and prosecuted for the crimes recorded on videotape. Those who go through the program and don't stay with their new job training or do commit a crime are also immediately arrested. Soon the word gets out that the authorities are serious about what they say. Then the mere threat of possible negative consequences becomes much more effective.

When All Else Fails, Punish

The implications here should be clear. There are times when you're simply going to have to punish others. A shot across the bow hasn't been enough. You've also tried incentives, exerted social pressure, and even appealed to the other person's sense of values, but the immediate gratification associated with the wrong behavior still remains victorious. It's time to make judicious use of discipline.

Consider the poor safety record of workers in the oil fields of Russia. With the fall of communism and the influx of demand for oil, Russian leaders cranked up their petroleum industry. Unfortunately, many of the new employees had not been trained in safe work practices nor did they appear to be the slightest bit interested in learning or applying them. Coming out of years of unemployment and depression, many new hires were drug and alcohol abusers. Combine poor safety practices, alcohol, and heavy equipment, and you have the perfect recipe for accidents.

Since the immediate danger was so high and employees had been used to heavy-handed methods before going to work in the fields, (and they had not responded to encouragements or hollow threats), company executives decided to punish behavior that led to accidents. Leaders notified employees that they could be randomly tested for drugs and alcohol at work — or while traveling to and from the job. Then authorities did exactly that and summarily fired anyone who was found to be under the influence. This direct application of punishment, coupled with safety training, helped dramatically decrease the number of accidents. Once again, the methods may seem harsh, but when compared to the loss of life or limb, leaders argue that it's worth it.

Consider the horrible cases of bride abduction in Ethiopia. Young girls were kidnapped on their way to or from school, raped, and then forced to marry the rapist in an effort to save face. This dreadful practice had survived in silence for generations. Nobody wanted to talk about or address the issue. However, that changed when a popular radio soap opera addressed the issue head on. Dr. Negussie Teffera—Population Media Center's country representative in Ethiopia—worked with a staff of writers and producers to create an enormously popular radio show titled *Yeken Kignit* ("Looking Over One's Daily Life"). In one story line, a much-admired character on the soap opera, a woman named Wubalem, was abducted and then eventually freed and able to marry the man she really loved. Immediately, this previously taboo topic became part of the public discourse. A letter from one female listener shows the impact the program had on the devastating problem in her community:

> *The story of Wubalem in your radio drama reflects clearly to the general public the harmful traditional practices in our country such as abduction and sexual violence. These practices have prevented us from sending our girls to school. . . . Our first child was married at the age of 14 after she was abducted. We were worrying for years as we thought that our second child would face a similar fate. At present, however, the radio drama focusing on abduction and sexual violence that you have presented to the public, and the discussions conducted on these topics, have aroused considerable popular indignation. The people have now strongly condemned such inhuman traditional practices. . . . Unlike in the past, special punitive measures have been taken by community people against offenders involved in such crimes. As a result, we have no worry in sending our girls to school. Our children go to school safely and return unharmed.*

According to Dr. Negussie, the problem has been solved in many places in Ethiopia once and for all—not simply as a result of the discourse, but by putting into place harsh punishment for what had previously been rewarded. Now, if a man assaults a young girl, instead of being allowed to keep the victim as his wife, he is put in prison.

Finally, a corporate example. One of the first questions we (the authors) ask employees in companies that complain about a lack of accountability is, "What does it take to get fired around here?" Almost always the answers have nothing to do with poor performance. "Embarrass the boss," is a common response. Another is a sarcastic, "Kill a really valuable coworker." In other words, only raging violations of ethics or political faux pas get the boot. When you hear these types of stories, you can bet that the *lack* of punishment for routine infractions is sending a loud message across the organization. The point isn't that people need to be threatened in order to perform. The point is that if you aren't willing to go to the mat when people violate a core value (such as giving their best effort), that value loses its moral force in the organization.

On the other hand, you send a powerful message about your values when you do hold employees accountable. For instance, the authors worked with a large consumer-goods company in Georgia where company leaders decided to take a harsh stance against racist behavior. To take on a norm that had lasted for a centuries, the leaders decided to pick a common racist behavior and annihilate it through the judicious use of punishment. They started with something simple. No longer would the company tolerate racist jokes.

To put the plan into action, the leaders explained their stance, the first behavior they were going to eliminate, and the action they would take. Anyone who told a racist joke would be fired on the spot, without any warning or grace period. The leaders then told their employees that they would be looking to make an example of anyone who dared violate the policy, and the first time someone did, they fired him. That was the end of racist jokes in that company.

SUMMARY: REWARDS

Administering rewards and punishments can be a tricky business. Consequently, when you look at the extrinsic motivators you're using to encourage or discourage behavior, take care to adhere to a few helpful principles. First, rely on personal and social motivators as your first line of attack. Let the value of the behavior itself, along with social motivators, carry the bulk of the motivational load.

When you do choose to employ extrinsic rewards, make sure that they are immediately linked to vital behaviors. Take care to link rewards to the specific actions you want to see repeated. When choosing rewards, don't be afraid to draw on small, heartfelt tokens of appreciation. Remember, when it comes to extrinsic rewards, less is often more. Do your best to reward behaviors and not merely outcomes. Sometimes outcomes hide inappropriate behaviors. Finally, if you end up having to administer punishment, first take a shot across the bow. Let people know what's coming before you drop the hammer.

9

Change the Environment

STRUCTURAL ABILITY

You are a product of your environment. So choose the environment that will best develop you toward your objective. Analyze your life in terms of its environment. Are the things around you helping you toward success—or are they holding you back?

—Clement Stone

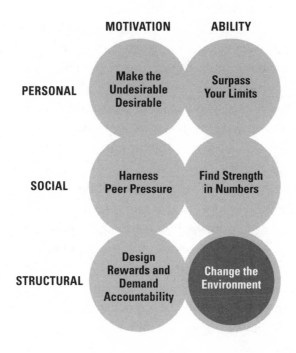

When it comes to *enabling* vital behaviors, we've already looked at two sources: improving personal mastery through deliberate practice, and gaining assistance from others by building social capital. For our third and final source for increasing our ability ("Can I do it?"), we move away from human influence altogether and examine how nonhuman forces—the world of buildings, space, sound, sight, and so forth—can be brought to bear in an influence strategy. To show how this might work, we start with an example that, when it comes to influence theory, is a genuine classic.

In the late 1940s, representatives from the National Restaurant Association asked William Foote Whyte, a professor at the University of Chicago, to help them with a growing problem. As World War II came to an end, the United States was in a period of incredible growth and prosperity. Along with this flourishing economy, Americans began eating out in unprecedented numbers. Unfortunately, the restaurant industry wasn't ready for the surge of customers.

Along with the return of soldiers came an awkward change in the restaurant pecking order. GIs returned from battle to take over the higher-paying job of cook, one that, along with "Rosie the Riveter," women had occupied for the first time during the labor-starved war years. Many of these displaced cooks, who had been forced to step down to the job of waitress, were upset with the new circumstance. When they shouted their orders, they weren't always polite. The gnarled veterans weren't always pleased to be taking orders from these women.

Given the increased workload and growing social tension, loud arguments often broke out at the kitchen counter. The results were predictable. Not only did the commotion annoy the patrons, but the power struggles often resulted in late or incorrect orders—sometimes out of confusion, often out of revenge. By the time Dr. Whyte entered the scene, both customers and employees were stomping out of restaurants in increasing numbers.

Dr. Whyte started his work by observing a sample of restaurants, doing his best to identify the behaviors behind the growing conflict. He noted that the waitresses would rush to the counter, shout an order, and then rush back to her customers. If the order was not ready when she returned, she would urge the cook to hurry, shouting expressions of encouragement such as, "Hey, hairball, where's the breaded veal? You got a broken arm or what?" The cooks usually responded in kind. Later, when the waitress received an incorrect order, the two would exchange still more unflattering remarks. After being yelled at a couple of times, the cooks often took revenge by slowing down. Dr. Whyte even observed cooks turning their backs on the servers and intentionally ignoring them until they left, sometimes in tears.

While many consultants might have been tempted to alter this unhealthy social climate by teaching interpersonal skills, conducting team-building exercises, or changing the pay system, Whyte took a different approach. In his view, the best way to solve the problem was to change the way employees communicated.

And now for Whyte's stroke of genius.

Dr. Whyte recommended that the restaurants use a 50-cent metal spindle to gather orders. He then asked servers to skewer a detailed written order on the spindle. Cooks were then to pull orders off and fill them in whatever sequence seemed most efficient (though generally following a first-in, first-out policy).

Whyte's recommendation was tried at a pilot restaurant the next day. Training consisted of a 10-minute instruction session that was given to both cooks and servers. Managers reported an immediate decrease in conflict and customer complaints. Both cooks and servers preferred the new structure, and both groups reported that they were being treated better.

The Restaurant Association distributed information about the new system to its membership. Whyte's spindle (which quickly transformed into the now-familiar order wheel) did not directly affect behavior. Whyte chose not to confront norms, history, or habit. Instead he simply eliminated the need for verbal communication and all its attendant problems. He did so immediately, and the improvements lasted forever by changing, not people, but *things*.

FISH DISCOVER WATER LAST

If you didn't think of Whyte's solution, you're in good company. Rarely does the average person conceive of changing the physical world as a way of changing human behavior. We see that others are misbehaving, and we look to change *them*, not their environment. Caught up in the human side of things, we completely miss the impact of subtle yet powerful sources such as the size of a room or the impact of a chair. Consequently, one of our most powerful sources of influence (the physical environment) is often the least used because it's the least noticeable. In the words of Fred Steele, the renowned sociotechnical theorist, most of us are "environmentally incompetent." If you doubt this allegation, just ask any of today's cooks and servers why they don't scream and curse at one another as did many of their predecessors a half century ago. See if any of them ever point to the order wheel as the source of their cooperation.

The impact of the physical world on human behavior is equally profound within the business world, and, as you might suspect, just as hard to spot. For example, the authors once met with the president of a large insurance company that was losing millions of dollars to quality problems that were widely known but rarely discussed. To turn things around, the president had decided to nurture a culture of candor within the organization. He declared: "We'll never solve our quality problems until every single person—right down to the newest employee on the loading dock—is comfortable sharing his honest opinion."

Despite the president's passion for candor, the heartfelt speeches he had given, the fiery memos he had written, and even the engaging training he had initiated, his efforts hadn't done much to propel people to share their frank opinions. When talking privately with his HR manager, he explained, "I keep telling people to open up, but it's not working." So he asked us (the authors) to help him come up with a plan to create a culture in which people, no matter their position or station, could comfortably disagree with anyone—particularly people in authority.

To reach the president's office, we had to traverse six hallways (each the length of an aircraft carrier), walk by hundreds of thousands of dollars of museum-quality artwork, and pass four different secretary stations. At each station we were visually frisked and subtly interrogated. Finally, we entered the president's office to find him seated behind a desk the size of a 1964 Caddy. Then, while seated in loosely stuffed chairs that slung us next to the floor and pushed our knees up and into our chests, we stared up at the president, much like grade-school children looking up at the principal.

The president's first words were, "I get the feeling that people around here are scared to talk to me." Perhaps he had missed the fact that his office was laid out like Hitler's chancellery. (Hitler demanded more than 480 feet of hallway so that visitors would "get a taste of the power and grandeur of the German Reich" on arriving.) Granted, there were several forces that had kept employees in this particular company from talking candidly. However, the physical features of the executive suite alone were enough to terrorize anyone.

"I'm not sure that you'll ever be able to overcome the intimidating effect of your office suite," one of us eventually shared, in a quivering voice.

From that point on, we developed a plan that contained a variety of features, starting with the strategy of placing decision-making groups in physical surroundings that didn't shout, "Behold, the great and mighty Oz!"

Consider the profound and yet mostly unnoticed effect of *things* on entire communities. Realizing that the physicality of a neighborhood can send out unspoken messages that encourage socially inappropriate behavior, George Kelling started a community movement that is largely credited for reducing felonies in New York City by as much as 75 percent. Few people are aware of how this influence expert manipulated *things* to achieve such impressive results.

Before the arrival of George Kelling, New York subways were a favorite venue for muggers, murderers, and drug dealers. Kelling, a criminologist and originator of the "broken windows theory" of crime, argued that disordered surroundings send out an unspoken but powerful message that encourages antisocial behavior. "A broken window left in disrepair," Kelling explains, "suggests that no one is in charge and no one cares." This relatively minor condition promotes more disorderly behavior, including violence.

Committed to lessening the effect *things* were having on the community, Kelling advised the New York Transit Authority to implement a strategy that others before him had simply ridiculed. He told community leaders that they needed to start sweating the small stuff. He pointed out small environmental cues that provided a fertile environment for criminal behavior.

Kelling's crew began a systematic attack against the silent force, attacking things like graffiti, litter, and vandalism. Officials organized crews in the train yard that rolled paint over newly applied graffiti the instant a car came in for service. Over time, a combination of cleanup and prosecution for minor offenses began to make a difference. Surroundings improved, community pride increased, and petty crimes declined. So did violent crime. Kelling taught people to sweat the small, silent, physical world, and he reaped great rewards.

All this talk about the powerful but often undetected influence of *things* is good news. It offers hope. If you can influence behavior by eliminating graffiti, shifting a wall, changing a reporting structure, putting in a new system, posting numbers, or otherwise working with *things*, the job of leader, parent, or change agent doesn't seem like such a daunting task. After all, these are inanimate objects. *Things* lie there quietly. *Things* never resist change, and they stay put forever once you change them.

There are two reasons that we don't make good use of *things* as much as we should. The first is the problem we've been discussing. More often than not, powerful elements from our environment remain invisible to us. Work procedures, job layouts, reporting structures, etc., don't exactly walk up and whisper in our ear. The effect of distance is something we suffer but rarely see. That's why Fred Steele, a social scientist and expert on the effects of physical space, suggests that most of us are "environmentally incompetent." The environment affects much of what we do, and yet we often fail to notice its profound impact.

Second, even when we do think about the impact the environment is having on us, we rarely know what to do about it. It's not as if we're carrying around a head full of sociophysical theories. If someone were to tell us that we need to worry about Festinger, Schachter, and Lewin's theory of propinquity (the impact of space on relationships), we'd think he or she was pulling our leg. Propinquity? Who's ever heard of propinquity?

So this is our final test. To complete our influence repertoire, we must step up to the challenge and become environmentally competent. To the extent that we (1) remember to think about things, and (2) are able to come up with theories of how changing *things* will change behavior, we'll have access to one more powerful set of influence tools.

LEARN TO NOTICE

If it's true that we rarely notice the impact of the physical environment that surrounds us because we simply don't think to look at it, it's time we change. The more we watch for silent forces from the physical world, the better prepared we'll be to deal with them. Equally important, the more we note how we fall prey to simple, silent things that surround us, the more likely it is that we'll extend our vigilance to other domains of our life.

To understand this concept more fully, let's start by sampling just one domain: our personal life. More specifically, our eating habits. How might understanding the power that things hold over us help here? What might we do to warn our friend Henry, who continues to struggle with his weight loss problem?

To answer this, consider the work of the clever and mischievous social scientist Brian Wansink, who manipulates *things* to see how a small change in physical features affects a large change in human behavior. For instance, he once invited a crowd of people who had just finished lunch to watch a movie. As subjects filed into the theater, Wansink's assistants handed them either a small, medium, or bigger-than-your-head bucket of very stale popcorn. The treat was so stale that it squeaked when eaten. One moviegoer described it as akin to eating Styrofoam packing peanuts.

Despite the fact that the popcorn tasted terrible and that the crowd was still full from lunch, when Wansink's crew gathered up the variously sized buckets at the end of the movie, it turned out almost everybody had mindlessly gobbled the chewy material. Even more interesting, the size of the container, not the size of the person or his or her appetite, predicted how much of the food had been consumed. Patrons with big buckets ate 53 percent more than those given the smaller portions. The distraction of the movie, the size of the bucket, and the sound of others eating around them all subtly influenced people to eat something they would otherwise have rejected.

Wansink has even more to teach Henry. For example, it turns out—contrary to what you and I might believe—that we don't tend to eat until we're *full*. We eat until small things from our environment make us *think* we're full. Wansink demonstrated this by constructing a magic soup bowl. The bowl could be refilled from the bottom without diners catching on to the trick. While people eating from a normal bowl ate on average 9 ounces and then reported being full, those with the bottomless bowls ate 15 ounces. Some ate more than a quart before reporting they'd had enough. Imagine, the two groups were equally satisfied, and yet one group ate 73 percent more than the other because diners were unconsciously waiting for their bowls to look more empty to cue them that they were full.

Wansink suggests that people make over 200 eating decisions every day without realizing it. This mindless eating adds hundreds of calories to our diets without adding at all to our satisfaction. If half of what Wansink suggests is true, we can profoundly influence our own eating behavior by simply finding ways to become more mindful of these "mindless" choices.

A mere glance at family, company, and community circumstances would reveal the same phenomenon. Much of what we do, for better or for worse, is influenced by dozens of silent environmental forces that drive our decisions and actions in ways that we rarely notice. So, to make the best use of your last source of influence, take your laserlike attention off people and take a closer look at their physical world. Step up to your persistent problem, identify vital behaviors, and then search for subtle features from the environment that are silently driving you and others to misbehave.

MAKE THE INVISIBLE VISIBLE

Once you've identified environmental elements that are subtly driving your or others' behavior, it's time to take steps to make them more obvious. That is, you should make the invisible visible. Provide actual cues in the environment to remind people of the behaviors you're trying to influence. For example, consider another Wansink experiment in which he gave cans of stacked potato chips to various subjects. Control subjects were given normal cans with uniform chips piled one on top of the other and were allowed to snack casually as they engaged in various activities. Experimental subjects were given cans in which every tenth chip was an odd color. The next nine chips would be normal and were followed by another odd-colored chip. Again, subjects were allowed to engage in other activities while snacking on their chips. Experimental subjects consumed 37 percent fewer chips than control subjects who were given no indication of how many chips they'd eaten.

What was going on here? By coloring every tenth chip, Wansink helped make the invisible visible. Nobody said anything about the chips or the colors. Nobody encouraged people to control their eating. Nevertheless, instructed by the visual cue, suddenly eaters were conscious of the volume of chips they were eating, and that awareness alone helped them make a decision rather than follow an impulse.

Business leaders have long understood the importance of making the invisible visible. For example, Emery Air Freight pioneered the use of containerized shipping in the 1960s. The company came up with the idea of using sturdy, reusable, and uniform-sized containers—and the whole world changed. Uniform containers were so much more efficient than previous methods that international shipping prices plummeted. Along with the unprecedented drop in price, industries that had previously been protected from global competition because of high transportation costs (steel, automobiles, etc.) suddenly found themselves competing with anyone, anywhere.

And yet, early on, Edward Feeney, the vice president of systems performance at the time, was frustrated because he couldn't get the workforce to use the new containers to their capacity. Containers were being sealed and shipped without being properly filled. An audit team found they were being properly filled only 45 percent of the time. The workers were extensively trained and constantly reminded of the importance of completely filling the containers, but they were still forgetting to do it more than half of the time. After exhausting these attempts to motivate the workforce, Feeney stumbled on a method that made the invisible visible. He drew conscious attention to the objective by having a "fill to here" line drawn on the inside of every container. Immediately, the rate of completely filled containers went from 45 percent to 95 percent. The problem went away the moment Feeney made the invisible visible.

Hospitals have been making similar improvements by restructuring their physical world. Savvy administrators help people understand the financial implications of their nearly unconscious choices by making invisible costs much more visible. In one hospital, leaders encouraged clinicians to pay attention to even small products that eventually cost a great deal of money. For example, a type of powderless latex gloves cost over 10 times more than a pair of regular, less-comfortable disposable gloves. And yet, in spite of regular pleas from senior management to reduce costs, almost everyone in the facility continued to use the pricey gloves for even short tasks. The powderless latex was more comfortable than the cheaper gloves, and besides, what were a few pennies here and there?

Then one day someone placed a 25¢ sign on the box of inexpensive gloves and a $3.00 sign on the box of pricier latex gloves. Problem solved. Now that the information was obvious at the moment people were making choices, the use of the expensive gloves dropped dramatically.

And speaking of hands in a hospital, we referred earlier to the appalling state of hand hygiene in U.S. hospitals. Remember Dr. Leon Bender and how he used Starbucks gift cards as an incentive to encourage doctors to use hand antiseptic? This influence method alone increased compliance from 65 to 80 percent. But this wasn't enough for the tenacious Dr. Bender. He wanted more. But what could he do next? After trying several other methods to motivate people to wash more thoroughly, he figured the hospital efforts had topped out until he too realized that he needed to make the invisible visible.

And what could be more invisible than the nasty little microorganisms that cause disease?

This particular problem of invisibility called for some minor theatrics. At a routine meeting of senior physicians, Rekha Murthy, the hospital's epidemiologist, handed each physician a petri dish coated with a spongy layer of agar. "I would love to culture your hand," Murthy told them while inviting each to press his or her palm onto the squishy medium. Murthy then collected the dishes and sent them to the lab for culturing and photographing.

When the photos came back from the lab, the images were frightfully effective. Doctors who had thought their hands were pristine when they submitted to the agar test were provided photo evidence of the horrific number of bacteria they routinely transported to their patients. Some of the more colorful photos of the bacterial colonies the lab had grown became popular screen savers in the hospital.

When it came to changing physicians' behavior, photos created poignant vicarious experiences and visual cues that reminded them of the need to properly wash their hands. Doctors didn't see their germs causing diseases, but they saw the next best thing. They saw whole colonies of the ugly micronatives they were hosting in their own fingerprints. After a few more opinion leaders were brought "face to colony" with the effects of their own inadequate hand hygiene, the hospital moved to nearly 100 percent compliance—and it stuck.

MIND THE DATA STREAM

The influence masters we just cited had one strategy in common: They affected how information found its way from the dark nooks and crannies of the unknown into the light of day. By providing small cues in the environment, they drew attention to critical data points, and they changed how people thought and eventually how they behaved. Since in these cases individuals weren't resisting the idea of washing thoroughly or wearing cheaper gloves or filling containers to the top—but were not thinking of the behaviors in the moment—merely putting the data in front of them was sufficient to change behavior.

The point here is the same one Bandura helped make for us earlier. Information affects behavior. People make choices based on cognitive maps that explain which behavior leads to which outcomes. The problem we're now exploring deals with our own lack of awareness of where we're getting our data, as well as how the data are affecting our behavior. Despite the fact that we're often exposed to incomplete or inaccurate data, if information is fed to us frequently and routinely enough, we begin to act on it as if it were an accurate sample of the greater reality, even when it often isn't.

For example, try this experiment. As quickly as you can, name every place in the world where armed conflict is currently taking place. If you're like most people, you can name an average of two to four places. Now ask yourself why you named these particular locales. Is it because these are the only places? Perhaps they're locations where there is the most bloodshed? Or is it because these are the places of most political significance?

It's probably because these are the sites that have received sustained media coverage. At any one time there are as many as two dozen armed conflicts taking place throughout the world, and it's not uncommon that some of the most horrific battles go largely unnoticed by the international audience. What's shocking about this is *not* that our mental agenda is so heavily influenced by a handful of news producers but that we are typically unaware that this is happening to us.

We frequently make this mental error because of a convenient heuristic we carry around in our head. It's known by cognitive psychologists as the "representative heuristic." To see how it works, take another quiz. What is the greater cause of deaths in the world each year? Suicide or homicide? Fire or drowning? Most people select homicides and fires because these are the catastrophes they see more often in the news.

Suicides are generally kept quiet for reasons of privacy, so we don't learn of them as often; and fires make for dramatic live coverage. The evening news team can hardly wait to show a reporter standing in front of a fiery blaze. And since we see homicides and fires on the news more often than we see suicides and drownings, we assume that this sample represents the underlying whole, when in fact it grossly distorts it. Death by flood and suicide are more common, but we apply a simple mental heuristic, fall victim to an inaccurate data stream, and rarely do we know that it's happening.

Influence geniuses understand the importance of an accurate data stream and do their best to ensure that their strategies focus on vital behaviors by serving up visible, timely, and accurate information that supports their goals. Instead of falling victim to data, they manage data religiously. For example, imagine what Dr. Donald Hopkins was up against when he kicked off the global campaign to eradicate Guinea worm disease. To get the campaign started, his biggest challenge was to move the parasite to the top of the agenda of developing-world leaders who typically worried a heck of a lot more about bloody coups, economic disasters, and corrupt politicians than they worried about parasites.

If competing priorities weren't enough to keep the worm problem out of the spotlight, the fact that most leaders had grown up in urban areas and were completely unaware of the pervasive effects of the Guinea worm in their own country didn't help. For example, Jimmy Carter, former U.S. president and founder of The Carter Center, told us that the first challenge leaders faced when attacking the Guinea worm disease in Pakistan was that the president of Pakistan had never even heard of the parasite. In addition to the worm's invisibility, even leaders who knew the plague was widespread paid little attention to the villages that were plagued because the leaders drew their political support from urban areas.

Consequently, Hopkins's first challenge was to escalate the importance of the Guinea worm plight in the eyes of the ruling forces by changing their data stream. That's why to this day the very first step any Guinea worm eradication team takes is to gather data.

"Data is extremely important in the campaign against Guinea worm," reports Hopkins. "We start by getting baseline information about nationwide infections." Actually, they're looking for counterintuitive, eye-popping statistics to catch people's attention. For instance, in Nigeria national leaders assumed that there were only a few thousand cases nationwide. In 1989, after village coordinators from around the country reported the number of infections in their region, leaders were horrified to discover that there were well over 650,000 cases. They had been off by as much as 3,000 percent! This made Nigeria the most endemic country in the world. With that new piece of information alone, support for eradicating the worm skyrocketed.

Since managing the data stream relies on numbers to change people's cognitive maps (as opposed to personal experience), the data have to be fresh, consistent, and relevant if they're going to have much of an impact. Hopkins is quick to point out that with such a small team working at The Carter Center, much of their influence comes from providing leaders with powerful information. Working closely with Dr. Hopkins is Dr. Ernesto Ruiz-Tiben, the technical director of the Guinea Worm Eradication Program. He oversees The Carter Center's efforts and has been key in tracking and communicating the status of the global campaign. Dr. Ruiz-Tiben makes Guinea worm eradication data available through publications such as the *Guinea Worm Wrap Up*, which is published every month by The Carter Center and The Centers for Disease Control and Prevention. This report summarizes the progress and setbacks in each country.

And here's where Hopkins grins a bit. "We publish lots of graphs, charts and tables. But none has been more influential than the Guinea worm race. We harness the natural competitive instincts of people by preparing a racetrack with the names of each country (or even the faces of the campaign leaders) on each runner. It's amazing to see how people respond not just to how many infections they have, but how many more or less they have than a neighboring country."

Do these data influence behavior?

"I was talking with the president of Burkina Faso," Hopkins reports, "and sharing some concerns about the campaign. I had all kinds of graphs and charts, but the one he wanted to look at the most was the Guinea worm race. They can't stand to be at the bottom. It gets their attention."

At the corporate level, it's easy to see how the flow of information affects behavior. The fact that different groups of employees are exposed to wildly different data streams helps explain why people often have such different priorities and passions. Different groups, departments, and levels of employees worry about very different aspects of the company's success, not because they hold different values, but because they're exposed to different data. For example, frontline employees who interface with complaining customers usually become the customer advocates. Top-level executives who are constantly poring over financial statements become the shareholder advocates. And sure enough, the folks who routinely take quality measures become the quality advocates. No surprise there.

The problem with passion for a single stakeholder group isn't that employees care greatly about someone or something; it's just that it's hard to expect people to act in balanced ways when they have access to only one data stream. For instance, members of a group of senior executives we (the authors) worked with were positively driven by their production numbers, which they reviewed weekly. When issues of morale came up (usually with the issuance of a grievance), they'd become rightfully concerned about "people problems," but generally only after it was too late. The same was true for customer satisfaction. This was also listed as a high priority, but nobody ever actually talked about customers or did anything to improve customer relationships until the company lost a major client to a competitor.

To change the executives' narrow focus, we changed the data stream. Alongside weekly production numbers, executives now enthusiastically pore over customer and employee data. If you watch their current behavior, you'll note that they spread their attention across more stakeholders than ever before. We also provided employees who had long shown passion for customer satisfaction with weekly cost and profit data, and they too broadened their interests. For instance, when faced with a dissatisfied customer, instead of simply throwing money at the problem (often the easiest solution), employees began to seek other, more cost-effective fixes. Before the intervention started, leaders and employees alike had talked about the importance of all their stakeholders, but nothing changed their parochial behavior until their data stream expanded.

One warning about data. When it comes to data, there is such a thing as "too much of a good thing." Corporate leaders often undermine the influence of the data they so carefully gather by overdoing it. The incessant flow of reports, printouts, and e-mails—one heaped upon the other—transforms into numbing and incoherent background noise. Influence masters never make this mistake. They're focused and deliberate about the data they share. They understand that the only reason for gathering or publishing any data is to reinforce vital behaviors.

SPACE: THE FINAL FRONTIER

As difficult as it can be to notice the effects of data on our behavior, it's much more difficult to notice the effects of physical space. Architects create space, and then we live with its effects for years on end, mostly unnoticed. When social psychologist Leon Festinger and others first started examining the effects of space (and its two-dimensional cousin, distance) on relationships, they had no idea that they had stumbled onto one of the most profound social-psychological phenomena of all time—propinquity. Simply put, *propinquity* is physical proximity, and Festinger and others spent a good amount of time studying how it affects our behaviors and relationships.

For instance, look at who marries whom and how they meet. Look at who collaborates on spontaneous group efforts at work. Examine who has the most friends and acquaintances in an apartment complex. Explore which employees are satisfied with their relationship with their supervisor. Surely most of these complicated interpersonal scenarios are largely a function of personal interests and interpersonal chemistry. Right?

Not really. Festinger discovered that the frequency and quality of human interaction is largely a function of physical distance. Apartment dwellers who are located near stairwells are acquainted with more people than individuals who have fewer people walking by their front doors. People who live across from the mailboxes are acquainted with more of their neighbors than anyone else in the building. At the corporate level, bosses who interact the most frequently with their subordinates generally have the best relationships. And who interacts most often? Bosses who are located closest to their direct reports.

But the opposite isn't necessarily true. That is, too much distance doesn't merely lead to inconvenience and loss of friendship. At the corporate level, when employees don't meet and chat (getting to know one another and jointly working on problems), bad things happen. Silos form and in-fighting reigns. Employees start labeling others with ugly terms such as "them" and "they"—meaning the bad people "out there" whom they rarely see and who are surely the cause of most of the problems they experience. If you want to predict who doesn't trust or get along with whom in a company, take out a tape measure.

But not everyone suffers from the negative effects of space and distance. Some people use it as a powerful influence lever. And when it comes to exploiting the use of space as a means of fostering vital behaviors, Delancey Street once again sets the standard. Dr. Silbert's goal, remember, is to foster two vital behaviors. She wants residents to be responsible for others rather than just themselves, and she wants to ensure that everyone confronts everyone with whom they have concerns. But how? These are people who are just as likely to punch each other out as anything else.

The first thing Silbert does is to stack previously mortal enemies on top of one another. She takes three guys—one new resident who's a card-carrying member of the Mexican Mafia, another who six months earlier was a Crip, and another who just a year ago was a leader in the Aryan Brotherhood—and makes them roommates. Nine such diverse folks will share a dorm. Someone from another background will be the crew boss. Perhaps a member of yet another race will be the minyan leader. It's like international spaghetti with every possible politically incorrect grouping tossed into the mix, and then they're asked to help and confront each other—in healthy ways.

We (the authors) watched the effects of placing former enemies in close proximity while eating in Delancey's restaurant. A fairly new employee named Kurt—a white man embroidered with tattoos from neck to fingertips—dropped a plate that smashed to pieces. Kurt had been at Delancey for just a couple of months and had been given the simple assignment of busing tables. Apparently he hadn't mastered the job yet.

And why should he? Kurt had come from a high-crime, largely black area of Richmond, California, where he had been schooled since age six in the hateful propaganda of the white-gang culture, not the restaurant business. He had been homeless for five years before joining Delancey, and for the first 60 days after entering the program he thought he'd die as his body adjusted to a life without drugs. He was hardly in any shape to be impressing customers.

When Kurt's plate shattered on the floor, he ducked his head in shame. A few dozen customers reflexively lifted their heads from their meals to look toward the source of the noise, only adding to his humiliation. Kurt was torn between wanting to curse at the onlookers and wanting to disappear entirely. What happened next was compelling evidence of the power of propinquity. The black maître d'—a former gang rival from Richmond and now a roommate—hurried over to where Kurt was kneeling over the broken plate and put his hand on Kurt's back in a gesture of support. He then knelt down and helped Kurt pick up the broken plate. He smiled at him and shrugged his shoulders, offering a look that said, "It happens." And with that, Kurt shook it off and returned to his duties.

While there's a lot going on at Delancey to influence change, you can't help but notice how propinquity is used to foster relationships. When you assign people interdependent roles and then put them in close proximity, you increase the chance that relationships that had once been the bane of their existence are now a big part of their personal transformation.

Families are also affected by how they make use of their space. For example, a recent study showed that the family dining table is vanishing from homes at a rapid rate. A parallel rise in family dysfunction and discontent suggests that familial unity is declining at a similar rate. Could there be a correlation here? The idea is not that a drop in furniture sales will harm family solidarity. It's that the dining room table is a significant facilitator of family togetherness. Do away with the table, and family members lose a fairly large portion of their time together.

But why would families stop buying and using dining room tables? Behold the microwave. There was a time when the preparation of the evening meal was such a significant undertaking that everyone, of necessity, ate at the same time and in the same place. The microwave changed all that by making it easy to prepare single portions for whomever whenever. Suddenly there was no need to prepare one big meal at one time.

Dining tables disappeared, and so did a regular ritual that brought people into face-to-face communication. Nowadays teenagers are as likely to have dinner alone or with their pals as they are to eat with their parents. Couple this trend with the creation of massive homes and separate TV rooms, and you'll see how space (the final frontier) has contributed to the average parent's loss of influence.

Within corporations, where friendships are less important than collaboration, propinquity also plays an important role in daily effectiveness. Distance keeps people from routinely interacting, and as we've suggested, it often leads to animosity and loss of influence. But it also leads to a loss of informal contact.

Most people don't lament this loss, but they should. When people casually bump into each other at work, they ask questions, share ideas, and surprisingly often come up with solutions to problems. The storied social scientist Bill Ouchi found that one practice at Hewlett-Packard greatly increased informal contact and collaboration. HP leaders demanded that employees keep, of all things, a messy desk. The goal wasn't to attract roaches; it was to attract humans. By leaving work visible and accessible, they found that it was much more likely that others wandering by would see, take an interest, and get involved in the work of a colleague.

As people bump into one another, take in the contents of a messy desk, and share ideas, they're also much more likely to work together on a formal project. Employees extend what starts out as a casual conversation into a shared task. In an area where multiple heads are required to solve most problems, this can be a real benefit. And once again, distance kills the chance of people running into each other and then working together on a shared project. In fact, in a study conducted at Bell Labs, researchers tested for factors that determine whether two scientists might collaborate. The best predictor was, you guessed it, *the distance between their offices.* Scientists who worked next to one another were three times more likely to discuss technical topics that lead to collaboration than scientists who sat 30 feet from one another. Put them 90 feet apart, and they are as likely to collaborate as those who work several miles away! The probability of collaboration sharply decreases in a matter of a few feet.

Given the overwhelming impact of proximity on informal contact and eventual collaboration, savvy leaders rely on the use of physical space as a means of enhancing interaction. Instead of simply telling people to collaborate, they move employees next to one another or provide them a shared common area or eating facility. At Hewlett-Packard, executives take it step further by mandating a daily break where everyone leaves his or her desk, retires to a common area, and drinks fruit juices while chatting with fellow employees about what's happening at work.

Over the years, this forced elbow-bumping has cost the company tens of thousands of dollars in food and drink, but many will argue that the benefits that come from informally chatting, collaborating, and eventually synergizing are well worth the investment. When it comes to corporate effectiveness, you can have propinquity work against you, or, as in HP's case, make it your ally.

Community leaders can benefit as well. For example, Muhammad Yunus discovered the importance of propinquity when working with poverty-stricken women in rural villages of Bangladesh. For generations women had been kept from venturing very far outside their own homes. When Dr. Yunus decided to give Bangladeshi women a hand-up by extending them microloans—in groups of five so they could support one another—he quickly learned that he would have to bring them together under the same roof, and frequently, or his plan would never work. Dr. Yunus wasn't merely changing his customers' financial circumstances when he started his banking business; he was turning the entire social community on end, and this had to be done in small, safe, social groups or not at all.

When we (the authors) were visiting a village called Gazipur in Bangladesh, here's what we learned about what Dr. Yunus had done to enlist the power of propinquity to create a new social order. In addition to promoting economic well-being, Grameen Bank asks that each borrower commit to 16 "Decisions." As we stood in the back of a small building containing a 30-member borrowing unit, we watched attentively as all 30 borrowers stood in unison and recited the 16 Decisions—one of which was: "I will neither give nor receive dowry."

This particular commitment is of grave importance to the group's economic well-being. The dowry—in which parents are required to pay a man to marry their daughter—can cause both social strife and economic disaster. Families are brought to penury as they try to scrape together enough money to induce a man to take their daughter in wedlock. Daughters are routinely berated by fathers who lament the fact that they fathered a girl who would later cost them so much money. Now, here stood 30 women at attention, loudly proclaiming their commitment to abolish the "curse of the dowry."

Later, as we chatted with the 30 women, we asked, "How many of you have had a son or daughter marry in the past year?" Five women proudly raised their hands. And then we sprung the follow-up question. "How many of you either gave or received dowry?" Three hands went sheepishly into the air. But two—Dipali and Shirina—didn't raise theirs. Here was evidence that this millennium-old practice was giving way. So we asked the two women to tell us how they had resisted the practice. They smiled broadly, looked at each other, and then Dipali said, "I had my son marry her daughter." With that the 30 women broke into spontaneous applause.

No longer did these women hide behind their own front door and simply take what fate had handed them. Now they met, talked, formed businesses, supported each other, signed for each others' loans, and became a genuine community, all within the confines of their own building where they met weekly.

Several forces are at play every time these intrepid entrepreneurs meet and fight their way out of poverty. Surely the social supports they provide one another help them make it through tough times, and they have plenty of tough times. The fact that they sign for each others' loans goes a long way toward ensuring that the businesses they create are well thought through. By forming 30-person units, they now offer as a group enough potential profit to command a bank's attention — something they never commanded individually.

And now we add one more feature. Yunus and his team had the good sense to design a simple space where this all happens. It wasn't easy. To come up with a building that was inexpensive enough to fit the budget of 30 poverty-stricken women called for a lot of work and careful planning. But they eventually did it, and the design ended up winning several international design awards.

So let's hear it for the architects out there who provide them (and us) with space. Now let's just hope we have the good sense to understand its effects.

MAKE IT EASY

For years there was a running debate concerning whether humans were the only animals that use tools. When scientists watched chimpanzees sit next to an anthill and place a stick in the entrance hole as a way of gathering ants — without having to dig — they decided that these creatures, with whom we share almost 95 percent of our DNA, were also using tools. So we now have our answer. Smart creatures, including Homo sapiens, use tools. Why? Because smart creatures do their best to find a way to make hard tasks easier.

Around a century ago, Frederick Taylor, the father of scientific management, decided that it was time that we tool users start using tools more wisely. After noticing that employees at Bethlehem Steel used but one shovel size for every task, he determined that the most effective load was 21½ pounds and set about designing and purchasing shovels of different sizes to ensure that no matter the medium, the weight employees hefted would always be the same. Never again would employees shovel slag and snow with the same instrument.

Nowadays you can't throw a rock without hitting someone who does similar time-study work. These folks aren't merely studying best practices; they study common practices and then through careful analysis make them better. Unfortunately, the principles of this discipline haven't always found their way into complex human problems such as divorce, obesity, drug abuse, credit card addiction, and AIDS transmission. Dr. Whyte (the innovator behind the restaurant spindle) brought an engineering solution to a social issue, but most people don't naturally think of industrial engineering as a resource for overcoming human challenges.

Influence whizzes don't make this mistake. They apply efficiency principles at the very highest level. Rather than constantly finding ways to motivate people to continue with their boring, painful, dangerous, or otherwise loathsome activities, they find a way to change *things*. Like an ape fashioning a stick to its needs, they change *things* in order to make the right behaviors easier to enact. And depending on whether the glass is half empty or half full, they also use *things* to make the wrong behaviors more difficult to enact.

For example, one of the main reasons the Guinea worm disease was eradicated so effectively across the sprawling subcontinent of India was that influence masters took steps to make it far easier to drink good water than to drink bad water. Here's the strategy they implemented.

In developing-world villages, women often spend several hours each day traveling to and from the local water source.

Hours that could have been spent in more fruitful or even enjoyable activities are expended walking back and forth to a pool while hauling a heavy pot. If this isn't bad enough, the pools these dedicated women hike to and from are often teeming with water fleas that are, in turn, filled with Guinea worm larvae.

Earlier we explained that change agents from The Carter Center had learned that villagers who filtered the water through their skirts had diminished the Guinea worm disease problem. Let's add some more detail to that project. In order to make it easier to filter the water effectively (many skirts didn't filter the water very well), The Carter Center set out on a campaign to develop an affordable and long-lasting cloth filter. People at the center knew that if they could find a way to get an effective, efficient, and durable filter into the hands of everyone who drew water, the parasite could be eliminated.

Former U.S. President Jimmy Carter, in his work with the center, explained how this all-important filter came about:

> *I went to see Edgar Bronfman, whose family owned about 20 percent of E.I. DuPont Company. I asked Edgar if he would donate $250,000 over a five year period, which in those days was a lot of money. He asked me, "What are you going to use the money for?" And I answered: "The best way to do away with the Guinea worm is to pour water through a very fine filter cloth." And he said, "Like this napkin on the table?" And I said, "Yes." "Then why don't you use napkins?" he asked. I explained, "Well, because if you take this napkin and wet and dry it eight or ten times a day, in the tropics it'll rot in a couple of weeks." And he responded, "Well, maybe we could help."*

Bronfman took the case to the DuPont board of directors, which knew of a company in Switzerland that produced a nylon fiber that would likely serve this purpose—a fiber that wouldn't rot in the tropics. DuPont provided these fibers to a company that does precision weaving, and they created the material for the filters. DuPont then donated 2 million square yards of this cloth to The Carter Center.

"This was the main resource we used to get rid of the Guinea worm," President Carter concluded.

Once the specialized cloth had been produced, the task of getting people to filter their water was made a great deal easier, and with the help of that simple invention the parasite began disappearing in hundreds of villages.

In India, there was an even more elegant engineering solution available than simply making it easy to filter the water effectively. Unlike sub-Saharan Africa, in India clear, clean water runs close to the surface of the earth. So engineers drilled and capped bore-hole wells in hundreds of villages across the country. This simple one-time strategy made safe water far more accessible and bad water much harder to get to. Guinea worm in India, robbed of its hosts, died off rapidly.

Much of Delancey's success also depends on making the right behavior easier while making the wrong behavior more difficult. This is particularly true when it comes to drug abuse. Imagine the challenge of ensuring that new residents succeed during their first few drug-free weeks. Withdrawing from heroin is described as one of the most excruciatingly painful trials you can experience. Addicts who come to loathe the drug, and who experience little benefit from the high after years of abuse, continue to use the drug just to avoid the pain of withdrawing.

And yet almost every heroin addict who comes to Delancey makes it through this agonizing period. Why? In part because they've changed their zip code. Minutes before walking through the front gate, new residents' environment had been filled with people who used, supplied, or supported their addictive behavior. Now they're in a dorm with eight other people who don't. And outside the dorm are another 50 residents on their floor who don't. And in their building are another 200 who don't. In order to get to drugs, residents would now have to go to much greater lengths and distances than ever before. And all of this happens because Dr. Silbert understands the importance of making the wrong behavior hard, and the right behavior easy—or at least easier.

If you're not a drug addict and don't have worms, what can this simple principle do for you? Or maybe for our friend Henry? Here's some more good news on the diet front. Brian Wansink has shown that if you make good eating choices a little easier and bad ones a little harder, you can make a substantial dent in your waistline.

For example, Brian Wansink found that plate size affects the amount of food a person will eat during a meal before deciding that he or she is satisfied. Smaller plates left people satisfied with smaller portions. If you want to eat fewer calories, change the dishes sitting in your cupboard. He also learned that the positioning of snacks and whether packaging is clear or opaque can increase or decrease consumption by 50 percent or more. A candy jar placed on a desk rather than a few feet away on a bookshelf can double the amount of candy consumed—once again, propinquity at work. Ice cream with a clear top in the freezer is much more likely to be eaten than the same treat in a cardboard box.

And when it comes to using your exercise equipment, you can bet that distance also takes its toll. Move your exercise bike from your TV room to your basement, and you've just dramatically cut your chances of using it. Travel to a gym for your routine cardiovascular exercise (as opposed to using a piece of home equipment), and this too will lessen your chances substantially.

So, if you're one who struggles to maintain a healthy lifestyle, do a quick inventory of things that affect your behavior. Take a count of how many bad food choices are within your reach at each hour of a typical day. Then take a count of how many good choices are within the same distance. Look at how difficult it is for you to exercise. Do you have to walk to a distant and socially isolated room to get to your equipment? Do you have to unpack something from a closet before you can get started?

Discover how many items in your home you can simply *move* to make the right behavior easier and the wrong behavior more difficult. Sure, you can always hunker down, gut it out, and suffer as a way of ensuring that you eat right and exercise regularly. You can always plug in a motivational tape to keep your spirits high in order to climb that mountain. Or you can just make the right things easier to do and the wrong things more difficult to do. It's your call.

Health-care institutions have also learned the importance of making the correct behavior easier. Consider what many institutions are doing to reduce medication errors. In the past, pills came in only a reddish brown bottle that offered no information about its content and looked just like the reddish brown bottle next to it. Oops. Couple this challenge with the fact that many people who fill medical orders do so after pulling back-to-back shifts while squinting to read that pharma-chicken-scratch that passes as a prescription, and it's easy to see why medication errors cause tens of thousands of deaths annually.

Nowadays progressive pharmaceutical companies and hospitals are teaming up to make the right choices obvious. By deft use of colored bottles and better labels, many hospitals have significantly reduced medication errors and subsequently needless deaths. It seems odd that something as important as *not killing patients* could be affected as recently as a few years ago with an intervention as simple as, well, making the right behavior simple. But, then again, when it comes to changing human behavior, most people would rather motivate the guilty—for instance, suing the blighters who spoon out the wrong drugs—than enable them. And when it comes to enabling others, we often turn to training before we look for ways to make the task easier to perform.

At the corporate level, companies are becoming more attuned to the concept of making the right behavior, such as buying their product, easier. For instance, consumer guru Paco Underhill helped increase the sales of doggie treats by making it just a little easier to take them off a shelf. Underhill found that young and middle-aged adults were more likely to buy animal treats than were the elderly and children. This piqued his curiosity. He videotaped customers on the pet aisle and quickly discovered what was keeping treat sales low among certain age groups. Typically the staple items like pet food were on the eye- and waist-level shelves, while treats were placed on higher shelves.

It turns out that the young and old find it significantly more difficult to reach items on a higher shelf. One video clip showed an elderly woman attempting to use a carton of aluminum foil to knock down a package of treats. Another revealed a child dangerously climbing shelves to try to reach the package. Moving the treats down one shelf made the behavior just easy enough to boost sales immediately.

But not everyone is listening. In fact, Bill Friedman, one of the biggest gurus on the effects of the environment on human behavior, is being systematically ignored. He studies gambling casinos. By watching thousands of hours of video of people gambling, he has discovered an interesting fact. The features that make a hotel attractive make gamblers miserable.

Las Vegas hotels compete on the basis of their size and splendor. The higher the ceilings and the longer the vistas, the more valued the hotel. Gamblers, in contrast, seek small, intimate places. When you think about it, sitting in front of a one-armed bandit and pulling a lever is actually quite boring. You'd have to pay production-line workers good money to do such things. What people find interesting at a casino is not the task of gambling, but the interactions they have with other people. The job of gambling is made more fun (a surrogate for easy), when other people are around. Consequently, when Friedman helps owners transform large unfriendly venues into cozy ones, profits soar.

But big Vegas hotels nowadays are competing as big *hotels*, so they ignore Friedman's advice and make massive, unfriendly casinos. Consequently, many modern hotels barely break even on their gambling (blasphemous in years past) and rely on entertainment, room costs, and restaurants to make money. Nevertheless, the principle is still the same. If you follow the guru's advice and make gambling more pleasant (that is, easy) by making it cozy and friendly, you'll make money hand over fist. But then again, maybe that's just too easy.

MAKE IT UNAVOIDABLE

Making use of *things* to enable behavior works best when you can alter the physical world in a way that eliminates human choice entirely. You don't merely make good behavior desirable, you make it inevitable. This is where structure, process, and procedures come into play, and, once again, the corporate world leads the way. Engineers, tiring of reminding employees not to stick their fingers in certain machines, build in mechanical features that prevent people from putting their hands at risk. Pilots follow lockstep procedures and rigid checklists that require them to double- and triple-check their takeoff and landing procedures.

When it comes to the fast-food industry, we've hardwired tasks that used to call for talent, and that often used to put customer satisfaction and profits at risk. For example, when it comes to taking an order, employees can simply push picture buttons, and of course, nobody has to know how to make change because the register does it automatically. It's all been routinized. When it comes to taking an order and making change, it's not only easy to do the right thing, it's now almost impossible to do the wrong thing.

However, when it comes to the profound and complex social problems we've been addressing, we're not as good at hardwiring successes through the manipulation of the physical environment. Fortunately, this is fairly easy to change. Often all that's required to make good behavior inevitable is to structure it into your daily routine. If we've learned only one thing about today's overscheduled world, it's that structure drives out lack of structure. Meetings happen. On the other hand, "I'll get back to you sometime later"—maybe that won't happen. So if you want to guarantee a positive behavior, build it into a special meeting or hardwire it into an existing meeting agenda.

For example, the CEO of a large defense contracting company the authors worked with saw a massive increase in innovative breakthroughs when he and his senior leadership team scheduled and met regularly with groups of employees to solicit ideas. This calendared practice created a forum that encouraged and enabled new behaviors, thereby making the right behavior inevitable. At Delancey, Silbert makes use of calendared events by taking them one step further and transforming them into *rituals*. These ordered procedures consist of hardwired meetings that are never missed and that are highly symbolic, quite volatile, and enormously effective at making the right behavior inevitable. Consider the Delancey ritual referred to simply as "Games." This particular ritual is not always fun, but it's always done.

Say you're a resident at Delancey. Three times a week you and members of your minyan get together to dump on each other. A disinterested person ensures that nothing gets physical, but beyond that it's pretty unstructured. During "Games" people learn the egalitarian approach to feedback that Delancey wants. Anyone can challenge anyone. If you think your crew boss is a jerk, you give him a slip of paper inviting him to a Game. He must show up. And when he's there, you can unload on him to your heart's content. Anyone from Silbert on down can be invited to a Game by anyone else.

Over time, the quality of Games increases as the volume decreases. Residents become better at sharing feedback. What doesn't change is that this long-standing ritual makes the right behavior inevitable. People don't like to confront others—particularly scary and powerful others. Left to their own proclivities, residents would do what anyone else would do—toggle from silence (holding our complaints inside) to violence (blowing up in a verbal tirade). So Silbert turns feedback into a ritual, calls it Games, and then lets the Games begin. Three times a week without fail.

SUMMARY: CHANGE THE ENVIRONMENT

When you first read that sociophysical guru Fred Steele thinks that most of us are environmentally incompetent, it's only natural to become defensive. That's a harsh term. Who died and left him in charge of measuring our competency? But then when you read of the dozens of environment-based strategies influence masters routinely employ as a means of bringing about change, you realize that most of us really don't turn to the power of propinquity or the data stream or any other physical factor as a means of supporting our influence efforts.

When it comes to developing a change strategy, we just don't think about *things* as our first line of influence. Given that things are far easier to change than people, and that these things can then have a permanent impact on how people behave, it's high time we pick up on the lead of Whyte, Steele, Wansink, and others and add the power of the environment to our influence repertoire. And who knows? Someday an everyday person may even be able to say the word *propinquity* in public without drawing snickers.

10

Become an Influencer

I was going to buy a copy of The Power of Positive Thinking, *and then I thought: What the hell good would that do?*

—*Ronnie Shakes*

This book started with a bold assertion. We claimed that if you bundle the right number and type of influence techniques into the right influence strategy, you can change virtually *anything*. At first blush this claim seems both cocky and unbelievable. Obviously there are thousands of things out there that none of us will ever change. Take gravity, for example. It's been around for a while and doesn't appear to be going anywhere. From there we explained that we're referring to the *behaviors* that cause most of the profound and persistent problems that we're currently experiencing.

There is a growing body of knowledge as well as an impressive supply of real-life success stories that teach exactly how to change almost any human behavior. Read the scholarly works of Dr. Albert Bandura. Then watch what Dr. Mimi Silbert does at Delancey Street. These two influencers alone demonstrate that, if you know what you're doing, you can indeed change remarkably resistant behaviors.

For example, today at Delancey, 500 former criminals and drug addicts are willingly immersed in an intense environment that employs every influence strategy we discussed. The strategies have been put into place to help each resident transform from a habitual offender into a productive citizen.

Naturally, bringing about the profound transformation of these 500 people isn't easy. It's never easy to get people to change deeply entrenched behaviors, and when you're working with people whose résumés include an average of four felony convictions, you're dealing with a population that has one unhelpful characteristic in common. The residents may come from different gangs, ethnic groups, or even criminal portfolios, but they have all failed to turn their lives around.

Before joining Delancey, each time these criminals matriculated into the penal system only to return to a life of crime, the penal system failed them. Each time some may have sworn to their family members that next time they'd get it right—and then got it wrong—they let down their loved ones. Each time some may have vowed to break their vile habits and promptly returned to their old ways, they let themselves down. And each time they failed to transform into a new person, they failed because not one of them brought together a comprehensive enough influence strategy to remake themselves.

All 500 of them had repeatedly failed before showing up at Delancey Street.

Yet Dr. Mimi Silbert's approach routinely transforms 90 percent of these habitual failures into law-abiding citizens. Dr. Silbert succeeds more than others not because she cares more than other change agents or because she spends more money. In fact, the operation funds itself through its own efforts. To date, Silbert has succeeded in turning around over 14,000 lives because she is a genuine card-carrying, four-star influencer. She knows how to help people change their thoughts and actions.

In 1992 when Dr. Don Berwick and IHI started the 100,000 lives campaign, they too were taking on one of the most entrenched establishments in the world—the U.S. health-care system. At that particular time in history, an estimated 100,000 patients were dying each year in hospitals as the direct result of a variety of preventable human errors. Berwick and his team set out to prevent these errors. That meant that they'd have to find a way to both enable and motivate health-care professionals to act in new ways.

As you might imagine, when Dr. Berwick and his colleagues started their campaign, some people in the health-care system were unconscious of how their own actions might be contributing to harm. Even those who were conscious of the dangers lurking in their systems were often incapable of building the influence strategies necessary to bring about profound and lasting change.

Fortunately, Berwick and his staff stuck with their campaign until they learned exactly what it would take to change deeply entrenched behavior. During the 100,000 lives campaign, 3,100 hospitals reduced total in-patient deaths by an estimated 122,000 over eighteen months. Today Berwick and his team are working on a 5 million lives campaign. Imagine the grief they'll be preventing and the joy they'll be bringing to the world. They're taking on a target that's 50 times larger than their original goal because they now know a great deal more about exerting influence.

For one final update, let's head to sub-Saharan Africa. For several decades well-intended anthropologists and health-care specialists did their best to encourage locals to read their worm brochures or attend their lectures or simply to follow their heartfelt advice. If the villagers would only listen to their ideas, they could rid themselves of the dreaded Guinea worm disease. But alas, few followed their advice, and the ugly scourge plagued tens of millions.

Enter Dr. Donald Hopkins and other influence masters from The Carter Center. Since the beginning of their campaign to eradicate Guinea worm disease, this small team of change agents has reduced the level of Guinea worm cases by 99.7 percent, completely eradicating the disease from 11 of the 20 endemic countries it originally targeted. The team is on schedule to completely eradicate the scourge by 2009. Team members have done this not through a medical breakthrough but by learning how to motivate and enable absolute strangers to alter their behavior. Like other influencers we've studied, these devoted change agents stepped up to an enormous challenge, left behind old and failed methods, and decided that if they wanted to solve the devastating Guinea worm problem, they would have to start with themselves. They would first have to learn what it would take to exert influence over human behavior.

So they did. They visited their target audience, studied positive deviance, and brought into play many of the methods we describe in this book. As a result, one day soon the very last Guinea worm will have been eliminated from the face of the earth. Forever. The horrible parasite will actually be extinct, and this is an extinction we can live with.

Bandura, Silbert, Berwick, Hopkins—in fact, all of the other practitioners and scholars we've studied—have made stunning contributions to the change literature. They have all succeeded where others have failed. They have all demonstrated that if you know how to make use of the right influence tools and bring them to bear on a carefully designed project, you can change anything.

And best of all, each of these geniuses has given us hope. We too can become master influencers—but not without some hard work. We have to stop tinkering with problems and learn how to build a comprehensive influence strategy. This, of course, raises the question of whether everyday people can actually put into play the principles influence masters use all the time. The answer, of course, is a resounding yes. None of the individuals we've studied were influencers by training, but all eventually learned what it took to wrestle persistent problems to the ground. To kick-start your personal efforts, you'll have to use this book as a handbook for change.

FIND VITAL BEHAVIORS

Start with vital behaviors. There's no use putting together several complex techniques all aimed at the wrong actions. That's where Dr. Ethna Reid's work comes into play. Dr. Reid taught us to look for best practice research that compares top performers to others, teases out the unique behaviors that separate the best from the rest, and then teaches these vital behaviors to lower-performing individuals. If they then make significant improvements, you have something worth trying.

When you find yourself sorting through a list of possible influence strategies, demand this same level of scientific rigor. Accept only those recommendations that have been proven through similar comparative analyses. Start your search by looking for scholastic work. Search for university publications, frequently cited research, and renowned practitioners who publish their results. Such scientific work can be found in respected journals and not necessarily in advertising brochures. In any case, take the time to explore the known universe, and don't merely accept the first plan that comes across your desk.

After identifying the vital behaviors that have worked for others, learn what works best for you by applying the principles of positive deviance. Examine the times when you have succeeded, and try to identify the force or strategy that led to your success. Once you've discovered the actions that have worked for you in the past, conduct short-cycle-time mini experiments to confirm your analysis. Don't head off on a lifelong trek. Instead, set short-term goals, try the behaviors within a low-risk environment, and then see what works for you.

ADD A SOURCE

Behind each vital behavior you'll find six distinct sources of influence. If you're lucky, any one of these sources might be enough to put your change strategy over the top. For example, you may have realized that if you simply build deliberate practice into your attempt to help your children love reading, you could make enormous strides. You may have been struck with the insanity of sending people off to corporate training programs and then dropping them back into a social climate where no one reinforces the concepts they were taught. So you've added social and structural reinforcement into the mix. Perhaps you have carted your treadmill from the basement up to your bedroom where you don't have to fight the deadly power of propinquity. In the odd event that your previous influence strategy was short one or two horsepower of what was needed to create change, picking and choosing from the influence concepts we've outlined could put you over the top.

DIAGNOSE BEFORE YOU PRESCRIBE

Be warned: If you're facing a more daunting challenge than those mentioned above, you'd do well to do what influence masters do. Diagnose before you prescribe. Figure out which sources of influence are behind the behavior you're trying to change. Most leaders fail to take this step and simply throw together an influence strategy they believe should work under any circumstances.

Skilled influencers do otherwise. For example, consider Dr. Warren Warwick of Fairview University Children's Hospital. He realized that his medicine was no better than his influence strategy. In one rather intriguing case, an 18-year-old cystic fibrosis patient he was treating wasn't conforming to her treatment plan. Rather than launch into a lecture about how she would suffocate in a few years if she continued to slack off, Dr. Warwick stopped and diagnosed the underlying cause. Rather than asking, "What the heck is wrong with her?" Dr. Warwick tried to understand why she would fail to do something that would save her life. As he probed and listened, he learned that there were several reasons behind the lapse.

The patient had a new boyfriend with whom she was staying half the time. Her mother had typically administered the treatments, but now the patient was often not at home at the prescribed times. She had started a job and was working nights. The school she attended changed policies and now required a nurse to administer her medicine. Deciding that this was a pain, she stopped taking the medicine. Worst of all, in spite of losing 20 percent of her lung capacity in the previous two months, she felt fine and concluded that fewer treatments were okay. The more Dr. Warwick talked with the patient, the more he realized that she was failing to follow standard procedure for several different reasons. When he understood the sources of influence he was up against, he and the patient were able to develop a plan that literally saved her life.

ADD MORE SOURCES

When the behavior you're trying to change is currently supported by several sources, you'll have to load up your influence strategy to address everything you're up against. The world is perfectly organized to create the results you're currently experiencing.

Draw on All Six Sources of Influence

To achieve new results, you're probably going to have to change several elements in order to both motivate and enable the new and healthier behaviors.

However, that's not how people tend to operate. Over the years we (the authors) have worked with corporate leaders who knew that they needed to change the very culture of their organizations. They knew that people's behavior across the company was sapping productivity, driving away customers, and swallowing profits. When we described the breadth of six-source strategies that would be required to create the results they wanted, the leaders often concluded that they could select from the various strategies we were recommending like so many items in a catalog. They wanted to purchase influence on the cheap, but the changes they were attempting to bring about couldn't be had at bargain-basement prices.

But desperate times lead to desperate actions, and people, more often than not, seek simplistic solutions, even when they're studying the world's best influencers. For example, Dr. Silbert explains that over the past three decades she has invested a great deal of time with people who have traveled halfway around the world to learn what she's done to help criminals and drug addicts become productive citizens. Silbert tells those who visit Delancey Street the *whole* story—emphasizing each of the elements required to make the venture succeed. She clarifies the exact vital behaviors the organization tries to encourage. She notes how she purposely creates direct and vicarious experiences to help residents change their minds. She goes to great pains to ensure that the influence strategy makes good use of all six sources of influence.

More often than not, the travelers leave Delancey Street filled with hope. Then they go home and select one idea to add to their existing ineffective effort. Of course, this single element rarely adds enough horsepower to create change, so their "new and improved" strategy fails, and the earnest change agents wonder why their effort didn't work.

These cafeteria-style change efforts—where people pick only a few elements from a broader array—happen all the time. For example, if you look at the diffusion of the North Carolina second-chance strategy we described earlier, you'll find that it follows a predictable and lamentable path. Remember the clever crime-reduction strategy where soon-to-be-arrested drug dealers were brought into a room filled with pictures of them committing crimes? At one point the local district attorney shows a video montage made up of criminal scenes taken of each of the subjects in action and then asks the subjects to raise their hand when they see themselves committing a felony. And they do.

This method for creating a sense of impending doom is coupled with family support, job training, and several other essential ingredients that have yielded encouraging results. In fact, the designers of second-chance programs go to great pains to ensure that all six sources of influence are affected by their change strategy.

The impressive results of the comprehensive effort have since been reported in the press. Police leaders enthusiastically read about the strategy and select a few of the elements they think their city council will approve, or a couple for which they can secure funding. Or perhaps they give extra attention to a strategy they are already implementing but can now call a second-chance program. And sure enough, after employing only one or two elements from the overall intervention, the change effort fails. In the end, eager would-be influencers search for another change plan that they then choose from selectively and implement poorly—thus failing all over again.

If One Source Doesn't Work, Try More Sources

The simplistic strategies that most people adopt from the cafeteria of choices are almost always the same. People realize that when it comes to motivating humans, a single motivator can be powerful enough to trump all other sources of motivation. For instance, say you don't like your job and aren't very fond of your coworkers, yet you show up to work every day. That's because you need the money. The money trumps your tedious job and abrasive colleagues.

In a similar vein, when people have power over others, they often trump all other sources of motivation by relying on threats. Now that others have been warned, surely they'll be motivated to do the right thing. Unfortunately, negative reinforcement yields mixed results and needs to be constantly monitored. Worse still, all abuses of authority transform those who rely on them into the parent or leader they swore they'd never become.

Ineffective influencers compensate for their weak influence repertoires by putting a megaphone to the one source they've already put in place. In contrast, influence geniuses tap new sources of influence rather than trying desperately to pump up their anemic single source.

For example, people who develop a change strategy based on a single extrinsic motivator typically miss the importance of creating circumstances in which intrinsic rewards carry their share of the motivational load. Savvy influencers increase their likelihood of achieving success by building in multiple sources. That means they co-opt rather than fight peer pressure. They link vital behaviors to the formal reward structure. In short, they align all the sources of motivation with the desired vital behaviors.

When it comes to *ability* problems, the importance of stacking the deck for success is equally essential. With ability barriers, no single enabling source can trump the other sources. In fact, quite the opposite is true. One barrier that disables a change project trumps all other enablers. For example, at work you may be able to complete your part of the job, but if those who provide you with materials and information you need can't do their part, you're stumped. If others can do their part but the computer system fails them, you're all stumped.

Consequently, when it comes to enabling a change effort, the common error made by naive influencers is *not* that they try to trump all the other disabling sources with one powerful megasource. Instead, the common mistake lies in surfacing a single barrier, fixing it, and then believing they're done. With six separate sources of influence behind any one barrier — and with dozens of forces lying behind each source — it's fairly likely that more than one disabler lies behind any persistent problem. That's often what has made it so persistent.

For instance, when it comes to your own health care, here's an interesting best practice. It's wise to talk with your personal physician with the idea that any lingering symptoms you experience might have more than one underlying medical cause. Recent research into how doctors think reveals that patients who say, "Yes, it sounds like I might have X, but could there be something else going on as well?" are more likely to resolve their overall health problems than those who hold to the belief that if they treat one source of the problem, they will be fine.

Left to our natural tendencies, most of us make poor use of the vast array of the tools that can help improve performance. When it comes to complex interpersonal skills, we rarely think to make use of deliberate practice. For instance, in the fields of leadership and interpersonal influence, students are rarely taught specific behaviors that they can then rehearse while receiving detailed feedback from a trained coach. Instead, students are taught "from the neck up" a set of ideas that rarely leads to changes in behavior.

The ability to withstand yearnings and temptations is rarely viewed as a skill. Instead, the ability to overcome enticements is routinely attributed to inherent, DNA-driven personality characteristics. Consequently, almost nobody actually practices methods for delaying gratification. When people don't believe that the ability to withstand cravings is skill based, they rely on every source of motivation imaginable. Eventually their inevitable failure leads to depression and helplessness rather than a search for newer and better skills.

Social capital also remains a largely untouched resource for enabling change. Often we're led to believe that battles need to be won within the confines of one's own heart. Heroes have first and last names, not collective descriptors such as "team" or "group." Consequently, asking for help is seen as a weakness rather as than a savvy strategy. Master influencers know better. They identify those who need to be added to the change effort in order to succeed. They make use of peer influence and ensure that social circles support the effort rather than get in its way.

When it comes to enabling performance by making use of the *physical world*, most people typically fail to even think about this powerful and yet largely untapped source of influence. Dr. William F. Whyte came up with the idea of building the restaurant order spindle when he was dealing with restaurant arguments, but nobody else thought of it. Dr. Frederick Steele explained this mental gaff by suggesting that most of us are environmentally incompetent. We rarely see the effect the physical environment is having on us, nor do we make use of environmental features when crafting an influence effort.

In short, you must address all six sources of influence when designing an influence strategy. Stop thinking of influence tools as a buffet, and recognize them as a comprehensive approach to creating systematic, widespread, and lasting change. Diagnose both motivational and ability sources of influence, and then lock in the results by applying individual, social, and structural forces to the solution. You now have a powerful six-source diagnostic tool at your fingertips. Use it liberally.

MAKE CHANGE INEVITABLE

Let's end on the concept of making change inevitable. More than anything else, this characteristic sets effective influencers apart from everyone else. Individuals who routinely hit their change goals *overdetermine* vital behaviors in order to make change inevitable, meaning that they routinely look at all six sources, find methods from within each source, and continue adding new influence strategies well after others have stopped searching for change levers. They do this for a good reason. Typically the change they're attempting to orchestrate is so audacious—so completely hopeless—that they pull out every influence tool available.

PUTTING IT ALL TOGETHER

To see how the principles we've studied can be used in combination in an actual business case, let's take a look at what we (the authors) once did when working with an executive team to solve a particularly destructive problem. The leaders attempted to use each influence method we've discussed to deal with the company's inability to deliver on commitments.

In this company, employees were good at making promises; it was *keeping* them that gave them fits. With each new project, senior managers set clear objectives, department heads agreed to detailed specs and deadlines, and then one or more groups fell miserably short of their goals and delayed the project. This habit of always missing deadlines caused enormous problems with customers. Delays and crisis recoveries caused costs to spiral out of control. And the company's growing reputation for being "long on commitment but short on fulfillment" was beginning to cost them dearly in the marketplace. Old customers were fleeing while new ones were becoming increasingly difficult to find.

To identify the self-defeating behaviors that were leading to failure, a team consisting of several senior managers and the authors conducted interviews with project managers and project team members. The research team quickly discovered that people were completely aware of consistent failures, as well as the reasons for them.

Fact-Free Planning. One manager told us that corporate executives would lay out plans without gathering facts about what the team was actually able to accomplish. If they did ask for input, it was just a joke because they already had the deadline in their heads. The manager explained, "More often than not, we know from the onset that we're going to fail because we don't have sufficient resources. Watching one of our projects unfold is like watching a 'slow-motion train wreck.' You know that your project is going to end in disaster, and all you can do is sit back and watch it tumble off the track."

Project Chicken. Another manager explained how the team played the same pernicious game we discussed earlier. "In every planning and follow-up meeting," she said, "project managers say they're right on spec and schedule, while in truth they're quietly praying that someone else will admit that he or she is behind schedule so that person will take the heat while everyone else is given a reprieve. It's a deadly game that pits managers against one another in a way that eventually crushes our customers."

AWOL Sponsors. Finally, we found that the organization's projects suffered when project sponsors were *absent without leave*. Each project was assigned a senior leader whose job it was to sponsor the project. The sponsor was supposed to help guide the project through the organization as they and other leaders competed for resources. If there was a problem, it was the sponsor's job to seek additional resources as required, update key personnel, and otherwise smooth the skids.

The trouble in this organization was that sometimes sponsors wouldn't show up for meetings, wouldn't enforce agreements with other departments, and would fail to align other leaders behind the teams' decisions. The project team was left hanging, and the project would inevitably come to nothing.

One project, for example, burned up thousands of person-hours and over a million dollars in precious resources, but ended up on the scrap heap at the end. The most painful part of the failure, however, wasn't just the loss of time and money. It was that halfway into the project everyone knew it was doomed because the sponsor was doing nothing to enforce commitments, gain support from stakeholders, and maintain accountability. Everyone would show up to project meetings, but they'd just play with their BlackBerries because they knew the meetings were irrelevant!

Search for Vital Behaviors

To discover what it would take to turn around this culture of fear and failure, we asked if there were any project managers or team leaders who consistently hit their deadlines, and if so, if we could watch them in action. It turned out there were. So we and the executive team studied these *positive deviants*.

While studying these accomplished project managers, we began to see why they hit their goals when others didn't. For instance, in one key meeting we watched a positive deviant deal with Fact-Free Planning. A senior executive had committed to a deadline without ensuring that the organization could deliver. When confronted with her misstep, the executive became very defensive. She threatened to outsource the project if the internal team "didn't have the commitment required."

That was when the magic happened. We watched this skillful project manager deal with the defensive executive, refuse to respond in kind, and calmly create a sense of shared purpose between the project team and the executive. The manager left the room with the backing of the executive for a far more realistic plan and, more importantly, with an agreement on how future project commitments would be made.

Watching this woman along with other positive deviants showed us that the *vital behaviors* for project success involved dealing with what we later called "crucial conversations." In fact, we've found that being able to successfully hold crucial conversations is frequently the vital behavior behind change. (Our book *Crucial Conversations: Tools for Talking when Stakes are High* teaches a very common set of vital behaviors—the ability to speak and be heard and encourage others to do the same, no matter how controversial, political, or unpopular one's views.)

Having found our vital behaviors in this particular organization (the ability to hold crucial conversations about Fact-Free Planning, Project Chicken, and AWOL Sponsors), it was our job to use every means within our control to ensure the results they wanted. What would it take to get everyone to enact these behaviors and eventually turn the culture around?

Change How You Change Minds

We knew one thing for certain: Verbal persuasion wasn't going to offer much help. Telling people that they needed to speak up when they disagreed with a person in authority or had bad news sounded more like, "You need to naively expose your problems, put your career at risk, and be seen as a whiney non-team player. So go ahead—who wants to be first?"

What we needed to do was find a way to help people change two specific views. First, they had to believe they could indeed speak frankly without looking like rebels or wimps. Second, they had to believe that if they did effectively share their contrary or controversial ideas, they and their colleagues would make the right choices about deadlines and resources, and eventually they'd be able to actually hit their goals.

MAKE CHANGE INEVITABLE

To replace their existing fears with a growing sense of confidence, employees didn't need a lecture; they needed to improve their actual skills (**Personal Ability**). To do so we took the rather complex behaviors demonstrated by those who knew how to make it safe to talk about just about anything, and followed the tenets of deliberate practice. We broke the skills into learnable parts and provided positive examples. As individuals practiced the new skills within a protected training environment, they were given immediate feedback from a coach. Finally, as they grew their competence they began to believe that they could indeed speak their minds without taking a huge risk.

But we didn't stop there. We took care to connect the newly acquired skill set to the trainees' sense of who they wanted to be as well as to their core values (**Personal Motivation**). People weren't being asked to learn skills merely because it was the latest "flavor of the month;" they were being given the chance to become the person they preferred to be. Nobody wanted to play project chicken—essentially lying about their readiness while wishing the worst on their peers. Consequently, as part of the training experience people openly discussed the existing culture, how it violated their values, and what it would take to become a functioning team composed of professionals rather than, well, a group of people who had originally described their culture as one built on lies and deception.

In addition, we gave team leaders a firsthand view of the human consequences of AWOL sponsorship and fact-free planning. We had them spend a weekend in development—seeing the problems thoughtless deadlines and lack of support from leadership created for the personal lives of those who had to meet the deadlines. At one point, an operations manager confessed that his marriage was about to collapse because he had not been home a full weekend for over a year. Members of the leadership team left with a whole new level of moral engagement.

To provide additional motivation to learn and implement the vital behaviors, we tapped into the social support system (**Social Motivation**). First we identified opinion leaders and asked them to help lead the influence effort. They were the first to go through the training. By learning firsthand that the training could help them resolve real problems they had been fighting for years—and then seeing the enormous benefit of learning and implementing the skills—opinion leaders openly encouraged their coworkers to take part in the training and put the skills into play. To transform mere words into a vicarious experience, several told stories of how the skills had helped them work through a touchy discussion.

To further enable each employee to routinely use the skills, the training was always taught in intact teams by the team's immediate supervisor (**Social Ability**). The supervisor would begin by forming participants into teams of three. After the training was complete, the teams met and discussed what they were doing to catch and solve problems early. They often gathered over lunch, where members helped each other prepare for an upcoming high-stakes conversation.

Managers provided additional incentive to routinely step up to and master the vital behaviors by including the target behaviors in performance reviews linked to the annual bonus (**Structural Motivation**). Employees were now measured against the skills that were taught in the training. In addition, 25 percent of senior executives' bonuses were pegged to whether or not they measurably improved the vital behaviors across the organization. That put real teeth into the intervention.

Finally, to make good use of the physical environment, every meeting room displayed a poster that reviewed the skills employees were supposed to bring into play when they faced problems with project management (**Structural Ability**). Leaders also included a short list of the vital skills at the top of their printed agenda as a way of reminding themselves to review one or more elements in each meeting. And then, to make good use of the power of propinquity, two groups that routinely went at it hammer-and-tong were moved to the same work area where constant interaction helped them become far more collaborative.

By carefully considering each of the principles we've covered in this book, this particular change team was able to overcome what had been an overwhelming problem. We know that they succeeded because we measured the results. By taking a pre-measure of the vital behaviors and then correlating improvements in the behavior with key performance indicators, the research team discovered that not only did the use of vital behaviors increase substantially, but for each percentage increase in the use of the vital behaviors, there was a $1.5 million improvement in productivity. Quality and customer satisfaction measures were similarly affected by improvements in the vital behaviors. By applying each of the influence principles and strategies we've studied—and not just one or two methods—the change team was able to resolve what had been a massive and resistant problem. They had become genuine influencers.

AN INVITATION FROM THE AUTHORS

Influencers not only overdetermine their results, but they also rarely work alone. Massive problems require a community of influencers working in concert. As an increasing number of people apply the works of Bandura, Silbert, Hopkins, Berwick, and other influence experts to problems of every kind, new and vibrant influence communities are springing up each day.

By working with others to bring every influence tool imaginable to bear on their problems, this growing community of experts has taught us not to be too quick to pray for serenity. They have shown us that the combined power of their influence tools is far greater than the sum of the individual parts. While turning criminals and addicts into healthy citizens, saving millions of lives, turning companies around, and annihilating deadly diseases, they have taught us one of the most important lessons we can ever learn. When you understand the forces behind any behavior, along with the strategies to change it, you hold within your grasp the power to change anything.

You too can find strength in numbers by joining the growing community of world-class influencers. Start by visiting our Web site at **influencerbook.com**, where we'll provide you with a worksheet to help you prepare for and organize your next influence project. At this site you can blog with other students of influence who are working to solve challenges similar to yours. You'll also be able to learn more about vital behaviors and six-source strategies, and view short segments of interviews with a few of the influencers you've already met in this book.

Finally, if you'd like to take a measure of your existing influence skills, the site offers a self-assessment that not only gives you a view into your existing influence repertoire but can also help you develop the next steps for becoming an effective influencer. Enjoy!

Additional Tools and Resources

Strengthen your influence skills today by visiting our Web site at **www.influencerbook.com**. There you'll find a variety of free resources that have been designed to help you transform this book into a tool for change. Resources include:

Worksheet. Download a worksheet that you can use to design and organize your next influence effort. This handy tool helps you select a problem, identify vital behaviors, explore six-source methods, and otherwise apply everything you've explored in the book to a problem you'd like to resolve once and for all.

Blog. Join a growing community of individuals who are doing their best to become the next generation of influencers. As you tackle the persistent problems you face every day, you can blog with other individuals who face challenges similar to your own.

Vital Behaviors and Six Sources. Discover what contemporary researchers and practitioners are learning each day regarding which behaviors lead to the greatest changes, as well as which six-source methods suit you best. As you read the practical suggestions of others, you can also contribute ideas of your own.

Video Interviews. View clips of some of the influence masters you've met in this book as they share their intriguing stories in candid, on-camera interviews. Use the video segments for your own personal review or to stimulate a group or community discussion.

Self-Assessment. Take the Influencer Self-Assessment, which will help you discover the strengths and weaknesses of your current influence style, as well provide you with helpful advice.

Works Cited

PART 1: THE POWER TO CHANGE ANYTHING

P. 6. YMCA pools: Kevin Trapani of Redwoods Insurance Group. Personal interview with the authors.

P. 7. Detroit jobs: Louis Aguilar, "Michigan Needs Auto Industry to Rebound to Help the State Out of Its Recession, Economist Says," *Detroit News*, June 12, 2007.

P. 7. Toyota: Charles Fishman, "No Satisfaction at Toyota," *Fastcompany.com*, 111 (January 2007): 82.

P. 8. Discussion of the proceedings of the 16th International AIDS Conference was taken from the conference program found at: http://www.aids2006.org/PAG/PAG.aspx?.

P. 10. Muhammad Yunus: Phil Smith and Eric Thurman, *A Billion Bootstraps: Microcredit, Barefoot Banking, and the Business Solution for Ending Poverty* (New York: McGraw-Hill, 2007), Foreword, p. x.

P. 10. AIDS cases in Thailand: Reported by Prime Minister Shinawatra in his opening speech at the 15th International AIDS Conference, Bangkok, Thailand, July 11, 2004. Can be found at: http://www.unaids.org/bangkok2004/docs/SP_ThaiPM_15thAIDSConference_11Jul04.pdf.

1: You're an Influencer

P. 13. Mimi Silbert: Personal interview with the authors, 2005. Any reference to Mimi Silbert or the Delancey Foundation is drawn from this interview unless otherwise cited.

P. 14. Delancey statistics: Ibid. Further discussion can be found at: http://portland.indymedia.org/en/static/prisonprograms.shtml, http://www.eisenhowerfoundation.org/grassroots/delancey/.

P. 14. Anonymous attendee of Delancey Street. Personal interview with the authors, 2005.

P. 15. Miguel Sabido: Arvind Singhal and Everett M. Rogers, *Entertainment Education: A Communication Strategy for Social Change* (Mahwah, New Jersey: Lawrence Erlbaum Associates, 1999), p. 55.

P. 17. Guinea worm: Donald Hopkins, personal interview with the authors, May 3, 2006. Any reference to Dr. Donald Hopkins, Guinea worm eradication, or The Carter Center is drawn from this interview unless otherwise cited.

P. 19. Bobo Doll study: Albert Bandura, Dorothea Ross, and Sheila A. Ross, "Transmission of Aggression through Imitation of Aggressive Models," *Journal of Abnormal and Social Psychology*, 63 (1961): 575–582.

P. 20. Albert Bandura: Personal interview with the authors, 2006. Any reference throughout the book to Albert Bandura and his work is drawn from this interview unless otherwise cited.

2: Find Vital Behaviors

P. 24. King's birthday present: Praphan Phanunphack, interview with authors, 2006. Dr. Phanumphack is the director of the Red Cross AIDS Research Center in Thailand. Additional information can be found at: http://www.csc-scc.gc.ca/ text/forum/bprisons/speeches/2_e.shtml.

P. 24. AIDS statistics: Anupong Chitwarakorn, Jai P. Narain, ed., "HIV/AIDS and Sexually Transmitted Infections in Thailand: Lessons Learned and Future Challenges," *AIDS in Asia: The Challenge Continues* (New Delhi, India: Sage Publications, 2004).

P. 24. Five million cases: Reported by Prime Minister Shinawatra in his opening speech at the 15th International AIDS Conference, Bangkok, Thailand, July 11, 2004. Can be found at: http://www.unaids.org/bangkok2004/docs/SP_ThaiPM_ 15thAIDSConference_11Jul04.pdf.

P. 25. Wiwat Rojanapithayakorn: Personal interview with the authors, 2006. Any reference to Dr. Wiwat or the 100% Condom Campaign in Thailand is drawn from this interview unless otherwise cited.

P. 25. Number of sex workers: K. Archavanitkul, "What Is the Number of Child Prostitutes in Thailand?" *Warasan Prachakon Lae Sangkhom*, 7 (1999):1–9.

P. 28. Relationship failure: Howard J. Markman, Scott M. Stanley, and Susan L. Blumberg, *Fighting for Your Marriage* (San Francisco: Jossey-Bass, 2001), p. 18.

P. 28. Divorce prediction: Howard Markman, personal interview with the authors, 2006. Any reference throughout the book to Howard Markman and his work is drawn from this interview unless otherwise cited.

P. 31. Ethna Reid: Personal interview with the authors, 2006. Any reference throughout the book to Ethna Reid or her work is taken from this interview unless otherwise cited.

P. 36. Regional medical center: This story is taken from a consulting project done by the authors with an anonymous medical center.

P. 41. Guinea worm statistics: Ruth Levine and the What Works Working Group with Molly Kinder, *Millions Saved: Proven Successes in Global Health* (Washington, DC: Center for Global Development, 2004), p. 91. Additional information is reported on The Carter Center's Web site: http://www.cartercenter.org/health/guinea_worm/index.html.

P. 42. Weight Control Registry: Jane E. Brody, "Personal Health: Weight Loss Is Possible," *New York Times*. September 16, 1997.

3: Changing Minds

P. 46. Snake phobics: Taken from interview previously referenced. For further info, see Albert Bandura, N. Adams, and J. Beyer, "Cognitive Process Mediating Behavioral Change," *Cognitive Therapy and Research*, 1 (1977): 287–310.

P. 54. *Ven Conmigo:* Arvind Singhal and Everett M. Rogers, *Entertainment Education: A Communication Strategy for Social Change* (Mahwah, New Jersey: Lawrence Erlbaum Associates, 1999), p. 55.

P. 54. *Twende Na Wakati* (Story of Mkwaju): Arvind Singhal, personal interview with the authors, 2006. Any reference throughout the book to Arvind Singhal or his work is taken from this interview unless otherwise cited.

P. 56. Results of *Twende Na Wakati:* Arvind Singhal and Everett M. Rogers, *Entertainment Education: A Communication Strategy for Social Change* (Mahwah, New Jersey: Lawrence Erlbaum Associates, 1999), pp. 152–171, 131–134.

P. 57. "Maude's Dilemma": Ibid., pp. 16, 17. For further discussion about "Maude's Dilemma," see: http://www.tvacres.com/censorship_maude.htm.

P. 59. Contaminated water: Elizabeth Rattine-Flaherty, personal interview with the authors, 2006.

P. 60 AIDS transmission: Arvind Singhal interview (details above).

P. 61. Lajos Egri. *The Art of Creative Writing* (New York: Kensington Publishing Corp., 1965), pp. 18–19.

P. 62. Mirror neurons: Giacomo Rizzolatti et al., "Premotor Cortex and the Recognition of Motor Actions," *Cognitive Brain Research*, 3 (1996): 131–141. For more info on the mirror neuron and the discovery thereof, see: http://www.biocrawler.com/encyclopedia/Mirror_neuron.

P. 66. *Scared Straight:* A. Petrosino, C. Turpin-Petrosino, and J. Buehler, "'Scared Straight' and Other Juvenile Awareness Programs for Preventing Juvenile

Delinquency," *The Campbell Collaborative Reviews of Intervention and Policy Evaluations* (Philadelphia: Campbell Collaboration, 2003).

P. 66. Gums: I. L. Janis and S. Feshbach, "Effects of Fear-Arousing Communications," *The Journal of Abnormal and Social Psychology*, 48 (1953): 78–92.

P. 68. Medical deaths: Don Berwick, personal interview with the authors, 2006. Information is taken from a report by the National Academy of Science: Linda Kohn et al., *To Err Is Human: Building a Safer Health System* (Washington, DC: National Academies Press, 1999).

P. 68. Don Berwick: Personal interview with the authors. Any reference throughout the book to Don Berwick or his work is taken from this interview unless otherwise cited. To learn more about Josie's story see: www.josieking.org.

P. 70. General Gowon: Personal interview with the authors, 2006.

PART 2: MAKE CHANGE INEVITABLE

P. 75. Information about the Guinea worm was taken from interviews with Dr. Donald Hopkins and other personnel at The Carter Center.

4. Personal Motivation

P. 85. Terri: Mimi Silbert, personal interview with the authors. Mimi told many stories of individuals who go through experiences similar to that of the fictionalized story of Terri.

P. 86. Scott Peck, *The Road Less Traveled* (New York: Simon and Schuster, 1978), pp. 213–214.

P. 87. Classical conditioning: I. P. Pavlov, translated and edited by G. V. Anrep, *Conditioned Reflexes: An Investigation of the Physiological Activity of the Cerebral Cortex* (London: Oxford University Press, 1927).

P. 88. Brian Wansink, *Mindless Eating: Why We Eat More than We Think* (New York: Bantam Books, 2006).

P. 90. Daniel Gilbert, *Stumbling on Happiness* (New York: A. A. Knopf, 2006).

P. 91. Miguel Sabido: Arvind Singhal and Everett M. Rogers, *Entertainment Education: A Communication Strategy for Social Change* (Mahwah, New Jersey: Lawrence Erlbaum Associates, 1999), p. 55.

P. 92. Mihaly Csikszentmihalyi, *Flow: The Psychology of Optimal Experience* (New York: Harper and Row, 1990), p. 51.

P. 94. Grigori Perelman: Greg Johnson, "The Math Was Complex, the Intentions, Strikingly Simple," *New York Times*, August 27, 2006.

P. 95. Lack of moral thinking: Patricia H. Werhane, "Engineers and Management: The Challenge of the Challenger Incident," *Journal of Business Ethics*, 10 (1991): 605.

P. 95. Ellen Langer, *Mindfulness* (Reading, Massachusetts: Addison-Wesley, 1989).

P. 96. Challenger launch: Micheal Gorman, *Transforming Nature* (Boston: Kluwer Academic Press, 1998).

P. 97. Moral disengagement: Albert Bandura, "Social Cognitive Theory of Moral Thought and Action," *Handbook of Moral Behavior and Development*, Vol. 1. (Hillsdale, New Jersey: Lawrence Erlbaum Associates, 1991). pp. 45–103.

P. 97. Pintos: Dennis Gioia, "Pinto Fires and Personal Ethics: A Script Analysis of Missed Opportunities," *Journal of Business Ethics*, 11 (1992): 379–389.

P. 97. Matthew T. Lee, "The Ford Pinto Case and the Development of Auto Safety Regulations, 1893–1978," *Business and Economic History*, 27 (1998), no. 2.

P. 97. M. Dowie, "Pinto Madness," *Mother Jones* (September/October 1977).

P. 99. Connect to values: Stanton Peele, *7 Tools to Beat Addiction* (New York: Three Rivers Press, 2004), p. 24.

P. 101. One-word label: Albert Bandura, et al., "Disinhibition of Aggression through Diffusion of Responsibility and Dehumanization of Victims," *Journal of Personality and Social Psychology*, 9 (1975): 253–269.

P. 104. Therapy length: William R. Miller and Stephen Rollnick, *Motivational Interviewing* (New York: The Guilford Press, 2002), p. 5.

P. 105. Therapy type: Ibid., pp 6, 7.

P. 105. Motivational interviewing results: Ibid., pp. 220, 226.

P. 106. Ralph Heath: Personal interview with the authors.

P. 106. Ginger L. Graham, "If you Want Honesty, Break Some Rules," *Harvard Business Review*, April 2002, pp. 42–47.

5. Personal Ability

P. 112. Fundamental attribution error: Lee Ross, "The Intuitive Psychologist and His Shortcomings: Distortions in the Attribution Process," *Advances in Experimental Social Psychology Education* (New York: Leonard Berkowitz Academic Press, 1977).

P. 112. Lack of training transfer: Mary Broad and John Newstrom, *The Transfer of Training: Action-Packed Strategies to Ensure High Payoff from Training Investments* (Reading, Massachusetts: Addison-Wesley, 1992), p. 7.

P. 114. Mindset: Carol S. Dweck, *Mindset: The New Psychology of Success* (New York: Random House, 2006).

P. 115. Marshmallow studies: W. Mischel, Y. Shoda, and P. Peake, "The Nature of Adolescent Competencies Predicted by Preschool Delay of Gratification," *Journal of Personality and Social Psychology*, 54 (1988): 687–696. See also Y. Shoda, W. Mischel, and P. Peake, "Predicting Adolescent Cognitive and Self-Regulatory Competencies from Preschool Delay of Gratification: Identifying Diagnostic Conditions," *Developmental Psychology*, 26 (1990): 978–986.

P. 116. SAT scores: Daniel Goleman, *Emotional Intelligence: Why It Can Matter More than IQ* (New York: Bantam, 1995), p. 82.

P. 116. S. S. Feldman and D. A. Weinberger, "Self-Restraint as a Mediator of Family Influences on Boys' Delinquent Behavior: A Longitudinal Study," *Child Development*, 65 (1994): 195–211.

P. 117. Mischel and Bandura: A. Bandura and W. Mischel, "Modification of Self-Imposed Delay of Reward through Exposure to Live and Symbolic Models," *Journal of Personality and Social Psychology*, 2 (1965): 698–705.

P. 118. Deliberate practice: K. A. Ericsson, R. Th. Krampe, and C. Tesch-Römer, "The Role of Deliberate Practice in the Acquisition of Expert Performance," *Psychological Review*, 100 (1993): 363–406.

P. 121. Thailand condom use: W. Rojanapithayakorn and R. Hanenberg, "The 100% Condom Programme in Thailand," *AIDS*, 10 (1996): 1–7.

P. 122. Skill development: K. A. Ericsson and A. C. Lehmann, "Expert and Exceptional Performance: Evidence on Maximal Adaptations on Task Constraints," *Annual Review of Psychology*, 47 (1996): 273–305.

P. 122. Ten years: Benjamin Bloom (ed.), *Developing Talent in Young People* (New York: Ballantine, 1985).

P. 122. Correlation between time and skill level: Karl Anders Ericsson, et al. (eds.), *The Cambridge Handbook of Expertise and Expert Performance* (New York: Cambridge University Press, 2006).

P. 123. Roger Bacon: Ibid.

P. 123. Olympic swimming: We compared Johnny Weissmuller's Olympic record times to times of current high school swimming champions. For more information visit: http://www.johnnyweissmuller.ro/main_eng.html.

P. 123. Deliberate practice techniques: Karl Anders Ericsson, et al. (eds.). *The Cambridge Handbook of Expertise and Expert Performance* (New York: Cambridge University Press, 2006), p. 699.

P. 124. Deliberate practice and feedback: Ibid., p. 532.

P. 124. Natalie Coughlin: M. Grudowski, "The Girl Next Door Is Hungry," *Men's Journal*, 12 (2003): 72–73.

P. 126. Pills: Albert Bandura, personal interview with the authors, September 7, 2005.

P. 126. Free throws: T. J. Cleary and B. J. Zimmerman, "Self-Regulation Differences during Athletic Practice by Experts, Non-Experts, and Novices," *Journal of Applied Sport Psychology*, 13 (2001): 185–206.

P. 127. Dating skills: S. L. Foster, et al., "Teaching Social Skills to Shy Single Men," *The Family Journal*, 5 (1997): 37–48.

P. 129. Hot/cool systems: J. Metcalf and W. Mischel, "A Hot/Cool System Analysis of Delay of Gratification," *Psychological Review*, 106 (1999): 3–19.

P. 129. W. Mischel, "Toward an Integrative Model for CBT: Encompassing Behavior, Cognition, Affect, and Process," *Behavior Therapy*, 35 (2004): 185–203.

P. 130. Children and delay of gratification: H. Mischel and W. Mischel. "The Development of Children's Knowledge of Self-Control Strategies," *Child Development*, 54 (1983): 603–619.

P. 132. Expectation and delay of gratification: W. Mischel and E. Staub, "Effects of Expectancy on Working and Waiting for Larger Rewards," *Journal of Personality and Social Psychology*, 2 (1965): 625–633.

P. 133. Distraction and delay of gratification: W. Mischel and E. Ebbesen, "Attention in Delay of Gratification," *Journal of Personality and Social Psychology*, 16 (1970): 329–337.

P. 133. Teaching skill of delay of gratification: A. Bandura and W. Mischel, "Modification of Self-Imposed Delay of Reward through Exposure to Live and Symbolic Models," *Journal of Personality and Social Psychology*, 2 (1965): 698–705.

P. 133. Focus and delay of gratification: W. Mischel and E. Ebbesen, "Attention in Delay of Gratification," *Journal of Personality and Social Psychology*, 16 (1970): 329–337.

P. 137. Willpower and delay of gratification: P. Peake, M. Hebl, and W. Mischel, "Strategic Attention Deployment in Waiting and Working Situations," *Developmental Psychology*, 38 (2002): 313–326.

P. 134. Cognitive reappraisal: J. J. Gross, "Emotion Regulation in Adulthood: Timing Is Everything," *Current Directions in Psychological Science*, 10 (2001): 214–219.

P. 134. Handwashing: Jeffrey Schwartz, *Brainlock* (New York: HarperCollins, 1996), p. 212.

6: Harness Peer Pressure

P. 139. Milgram obedience studies: Stanley Milgram, "Behavioral Study of Obedience," *Journal of Abnormal and Social Psychology*, 67 (1963): 371–378.

P. 139. Phil Zimbardo discusses Milgram's experiments on the Web site http://thesituationist.wordpress.com/2007/02/16/when-good-people-do-evil-%E2%80%93-part-i/

P. 143. Obedience study with confederate: Stanley Milgram, *Obedience to Authority: An Experimental View* (New York: Harper and Row, 1974).

P. 148. Everett Rogers and diffusion of innovations: Everett Rogers, *Diffusion of Innovations*, 3rd ed. (New York: Free Press, 1983), pp. 15, 32–34, 54–56, 247, 258, 266, 271. The story about the "Guy in the Bermudas" was told by Rogers in a lecture at Stanford University in the fall of 1982.

P. 148. Limey story: Don Berwick, "Disseminating Innovations in Health Care," *JAMA* (2003): 1969–1975.

P. 150. *Tinka Tinka Suhk*: Arvind Singhal and Everett M. Rogers, *Entertainment Education: A Communication Strategy for Social Change* (Mahwah, New Jersey: Lawrence Erlbaum Associates, 1999), pp. 1, 176, 58, 137.

P. 151. Barefoot doctors: Everett Rogers, *Diffusion of Innovations*, 3rd ed. (New York: Free Press, 1983), pp. 326–328.

P. 152. E-mail support: Personal interview with Albert Bandura, 2006.

P. 152. Diabetics and social support: C. Y. Wang and M. M. Fenske, "Self-Care of Adults with Non-Insulin-Dependent Diabetes Mellitus: Influence of Family and Friends," *Diabetes Education*, 22 (1996): 465–470.

P. 152. Social commitments: Kurt Lewin, "Forces behind Food Habits and Methods of Change," *The Problem of Changing Food Habits: Bulletin of The National Research Council* (National Research Council and National Academy of Sciences, Washington, DC, 1943), pp. 35–65.

P. 153. Parents' influence: Brent L. Top and Bruce A. Chadwick, *Rearing Righteous Youth of Zion* (Salt Lake City: BookCraft, 1998).

P. 153. Qualities of opinion leaders: Everett Rogers, *Diffusion of Innovations*, 3rd ed. (New York: Free Press, 1983), pp. 15, 32–34, 54–56, 247, 258, 266, 271.

P. 157. *Tinka Tinka Sukh*: Arvind Singhal, personal interview with the authors, 2006.

P. 159. Silence Fails study: For more info, see VitalSmarts/Concourse Group. http://silencefails.com.

7: Find Strength in Numbers

P. 168. Tanika's story: A story told to one of the authors as a microcredit industry leader.

P. 171. Muhammad Yunus and the Grameen Bank: Muhammad Yunus, *Banker to the Poor* (Dhaka, Bangladesh: University Press, 1998), p. 12.

P. 172. Borrower stats: Grameen Bank at a Glance: http://www.grameen-info.org/bank/GBGlance.htm.

P. 173. Statement of Professor Muhammad Yunus at the ITU World Information Society Award Ceremony, May 17, 2006. Accessible at: http://www.itu.int/wisd/2006/award/statements/yunus.html.

P. 174. Friends: John Lennon and Paul McCartney, "With a Little Help from My Friends," *Sgt. Pepper's Lonely Hearts Club Band*, 1967.

P. 175. Weight of ox: James Surowiecki, *The Wisdom of Crowds* (New York: Doubleday, 2004), p. xiii.

P. 179. *Soul City*: Garth Japhet, personal interview with the authors, 2006.

P. 187. Network quotient: Don Cohen and Laurence Prusak, *In Good Company: How Social Capital Makes Organizations Work* (Cambridge, Massachusetts: Harvard Business School Press, 2001).

P. 188. Physicians: Atul Gawanda, *Complications: A Surgeon's Notes on an Imperfect Science* (New York: Picado, 2002), pp. 11–24.

P. 189. Tragedy of the Commons: William Forester Lloyd, *Two Lectures on the Checks to Population* (Oxford, England: Oxford University Press, 1833).

P. 191. HIV/AIDS in Thailand: Wiwat Rojanapithayakorn, "100% Condom Use Programme," manuscript presented in Provo, Utah, 2006.

P. 191. Five million saved: As reported by Prime Minister Shinawatra in his opening speech at the 15th International AIDS Conference, Bangkok, Thailand, July 11, 2004. Can be found at: http://www.unaids.org/bangkok2004/docs/SP_ThaiPM _15thAIDSConference_11Jul04.pdf.

8: Design Rewards and Demand Accountability

P. 194. Rewarding Children: M. R. Lepper, D. Greene, and R. E. Nisbett, "Undermining Children's Intrinsic Motivation with Extrinsic Reward: A Test of the 'Over-Justification' Hypothesis," *Journal of Personality and Social Psychology*, 28 (1973): 129–137.

P. 197. Soviet Union: Marshall Goldman, *U.S.S.R. in Crisis: The Failure of an Economic System* (New York: W. W. Norton & Co., 1983), p. 32.

P. 199. Privileges and alcohol: Stanton Peele, *7 Tools to Beat Addiction* (New York: Three Rivers Press, 2004), p. 95.

P. 199. Cocaine and vouchers: Ibid., p. 96.

P. 200. Frequent flier mileage: "Frequent Flyer Miles: In Terminal Decline?" *The Economist*, January 6, 2006.

P. 201. Teen suicide: Karen M. Simon, personal communication with the authors, 1976.

P. 202. Colored stars as rewards: http://www.grameen-info.org/bank/bank2.html.

P. 204. Hand hygiene: Stephen Dubnar and Steven Levitt, "Selling Soap," *New York Times*, September 24, 2006.

P. 205. Employee polls: Employee poll taken from 20 years of polling done at VitalSmarts.

P. 208. Tea leaf consumption: Masaaki Imai, *Kaizen* (New York: McGraw-Hill, 1986), p. 20.

P. 209. Soldiers in Vietnam: Steven Kerr, "On the Folly of Rewarding A, While Hoping for B," *Academy of Management Executive*, 9 (1995): 7–14.

P. 211. Learned helplessness: Martin Seligman, Christopher Peterson, and Steven Maier, *Learned Helplessness: A Theory for the Age of Personal Control* (New York: Oxford University Press, 1993).

P. 212. Crime prevention program: Mark Shoofs, "Novel Police Tactic Puts Drug Markets Out of Business," *Wall Street Journal*, September 27, 2006.

P. 214. Russian oil: Jerome Dumetz, personal communication with the authors, 2006. Jerome is a consultant to many Russian oil firms.

P. 215. Ethiopia: Negussie Teffera, personal interview with the authors, 2006.

9: Change the Environment

P. 220. Order spindle: W. F. White, *Human Relations in the Restaurant Industry* (New York: McGraw-Hill, 1948).

P. 222. Environmentally incompetent: Fred Steele, *Physical Settings and Organization Development* (Reading, Mass: Addison-Wesley, 1973), pp. 11, 113.

P. 223. Hitler's hallway: Albert Speer, *Inside the Third Reich* (New York: Macmillan, 1970).

P. 224. Broken windows: George Kelling and Catherine Coles, *Fixing Broken Windows: Restoring Order and Reducing Crime in Our Communities* (New York: Simon and Schuster, 1996), p. 152.

P. 226. Food studies: Brian Wansink, *Mindless Eating: Why We Eat More than We Think* (New York: Bantam Books, 2006).

P. 229. Fill-to-here line: Fred Luthans, *Organizational Behavior* (New York: McGraw-Hill, 1981.)

P. 229. A. M. Dickinson, "The Historical Roots of Organizational Behavior Management in the Private Sector: The 1950's–1980s," *Journal of Organizational Behavior Management*, 20 (2000): 9–58.

P. 229. Latex gloves: Occurred on a consulting project of the authors.

P. 229. Starbucks cards and screen saver: Stephen J. Dubner and Steven Levitt, "Selling Soap," *New York Times*, September 24, 2006.

P. 231. Representative heuristic: For reading on the topic, see A. Tversky and D. Kahneman, "Judgement under Uncertainty: Heuristics and Biases," *Science*, 185 (1974): 1124–1130.

P. 233. Jimmy Carter, personal interview with the authors, 2007.

P. 236. Effects of space and propinquity: L. Festinger, S. Schachter, and K. Back, *Social Pressure in Informal Groups* (Stanford, California: Stanford University Press, 1950), Chapter 4.

P. 238. Dining room table: This phenomenon is discussed in "Dining Room Table Losing Central Status in Families," *USA Today*, December 18, 2005.

P. 240. Desk proximity: Robert Kraut and Carmen Egido, and Jolene Galegher, *Patterns of Contact and Communication in Scientific Research Collaboration* (New York: ACM Press, 1988).

P. 240. Hewlett-Packard daily break: Personal communication with Ray Price, 1980.

P. 243. Frederick Taylor: Robert Kanigel, *The One Best Way: Frederick Winslow Taylor and the Enigma of Efficiency* (New York: Viking, 1997).

P. 246. Food container: Brian Wansink, *Mindless Eating: Why We Eat More than We Think* (New York: Bantam Books, 2006).

P. 247. Medication bottles: Adrienne Berman, "Reducing Medication Errors through Naming, Labeling, and Packaging," *Journal of Medical Systems*, 28 (2004): 9–29.

P. 248. Dog food: Paco Underhill, *Why We Buy: The Science of Shopping* (New York: Simon and Schuster, 1999), Chapter 1.

P. 248. Casinos: Bill Friedman, *Designing Casinos to Dominate the Competition: The Friedman International Standards of Casino Design* (Reno, Nevada: The Institute for the Study of Gambling and Commercial Gaming College of Business Administration, 2000).

10: Become an Influencer

P. 258. Cystic fibrosis: Atul Gawande, "The Bell Curve," *The New Yorker*, December 6, 2004.

P. 263. It sounds like X: Silencekills.com.

P. 265. Putting It All Together case study: Silencefails.com.

Index

Acknowledgments

We are deeply grateful to many who have helped us throughout the years in our research, teaching, testing, and learning.

First, to our families for your influence on us. Thanks for the love and support that has changed us, inspired us, and enabled us. Thank you particularly for your sacrifice and patience when we were far from home—or at home, but overly focused, head down over a keyboard.

Second, thanks to our colleagues, associates, and team members at VitalSmarts who help in hundreds of ways—working to achieve our mission, serving customers, training the skills to help change lives, and supporting one another with care, loyalty, and competence. To all (all is now a large number) we say thanks. Highlighting just a few is tough, but necessary. So an additional thanks to James Allred, Brad Anderson, Mike Carter, Mary Dondiego, Jeff Gibbs, Todd King, Emily Moss, Joanne Staheli, Brett Walker, Yan Wang, and Steve Willis.

Third, a special thanks to Bob Foote, Chase McMillan, and Mindy Waite, who continuously provided us with extraordinary logistical support, attention to detail, and insight.

Fourth, we express appreciation for our extended team of supporters. To our agents, Jan Miller and Shannon Miser-Marvin, thank you. Our publisher, McGraw-Hill, has been an exceptional partner. We especially acknowledge Mary Glenn, Lynda Luppino, Philip Ruppel, Herb Schaffner, and Cheryl Hudson. They have been consummate professionals in all our dealings.

About the Authors

This award-winning team of authors—now joined by leading researcher David Maxfield—previously produced the two *New York Times* bestsellers *Crucial Conversations: Tools for Talking When Stakes Are High* (2002) and *Crucial Confrontations: Tools for Resolving Broken Promises, Violated Expectations, and Bad Behavior* (2005).

Kerry Patterson has authored award-winning training programs and led multiple long-term change efforts. He received the prestigious 2004 BYU Marriott School of Management Dyer Award for outstanding contribution in organizational behavior. He did doctoral work in organizational behavior at Stanford University.

Joseph Grenny is an acclaimed keynote speaker and consultant who has designed and implemented major corporate change initiatives for the past 20 years. He is also a cofounder of Unitus, a nonprofit organization that helps the world's poor achieve economic self-reliance.

David Maxfield is a leading researcher and frequent conference speaker on topics ranging from dialogue skills to performance improvement. He did doctoral work in psychology at Stanford University, where he studied personality theory and interpersonal-skill development.

Ron McMillan is a sought-after speaker and consultant. He cofounded the Covey Leadership Center, where he served as vice president of research and development. He has worked with leaders ranging from first-level managers to corporate executives on topics such as leadership and team development.

Al Switzler is a renowned consultant and speaker who has directed training and management initiatives with dozens of Fortune 500 companies worldwide. He is on the faculty of the Executive Development Center at the University of Michigan.

About VitalSmarts

An innovator in corporate training and organizational performance, VitalSmarts helps teams and organizations achieve the results they care about most. With award-winning training products based on more than 30 years of ongoing research, VitalSmarts has helped more than 300 of the Fortune 500 realize significant results using a proven method for driving rapid, sustainable, and measurable change in behaviors. VitalSmarts has been ranked twice by *Inc.* magazine as one of the fastest-growing companies in America and has taught more than 2 million people worldwide.

VitalSmarts is home to multiple training offerings, including Crucial Conversations®, Crucial Confrontations™, and Influencer Training™. Each course improves key organizational outcomes by focusing on high-leverage skills and strategies. Along with *Influencer*, their latest book, the VitalSmarts authors have written two *New York Times* bestsellers, *Crucial Conversations* and *Crucial Confrontations*. VitalSmarts also offers on-site consulting, research, executive team development, and speaking engagements.

www.vitalsmarts.com

Award-Winning Training from VitalSmarts

VitalSmarts is home to multiple training offerings, including Crucial Conversations®, Crucial Confrontations™, and the brand new Influencer Training™.

Based on more than 30 years of ongoing research, VitalSmarts training helps people transform ideas into action and action into results. Each course improves key individual, team, and organizational outcomes by teaching high-leverage skills and strategies.

Crucial Conversations® Training

Drive results by learning to speak with complete candor and complete respect, no matter the issues or the individuals involved. Create alignment, resolve disagreements, surface the best ideas, and make decisions with unity and conviction.

Crucial Confrontations™ Training

Ensure flawless execution with a step-by-step process for improving accountability and addressing performance gaps. Achieve the results you want by learning to motivate without using power and to enable without taking over.

NEW—Influencer Training™

Diagnose the real reasons behind the problems most organizations face. Use eight powerful principles to create sustainable behavior change and overcome persistent problems.

To receive more information on training from VitalSmarts, mail in the card found in the back of this book, call 1-800-449-5989, or go online to www.vitalsmarts.com.